Collected essays

Also edited by G. Singh

Q. D. Leavis, *Collected Essays:*
Volume 1: *The Englishness of the English Novel*

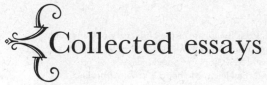

Collected essays

Volume 2
The American novel and reflections on
the European novel

Q. D. LEAVIS

EDITED BY G. SINGH

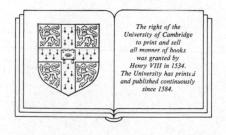

The right of the
University of Cambridge
to print and sell
all manner of books
was granted by
Henry VIII in 1534.
The University has printed
and published continuously
since 1584.

CAMBRIDGE UNIVERSITY PRESS

CAMBRIDGE
LONDON   NEW YORK   NEW ROCHELLE
MELBOURNE   SYDNEY

86-368

Published by the Press Syndicate of the ·University of Cambridge
The Pitt Building, Trumpington Street, Cambridge CB2 1RP
32 East 57th Street, New York, NY 10022, USA
10 Stamford Road, Oakleigh, Melbourne 3166, Australia

© Cambridge University Press 1985

First published 1985

Printed in Great Britain by
the University Press, Cambridge

Library of Congress catalogue card number: 83-1978

British Library Cataloguing in Publication Data

Leavis, Q. D.
Collected essays.
Vol. 2: The American novel
and reflections on
the European novel.
1. English literature – 19th century –
History and criticism
I. Title   II. Singh, G.
820.9′008   PR461

ISBN 0 521 26702 1 hard covers
ISBN 0 521 31825 4 paperback

UP

Contents

Sources and acknowledgments

'The American novel', 'Henry James and the disabilities of the American novelist in the nineteenth century', 'James, Trollope and the American–English confrontation theme', 'The fox is the novelist's idea: Henry James and the house beautiful' and 'Edith Wharton: *The House of Mirth*' as well as the text of Q. D. Leavis's lectures on the French, the Russian and the Italian novel delivered at Queen's University, Belfast, in 1980, are published for the first time. 'Hawthorne as poet' (parts 1 and 2) by Q. D. Leavis was first published in the *Sewanee Review*, LIX (spring and summer 1951). Copyright 1951, 1979, by the University of the South. Reprinted with the permission of the editor. 'Melville: the 1853–6 phase' was included in *New Perspectives on Melville*, ed. Faith Pullen (Edinburgh University Press, 1978). 'A note on literary indebtedness: Dickens, George Eliot, Henry James' appeared in the *Hudson Review*, VIII, 3 (autumn 1955). 'Henry James: the stories', 'The institution of Henry James' and 'Henry James's heiress: the importance of Edith Wharton' were first published in *Scrutiny*, vols. XIV, XV and VII respectively.

The editor and publishers are grateful to the *Sewanee Review* for permission to reprint 'Hawthorne as poet', to the *Hudson Review* for permission to reprint 'A note on literary indebtedness: Dickens, George Eliot, Henry James' and to Edinburgh University Press for permission to reprint 'Melville: the 1853–6 phase'.

Editor's introduction

Given her close interest in and her critical authority on the English novel, it was natural that Q. D. Leavis should have turned to examine the tradition of the American classical novel – especially Hawthorne, Melville and Henry James. She published some critiques in her lifetime, and left further unpublished essays on the American novel which are now collected in this volume.

In her lecture on the American novel – part of the series of lectures on the European and American novel given at Queen's University, Belfast – Q. D. Leavis links the growth and development of the American novel with two conditions: the emancipation of a former colony from the mother-country; and the naïve Utopian theory on which the settlement of the new continent was originally based. But even by the time of the first novelists such as Fenimore Cooper and Hawthorne, a sense of disillusion and dissatisfaction had set in as the confident hopes of the first American pioneers were dashed and 'their Calvinist theocracy turned into a Philistine commercial society with all the added drawbacks of a built-in Puritanism'. In her general critique of the American novel as well as in her particular dealings with aspects of Hawthorne, Melville and Henry James, Q. D. Leavis examines the nature and implications of these two conditions in creative terms – conditions that form the theoretical basis of what she has to say. What emerges from these essays on the American novel is an illuminating and challenging account of what is creatively fruitful in the confident hopes of the first American pioneers and in the successive American novelists' reaction to their country's failure to achieve 'the intended (moral and spiritual) goal'.

From among what she calls 'an embarrassing quantity of novels and novelists' in the history of American literature in the last century and a half, Q. D. Leavis chooses six to illustrate her thesis – Fenimore Cooper, Hawthorne, Melville, Mark Twain, Henry James and Edith Wharton. Part of her discussion centres round the question as to what the American novelists owed to the English novel, and how they reacted to it or moulded what it had to teach to their own particular scope and method.

In the evolution of American prose and its creative use by novelists, Q. D. Leavis presents Henry James as a typical example. In James's youth, the English he heard was the spoken language of the educated, and at first his American characters speak an appropriate idiom, with much more life and individuality in their speech than there is in that of his English characters. But by the time of his last phase, James had lost his ear for American idiom and vocabulary – that idiom which Mark Twain had fully developed, even though it was unacceptable to the genteel American reading-public.

Along with this linguistic development, there was in the history of the American novel the development of a social conscience in part due to awareness of national history and its inherent shortcomings. Q. D. Leavis analyses the sense of guilt this engendered in major American novelists as they came to recognize 'an irrevocable process of corruption of the land and of society...due to the fallacies and flaws in the confident American theory'.

Cooper too, with his conflicting sympathies, at once English and American, is seen as being both proud of America's democracy and practical achievements, and highly critical of 'the other results' – a conflict that, for Q. D. Leavis, characterizes all the classical American novelists. Thus, for instance, in *The Pioneers*, Cooper mythologizes the conflict between the Red Indians and the settlers, between Nature and the white despoiler of the land. Another theme Cooper deals with, even before James, is that of the Anglo-American confrontation – a theme treated also by Melville, whose attitude Q. D. Leavis finds more balanced and more mature than that of James, because Melville had no anti-English feeling or social prejudice, had 'no reservation about registering his respect for such purely English qualities as he found admirable', and, unlike other novelists, did not shift 'the responsibility for American troubles on to the shoulders of England'.

In her long two-part essay on 'Hawthorne as poet', which she wrote for *The Sewanee Review* in 1951, she observes at the outset that 'for an English person to offer an opinion on Hawthorne, much more an evaluation of his *oeuvre*, must be felt in America to be an impertinence'. This did not prevent her – 'a tremendous admirer of long standing of much of Hawthorne's work' – from offering a full-fledged, frank and balanced critical appraisal of Hawthorne to whom she applied the critical standards and criteria that she had applied to the English novel.

Arguing against the then current evaluation of Hawthorne in the hands of Yvor Winters and Henry James, who relegated him, along with Bunyan, to 'an inferior class of writer who depends for his effect on "allegory"', Q. D. Leavis argued that while Hawthorne's less interesting work bulks large, it was 'easily cut free' from his essential contribution to American literature in which he decidedly emerges 'a great genius, the creator of a literary tradition as well as a wonderfully original and accomplished artist'. And if much of Hawthorne's writing is allegorical, it is in the manner of Shakespeare – the Shakespeare of the tragedies each of which may be regarded, as G. Wilson Knight regards them, as 'an expanded metaphor' – rather than in the style of Spenser, Milton or Bunyan. For in Hawthorne's work too, the symbol 'is the thing itself, with no separable paraphrasable meaning as in an allegory: the language is discreetly evocative'. Even more than the allegorical quality, what interests Q. D. Leavis is that Hawthorne was above all else the critic and interpreter of American cultural history and hence the finder and creator of a literary tradition from which sprang both Henry James and Melville. In discussing this aspect – in some respects the core of this and other essays in the present volume – Q. D. Leavis examines not only the creative and artistic aspects of the novel but the historical and sociological factors which constituted the cultural climate in which the novel grew, and which the novel in turn reflects.

Thus Hawthorne's work shows how 'a distinctively American society developed and how it came to have a tradition of its own'. Q. D. Leavis quotes Hawthorne as saying that 'A work of genius is but the newspaper of a century, or perchance of a hundred centuries.' She explicitly endorses this view and sets out to demonstrate why Hawthorne is to be regarded as a sociological novelist who employs 'a poetic technique which communicates instead of stating his findings'.

Hawthorne's principal theme was the significance of the American past and present in the light of the conflict between the Puritans who became New England and thus America, and the non-Puritans who were for Hawthorne 'merely the English in America and whom he partly with triumph but partly also with anguish sees as being cast out'. Q. D. Leavis defines the theme as 'a kind of spiritual and cultural casting-up of accounts: what was lost and what gained, what sacrificed to create what? he is perpetually asking, and showing'. In dealing with it Hawthorne achieves a moral depth and maturity and 'a corresponding form of sensitiveness' which, for Q. D. Leavis, is the hall-mark of his distinction and originality.

Although she had long been interested in Melville it was only towards the end of her life that Q. D. Leavis wrote on him. In her essay 'Melville: the 1853–6 phase', she is concerned with what makes Melville's writings of this phase 'more accomplished art, more varied...noticeably more condensed, controlled and mature than either *Moby Dick* or *Pierre*'. She takes up *The Confidence Man* (a 'difficult and still highly controversial work' and 'an ironic masterpiece') for a full-scale evaluative critique, analysing what she calls the 'shape-shiftings of the confidence-man', the 'indigestibly rich' intellectual fare of the tale, the doubts, exploration and speculation of one who was not so much a 'village atheist' (as he has been sometimes labelled) as 'a truth-seeker with an open mind', as well as the novel's 'pugnacious style and strongly presented moral values implicit and explicit'. In her analyses she shows how these values are so presented as to become both creatively relevant and morally pregnant by means of double-faced ironies 'both local and total' and through the many 'avatars' of the confidence-man which are interpreted as so many 'disguises of the Devil in contemporary forms of humbug or cant or dishonesty'. By virtue of this technique – and the sociological ideas and moral concepts behind it – *The Confidence Man* is to be regarded as a novel of philosophical speculation, and so in the same category as *Rasselas, Candide, Gulliver's Travels, The Tale of the Tub* and Peacock's novels. And in virtue of the moral irony and social criticism Melville embodies in his novel, he is compared with Solzhenitsyn and Tolstoy on the one hand, and with George Eliot on the other.

Thus, because they were critical of American society with its indifference to spiritual values and literary art, Hawthorne and Melville forged the tradition of what Q. D. Leavis calls 'great and truly American novels and tales'.

As Jane Austen occupied the central as well as the bulkiest part of the first volume of Collected Essays (The Englishness of the English Novel) so does Henry James of the second. Q. D. Leavis published three critiques in her lifetime, and wrote three long hitherto unpublished essays, all of which are included in this volume. In 'Henry James and the disabilities of the American novelist in the nineteenth century' she deals with the emergence of the American novel as a national literature, partly through reaction against the English novel, and with the complex problems the process entailed. James, we are told, had an uneasy conscience for not having cultivated the American language and for developing a literary English interest, for he felt like a Tolstoy 'who had chosen to write in French instead of working in, and therefore improving in fact, Russian – a form of artistic treachery'. This was the penalty James had to pay for his expatriation and for 'opting out of his native idiom in favour of a higher form of the same language'. Thus part of James's greatness as an artist lies in the way he transcended his disability and created an art-form – the novel – 'that does not appear except in a sophisticated society'.

In 'James, Trollope and the American–English confrontation theme', Q. D. Leavis evaluates the nature of the debt James owed to Trollope. James depended on literature and art for his knowledge of English society and hence he habitually used 'patterns and situations that were congenial to him, or struck him as fine'. But it was Trollope who forced James to reconsider his own American hostilities, prejudices and assumptions. Q. D. Leavis compares the way Trollope and Henry James deal with the American–English confrontation theme, and shows that even though Trollope had 'no sense of form and little respect for diction in his use of the novel', the contents of parts of many of his novels were very useful to James 'the way irritants are to the pearl oyster (at any rate, from the point of view of the collector of pearls)'. And it was Trollope's treatment of 'the most sensitive areas of American feeling', especially in connection with love and marriage, that made James 'take up seriously the question of Anglo-American confrontation in its most testing and dramatic form, that of inter-marriage'.

'A note on literary indebtedness: Dickens, George Eliot, Henry James' as well as the three *Scrutiny* reviews ('Henry James: the stories', 'The institution of Henry James' and 'Henry James's heiress: the importance of Edith Wharton') are the only things Q. D. Leavis published on James in her lifetime.

In 'The fox is the novelist's idea: Henry James and the house beautiful' Q. D. Leavis discusses the idea of the novel James wanted to write, and its key-theme – the House Beautiful – which 'reveals and perhaps explains his development or changes of attitude up to the end almost of his career'. In her analytical comment on the obsession of the American with acquiring the English heritage without forfeiting his Americanness, Q. D. Leavis's insight into the characters' sociology and psychology is seen to be as impressively operant as her grasp of realistic and sociological detail and her unfailing sense of relevance, moral and psychological as well as artistic. She finds *The Tragic Muse*, as the climax of James's work, 'the fullest, most ambiguous, and most pregnant statement of his position' and deals with it at some length. She also comments briefly on other novels which represent James's concept of and attitude to a 'change in social assumptions and values which is indispensable to the survival of the creative practitioner of the arts'.

In 'Henry James: the stories' (review of *Fourteen Stories by Henry James*, selected by David Garnett) she criticizes the choice of stories – 'half of which are not worth owning (some worth reading once, some not)' – but also pinpoints the salient qualities of James's narrative art – 'his deliberate stylization of life...the techniques he devised for conveying his special interests, his recurrent symbols, his preoccupation with the ideal social life and the function of the artist in it'. One of James's favourite techniques is 'the structure built on alternative values' which Q. D. Leavis discusses in relation to the story 'The Jolly Corner': 'The series of surprises in the structure are not the surprise of the trick plot of the well-made story of the Maupassant–Kipling–W. W. Jacobs type. The ambivalence, which is personal and inside James himself, conditions the structure: the uncertainty Henry James felt remains to the end and is expressed in the final ambiguity – what indeed was the lesson of the Master? It is one of the most remarkable of works of art.' It is by virtue of these qualities – present in the short stories no less than in the novels – that she ranks Henry James together with Tolstoy and Conrad.

In 'The institution of Henry James' (a review of *The Question of Henry James* ed. by F. W. Dupee) she examines the critical views on Henry James collected in this volume, distinguishing those of Eliot, Conrad and Pound – 'creative writers who were also literary critics' – from those of journalists and academics and social men of letters. Quoting Edmund Wilson and Stephen Spender (as belonging to the latter group) to the effect that James's works offer 'a Freudian field-day', she observes: 'Of course every great writer is interpreted in the light of contemporary interests (and fashions), but how sound the more recent presentations of James will look tomorrow is still to be decided.' This – and what she has to say about Edmund Wilson ('Mr Wilson's criticism is tough as opposed to the "aesthetic" apprehensions of Mr Matthiessen, but, being alive and disinterested, he succeeds in infusing a new sense of reality into James's works whereas the other's kind of attention seems to empty James's art of significance') – clearly suggests in which direction Q. D. Leavis's own critical inclinations and methodology lay, and how her own criticism was to eschew, as it did, both contemporary interests and fashions on the one hand, and 'aesthetic' apprehensions on the other.

Q. D. Leavis wrote twice on Edith Wharton. She reviewed the unfinished posthumous novel of Edith Wharton (*The Buccaneers*) in *Scrutiny* under the title 'Henry James's heiress: the importance of Edith Wharton'. And she left an unpublished critique of another novel by Edith Wharton, *The House of Mirth*. Her own interests as sociologist-cum-literary critic and historian meant that Edith Wharton's personality was particularly congenial to her, even though she had some reservations. While examining what made Edith Wharton both an original writer and an extraordinarily acute and far-sighted social critic, Q. D. Leavis brings out Edith Wharton's indebtedness to and her affinity with Henry James. The American novel, she tells us, 'grew up with Henry James and achieved a tradition with Mrs Wharton'. Q. D. Leavis also compares Edith Wharton with

George Eliot – George Eliot, 'a simple-minded woman except where great sensitiveness of feeling gave her a subtle insight' and 'Mrs Wharton with a more flexible mind...both socially and morally more experienced than George Eliot and therefore better able to enter into congenial states of feeling and to depict as an artist instead of a preacher distasteful kinds of behaviour...George Eliot...lacking grace rarely achieves the economy of language that Mrs Wharton commands habitually.'

In her critical comment on *The House of Mirth* Q. D. Leavis's analysis of and insight into Lily Barton's character are comparable to Lawrence Seldon's critical though appreciative awareness of her, and are buttressed by critical comments that are both morally pregnant and psychologically illuminating – comments on the social ambiance and ethos of the protagonists of the novel. For instance, in analysing Lily's fastidious tastes and her life-style Q. D. Leavis points out how 'The exquisiteness inevitably goes with weakness – always implicit in aestheticism – which can't always grasp the nettle or embrace and defeat hardships.' Her comments on Lily's character and personality are dictated both by literary and artistic considerations, and by a concern for moral values which for Q. D. Leavis ultimately represents the essential core of the novel. 'It is hard to have any sympathy', she observes, 'for a woman (far from being a young girl now) who has no desire for any better life than the smart set's and whose hardship is in not being able to pay her gambling debts and dressmakers' bills and to satisfy her ambition to have smarter gowns and "far more jewels than her hostesses"'. Q. D. Leavis's view of this novel is summed up by her observation that 'When a novel fails to convince the reader of the inevitability of the conclusions the author has laid out for us, then it must be due to a discrepancy in the values that have been the basis for the fiction; or to the reader's inability to accept the author's value-judgments.'

Q. D. Leavis's interest in the European novel was the outcome of her critical, cultural and sociological curiosity, which extended to traditions of the novel other than the English, the American and the Anglo-Irish novel, and which led her to ask why, among those traditions, the Russians and the French had achieved what the Italians could not. Hence her comparative evaluation of the European novel was motivated by the question, which often emerged in the course of her numerous conversations with me during the last years of her life: 'Why did Italy not produce a distinctive novel tradition of its own?' I was fascinated by the prospect of that question being answered by Q. D. Leavis herself if she could be persuaded to undertake the task. So one day I asked her if she would care to come to Belfast and give a series of lectures and seminars on the European novel. Much to my delight, she accepted the invitation, flew over to Belfast, and during her one-week stay gave five lectures – one each on the English, the American, the Anglo-Irish, the French, the Russian and the Italian tradition of the novel – two seminars, and one public lecture ('Jane Austen: novelist of a changing society', now included in *Collected Essays*, vol. I : *The Englishness of the English Novel*).

While analysing the reasons why Italy, unlike France or Russia, had not produced a distinctive novel tradition of its own, Q. D. Leavis did not deal – nor, given the time limit, could she have dealt – with all the major novels or novelists in any particular tradition. However, through a series of intensely personal convictions and insights and challenging formulations and assessments, she identified the social, cultural and moral factors which accounted for the growth and development of the kind of novel which each European tradition produced, and also cast a critical glance at some of the novels or novelists she mentioned.

She died a few months after giving these lectures and the original, hand-written draft of the text was never revised for publication. As editor I was therefore faced with a difficult choice, whether to publish the material or not. After a great deal of thought, and having gone through the material a number of times, I decided to include it in this volume because, on balance, the grounds for publishing prevailed over those for not publishing. It is not that Q. D. Leavis was an authority on French, Russian or Italian literature – she would have been the first to disclaim such a title – but because in my view her unique authority as a critic of the novel makes what she has to say about the European novel interesting and thought-provoking, even if one does not always agree with her. Another reason for the publication of this material is that Q. D. Leavis's attitude to and conclusions about the European novel are already adumbrated in her Cheltenham Festival Annual Literature Lecture on 'The Englishness of the English Novel' (*Collected Essays*, vol.1), so that the Belfast lectures on the European novel interestingly corroborate and expatiate upon those conclusions. The lectures have been printed as Q. D. Leavis delivered them, and with minimal editing.

G. SINGH

The American novel

I see the American novel as resulting from two conditions. The first is the reaction of a former colony having emancipated itself successfully by war from the mother-country, determined to show it then stood on its own feet culturally as well as politically. The self-respect of these ex-colonials demanded that they should aim at superior material achievements and a higher general standard of living, to prove the superiority of American democracy. Untrammelled by royalty, an aristocracy, feudal institutions or an Established Church, they owed it to themselves, they felt, to produce an Instant Great Literature, to prove a consequent *cultural* superiority. One can see from Henry James Senior's comment on Emerson's *English Traits* how the American citizen of that generation thought of his country in comparison with Europe:

His [Emerson's] own standpoint is too high to do justice to the English. They are an intensely vulgar race, high and low; and their qualities, good or evil, date from most obvious causes. They are not worth studying. The prejudices one has about them, even when they are unjust, are scarcely worth correcting. They belong, all their good and their evil, to the past humanity, to the infantile development of the mind, and they don't deserve, more than any other European nation, the least reverence from a denizen of the new world... I see that they (European peoples) are all destined to be recast and remoulded into the form of a new and *de-nationalized humanity*... American disorder is sweet beside European order: it is so full of promise. The historical consciousness rules to such a disordered excess in Europe that I have always been restless here, and ended by pining for the land of the future exclusively.

Particularly notice the animus against the English, though Henry James Senior came of English and Scottish-Irish stock. Note also the conviction that the future of civilization belonged to Americans exclusively. This is the more remarkable since this writer claimed to be a philosophic and religious thinker.

The second condition which gave the American novel its unique character was the naïve *Utopian* theory on which their settlement of the new continent was originally based. This had soon, even by the time of the first novelists such as Fenimore Cooper and Hawthorne, produced in creative writers a bitter sense of disillusion and dissatisfaction with the American present which was so far from Utopian for them at least, in contrast to the confident hopes of the first American pioneers, as their Calvinist theocracy turned into a Philistine commercial society with all the added drawbacks of a built-in Puritanism. Hence the American novelist was characteristically both a patriot and a dissident and the failure to achieve the intended (moral and spiritual) goal could not be blamed on the English, but, as these writers recognized, was innate, owing to the facts of human nature. Hence a radical bitterness from loss of faith in man characterized the American novel from its early days and up to the present day, so that its prevailing and indeed inevitable style has always been ironic – ironic not only in tone but in essential structure. It is a totally different irony from that of any European novelists, whose traditions have attuned them to the realities of the human condition and provided them with a fund of social compensations for its disadvantages. But without these two conditions there would not have been the strong motivation of creative American writers to make the distinctively American Novel.

Though there is an embarrassing quantity of novels and *nouvelles* in the history of American literature in the last century and a half, it is possible to represent its best and distinctive contribution to the novel by a quite short though not of course exhaustive list. The classical line that I am going to discuss is indicated by the names of Fenimore Cooper, Hawthorne, Melville, Mark Twain, Henry James and incidentally his pupil and close successor Edith Wharton, and as representative novels of the succeeding two generations to Edith Wharton, Scott Fitzgerald's *The Great Gatsby*, which was a product of the Prohibition Era and said by T. S. Eliot to be the first step forward in the American novel since Henry James, and Randall Jarrell's brilliant university novel of the mid-1950s, *Pictures from an Institution*, which is an examination of the culture of modern

American prosperity. There are, of course, other kinds of American novel, such as regional novels like H. L. Davis's *Honey in the Horn* (in the Mark Twain tradition) or social propaganda like Upton Sinclair's novel, or *Grapes of Wrath*, and a line of complacent Americanism like the novels of Henry James's patron W. D. Howells; but these are of marginal interest. Even the three novels Dos Passos published in the 1930s and then collected in one volume called *U.S.A.*, which was an attempt to chart wholly objectively the rise and fall of modern America by techniques related to the advanced cinema of the age, and uses the popular press and songs, which was hailed as a substantial achievement, one now feels is too external, like French naturalism, to give satisfying results.

But the novels of the line of Americans I have indicated are quite other than naturalistic, and we can see why they had to be. The English novels of the eighteenth century, which culminated artistically in the work of Jane Austen, were concerned with a social realism examined in the drawing-room, or, even if picaresque novels (the alternative), they were realistic, but the reality was of a class society and one seen from above. Such literary traditions were useless to Americans whose social realities were completely different, and who had had to probe the heart of their reality. We see this necessary rejection of writing in the English modes put with conscious aggressiveness by Melville, but with intelligence too, in his pioneer essay on Hawthorne in 1850, where he argued the case against a 'colonial' literature, however accomplished, and stated the requirements for a national one. He saw in Hawthorne the desired type of distinctively American creativity. As 1850 was also the year of the publication of *The Scarlet Letter*, the achievement of that idea had already been effected, as it had been much earlier in the many substantial tales about the American past which Hawthorne had been writing on since his youth. Rejecting the Boston school of genteel or Anglophile writers, Melville declares:

Intolerance has come to exist in this matter. You must believe in Shakespeare's inapproachability, or quit the country. But what sort of a belief is this for an American, a man who is bound to carry republican progressiveness into Literature as well as in Life? Believe me, my friends, that men not very much inferior to Shakespeare are this day being born on the banks of the Ohio. And the day will come when you shall say, Who reads a book by an Englishman that is a modern? Now I do not say that Nathaniel of Salem is a greater man than William of Avon, or as great. But the difference between the two men is by no means immeasurable. Let America, then, prize and cherish her writers; yea, let her glorify them. And while she has good kith and kin of her own to take to her bosom, let her not lavish her embraces upon the household of an alien...

Let us believe then that there is no hope for us in these smooth, pleasing writers who owe their chief reputation to the self-acknowledged imitation of a foreign model... They but furnish an appendix to Goldsmith and other English authors. And we want no American Goldsmiths, nay, we want no American Miltons. Let us away with this leaven of literary flunkeyism towards England. While we are rapidly preparing for that political supremacy among the nations which prophetically awaits us at the close of the present century, in a literary point of view we are deplorably unprepared for it. Let us boldly condemn all imitation, though it comes to us graceful and fragrant as the morning; and foster all originality, though at first it be crabbed and ugly as our own pine knots. The truth is, that in one point of view this matter of a national literature has come to such a pass with us, that in some sense we must turn bullies. And now, as an excellent author of your own flesh and blood – an inimitating, and, perhaps, in his way, an inimitable man – whom better can I commend to you than Nathaniel Hawthorne?

He shared the chauvinism of Henry James's father, but he has also put a sound case for an American literature, and he ends with an undeniable truth: 'Great geniuses are a part of the times; they themselves *are* the times, and possess a correspondent colouring.'

Melville himself was stimulated by Hawthorne's achievement to follow his lead as a novelist. They both expressed American insights and attitudes in fictions embodying American types of character, in typically American situations and settings, characters speaking an American idiom with the object of examining the American past which had produced their prose. For Hawthorne this meant going back to the early settlers to find out how the deplorable contemporary America had come about. Fenimore Cooper had long been working on these lines, questioning, like Hawthorne, the quality and values of the American achievement. For already by their prime it had become evident to these first American novelists that the development of their nation had been in a direction fatal to creative writers: Hawthorne and Melville soon dried up in despair of support and countenance; Cooper, the American Scott as he was known, visiting England saw with bitterness the difference between the success and esteem Scott had earned and the indifference of America towards its creative writers. In the next generation Henry James fled the country, justified by Coopers's dictum: 'If any man is excusable for deserting his country, it is the American artist.'

But in the age of Cooper and Hawthorne, in James's youth in New York and a generation later in Edith Wharton's society of the New York rich old families, English was still the spoken language of the educated, as French was in Tsarist Russia. So these writers wrote standard English though their American characters spoke an appropriate American idiom – and one notices in Henry James's novels how much more life and individuality there is in his American characters' speech than there is in his English characters, as in *The Bostonians*, *The Portrait of a Lady*, and other early and middle-period works, while by his last phase he had lost his ear for American idiom by living in England. It was the uncultured frontiersmen, the pioneers of the Middle and Far West and the South-West, who developed a thoroughly American idiom and vocabulary, spoken with such effect by Melville's whalemen and Mark Twain's southern characters. Mark Twain, who came from the frontier world, systematically adopted his regional dialects and exploited their richness and humour, not only for his characters' dialogues but also as himself the narrator, achieving by this means a masterpiece in *Huckleberry Finn*, and other brilliant successes like *Pudd'nhead Wilson*, *Roughing It*, and *Life on the Mississippi*. But these were therefore unacceptable to the genteel American reading-public, consistently discouraging American artists as Edith Wharton notes in her autobiography, and I remember my husband telling me that T. S. Eliot – who came from Mark Twain's own home-town – told him that he had not read Mark Twain because the Eliots considered him 'low' when *he* was a boy.

But the American novel had started with hopeful prospects for a literature. Hawthorne, born in 1804, was the right man at the right time. He himself, in his family history and his college education, his wide reading, his sensitive conscience and habit of introspection, combined the stresses of national history with an understanding of its inherent shortcomings. He suffered from the discovery that in a Puritan society the artist had no recognized function. The sins of these intolerant settlers lay on his conscience, as other national sins tormented the minds of the other American novelists – slave-owning for Mark Twain, the destruction of virgin America and of the Redskins for Fenimore Cooper, the deathly materialism of the American wealthy for Edith Wharton, for instance. This sense of guilt in the major American novelists is quite different from European guilt, for instance that which possessed our Early Victorian novelists because of the slums and other inhumane developments of their nineteenth-century industrial society, for *they* could suggest remedies and believe they would be implemented – that is why they wrote novels – whereas the bitterness of Hawthorne and his successors was due to their recognition of an irrevocable process of corruption of the land and of society that, they now saw, was due to the fallacies and flaws in the confident American theory.

Already Hawthorne had opened his first novel with a short chapter that is a symbolic statement of the fallacy and which points to the dreadful consequences, with a profound irony. He was able to escape from the prosaic realism of English eighteenth-century and Regency novels, which dealt with a sophisticated class-culture, and to invoke instead suitable primitive superstitions and beliefs, the supernatural figure of folk-religion and of historical legend, and the dreams and visions of folk-lore, to give his allegories an imaginative density, emotional overtones and a more profound layer of meanings, combining the sophisticated intellectual content with primitive elements which, though universal, are given by Hawthorne a national character. This combination we find characteristic of all major novels – even the work of such an intellectual novelist as George Eliot.

At the time Hawthorne was working on his remarkable early tales, Fenimore Cooper had also been publishing novels to characterize the settlement of the American continent and to assess its cultural and moral consequences. Like Hawthorne, he was the descendant of a family with traditions of involvement with colonial and post-colonial history, as land-owners of conflicting loyalties – like W. H. Prescott, the American historian, who wrote in his study under the crossed swords of his two grandfathers who had fought on opposite sides in the War of Independence. Thus Cooper had conflicting sympathies, at once English and American, in his traditions, which made him peculiarly sensitive to the American situation, and though proud of its democracy and practical achievements, he was highly critical of the other results. *The Pioneers*, a novel so much admired by D. H. Lawrence, was the first of the series in which Cooper mythologized the conflict between the Red Indians and the settlers, between Nature and the white despoiler of the land, and it was published as early as 1823. Cooper saw that the native hunting peoples were doomed before the advance of the white settlers who must, in order to farm, clear the forests and plough up the prairies; but he could not forgive them for wasting the natural resources, which the Red Indians had religiously preserved, and as even farming became subordinate to urban life, which Cooper felt to be alien to America, his hero, the white hunter, the Leatherstocking, takes refuge from the progress of civilization by joining the thronging Indians and dying among them. Cooper's divided feelings about his America and his inner conflict are characteristic of all the classical American novelists.

But Cooper manifested these conflicts also in other kinds of novel, the kinds that, I think, are the reason for Conrad's expressed admiration for Cooper, whom he described in a letter as 'a great novelist and my master'. A very early novel of Cooper's *The Spy* (1821) focuses on the moral anguish and the ambiguities of the colonials in the War of Independence who were patriots from one point of view and traitors from the other, a difference of outlook which split American families and which made the War of Independence a kind of civil war. Cooper continued to work on this theme of moral conflict and doubt as to right and wrong in political issues by novels located in other settings than those of American history, such as *The Bravo* and *Wing and Wing*, this last being an adventure on the seas, strikingly reminiscent of Conrad's novel *The Rover*. Cooper's interest in the moral aberrations and violence that were problems in a lawless pioneer society as well as in the Indian and other American Wars, anticipated Dostoevsky's novelistic use of these themes. Yet a third variety of Cooper's novels, written in the late 1830s, deals with the Anglo-American confrontation – a subject we are apt to assume was invented by

Henry James; but though James is the supreme artist of this subject, he inherited a tradition of it, both popular and literary.

To anticipate, we should notice that the American novelists have different choices of folk-heroes: Hawthorne's are the dissidents in the cause of humane tolerance but also American early patriots who defied and defeated England; Cooper's are primitive settlers respectful towards American Nature, like the Leatherstocking, the professional bee-hunter, the sailors on the Great Lakes, and the good Indians – all those who maintained the life-style of the virgin continent of forests, lakes and prairie. Melville's are those who confront and wrestle with Nature, like his bold but disciplined whalemen and sailors (notice the panegyric in *Moby Dick* to the intrepid helmsman Bulkington) and the handsome sailor Billy Budd whose guileless nature makes him fall a victim to the sophisticated evil nature which cannot bear goodness – a truly American symbol; while in Melville's *Contes* (condensed novels rather than short stories) of his last writing phase in the mid-1850s, about life on land, his heroic protagonists are those who resist, but are defeated by, the commercial America that killed Melville himself as a writer, tragic characters like Billy Budd, the invalid Titan and Charlemont of *The Confidence Man*, Bartleby, Merrymusk of *Cock-a-Doodle-Doo!*, Benito Cereno. But with Henry James, in a later phase of American Society, now more sophisticated but with visibly fewer prospects of achieving a better and finer organization than that of the Old World, we find a self-protective myth of pathetic figures of American innocence defeated or corrrupted by Europeans. The concept of the naïvely good American who, though self-made as to fortune, is emotionally guileless and honourable, survives from Henry James to its contemporary version for Scott Fitzgerald of the 1920s in Jay Gatsby, even though Jay has risen by dubious means to great wealth made by organizing illegal supplies of alcohol in the Prohibition Era. Mark Twain in *Huckleberry Finn* sponsored *social* innocents – the runaway and ill-used slave Jim and his friend the outcast Huck, both primitives – to play off their unconscious innate right feeling against the baseness and vices of the civilized inhabitants of the country as they encounter these on the land or on the river, whether they are Southern gentlemen, farmers, town mobs or religious villagers. This general recognition by the creative writers of a failure in their society in human development and in its institutions, shown in their having become the enemy of all that Americans had thought of as good and admirable in their past, was a permanent source of irony and despair, reinforced by a belated awareness – though of course to be resisted in the interests of patriotism – that the mother-country had done better in these respects. Melville, who alone had no anti-English feeling or social prejudice, often registered in short stories and novels his respect for such purely English qualities as he found admirable, noting, for instance, that there was much less flogging in the English Navy than in the American because, he said, of the greater self-confidence in their authority of the English captains, owing to their habit of command in an aristocratic society. Though Melville, like Hawthorne, chose symbolic situations from history and chose distinctively American types (such as the American pragmatist, Captain Delano, in the short novel *Benito Cereno*), he moved their cases into the larger world of ethical questions, for his mind was philosophical in bent though working as an artist in the concrete of social as well as psychological realities.

Shifting the responsibility for American troubles on to the shoulders of England and measuring themselves against the Old World generally, became early a necessity for American writers (other than Melville), and Cooper in the 1830s had based novels on the confrontation of American types with English and Europeans, as Hawthorne did in a last novel *The Marble Faun*, as did also Henry James and Edith Wharton subsequently – confrontations enacted in England, Europe and America. This was made inevitable because most prosperous nineteenth-century Americans travelled to England and Western Europe as a duty, for cultural improvement and in search of pictures and other symbols of culture to take home. They thus encountered high cultures of the past embodied in visible forms (as George Eliot's puritan-formed Dorothea Casaubon did on her honeymoon in Rome in *Middlemarch*), but, more painfully, they met also a present culture embodied in superior manners and a finer social life, and in England, as even William James and Mark Twain ruefully noted, not merely internal beauty but a countryside landscaped and gardened, as well as productively farmed, and with the considerable charm of countless picturesque towns and villages, an aesthetic beauty America had never achieved. For patriotic Americans, the fact that the evils of feudalism and aristocracy had resulted in immemorial beauty still being maintained and added to at that, whereas American democracy had pioneered only ugliness and destruction, was morally distressing to them. It helped provoke American writers into a tradition of using the novel to question their ideas of progress: Randall Jarrell in the 1950s was still making his novel an enquiry of why such a rich and powerful country as his United States did not foster creative genius, and produce an educated and appreciative public for it, as the comparatively poor European countries and even tiny states in the Old World had done, and were still doing. Why, he asks, didn't America produce great artists, composers, writers and dramatists, painters and sculptors – the well-being of a great nation – though rich Americans have been historically collectors of European artifacts and housed them in endowed museums for public improvement? Why, since American democracy has provided abundantly endowed universities, and based on the ideas of progressive education too, for the education of all citizens and not merely an élite, why has no educated public for the arts existed? (We remember Melville's and Henry James Senior's confident predictions of American superiority in every respect.) All these are urgent questions for a poet and critic and university teacher as Jarrell was.

The inhospitality of northern Puritanism to the artist, as distinct from the aristocratic society which had been the traditional context that sustained the arts, was next examined in *The Europeans*, thus pursuing the subject known as the International Theme. A European-bred couple, of American parents, typically the one a gay young painter and his elder sister, a fascinating baroness married morganatically to a German prince, visit their rich, New England cousins as a speculation, he more innocently hoping to be commissioned to paint their portraits, she hoping for a rich American husband since her prince is trying to shed her. They are doomed to disappointment: the graces of life as understood in Europe are unknown to even the rich in New England, where gaiety, good conversation, and spontaneous feeling (instead of created feelings) are as ill-regarded as the arts. Except for the younger daughter of the house, who felt dissatisfied with her home, the simple-minded natives shrink from the sophisticated European-ized couple as frivolous, immoral and disturbing. They all talk

at cross-purposes, giving rise to a good deal of social comedy
that Jane Austen would have appreciated: by this technique,
each set of people is seen through the eyes of the other, allowing
James to weigh the merits and disadvantages of each culture,
and thus investigating also his own ambivalent feelings towards
his native country and the Old World. In the novel the outcome
is that the Baroness, who represents only a court society, is
utterly defeated and repulsed, while her brother, the artist,
triumphs by winning his younger cousin and her fortune and
carrying her off to Europe, where her love of laughter and moral
liberty is understood to find fulfilment. The tone of this little
drama is wittily ironic but James's mature treatment of the
general subject of the position of the artist in a Puritan and
Philistine society, *The Tragic Muse*, is conveniently removed
from America and takes place in a contrast between Late
Victorian England and late nineteenth-century France, and is
much more thorough.

But James was far from being merely an intellectual or
physical novelist. He was radically influenced not only by
popular American attitudes as we have seen, but by the crude
folk-myths which he developed in a more refined form, and
which form the basis of many stories and situations around
which his novels were constructed. James had absorbed them
in his youth in New York from the popular drama and tales.
All over America, from the 1820s onwards and for a century
later, plays were being performed which, like the similar tales,
had arisen from the American self-dramatization in relation to
England. James as a boy would have seen the 'Uncle Sam' or
'Brother Jonathan' plays, as they were called, which featured
an uncouth New England or Western character defeating, by
his rustic wit and shrewdness, the typical Briton, who is drawn
either as nefarious or ridiculously effete, the situation being a
patriotic stereotype. This developed into what Hawthorne
himself described as 'The American myth' when, as American
consul in England, he constantly met in real life Americans
demanding his help to pursue illusory claims to English titles
and estates. The Yankee plays, which developed out of the
earlier types I have described, showed a resourceful Yankee
come to England to prove himself the rightful heir to a title and
mansion, thus superseding the English holder, a daydream that
is the subject of one of James's very earliest published tales, *The*

Passionate Pilgrim, and in less crude forms it produced his American 'princesses' like Isabel Archer and Milly Theale and Maggie Verver, who are shown morally and personally superior to the English nobility, and often richer.

But the characteristic irony of the home-keeping American novelist is also painful – 'these probings at the axis of reality' Melville called them. The 'blackness' which he said he found in Hawthorne's work as characteristic of the truly American writer and which, he said, 'so fires and fascinates me' is inescapably mordant in Mark Twain, even in his brand of humour. *Huckleberry Finn* is a tissue of local ironies over profounder underlying ironies. For instance, Huck has to struggle to resist his acquired deplorable morality, in order to obey his innate moral sense or right feeling, when he decides to help Jim, the runaway slave, to reach the free states; for Huck, brought up in a slave-owning society, even though he shares none of its benefits, knows that a negro is someone's property and that it is wicked to rob that owner – this is the only morality he has learnt. 'All right then, I'll go to hide', he says desperately, having decided not to hand Jim over to his 'owner'. So he is shocked to find that Tom Sawyer, of respectable family and not a pariah like himself, is willing to help in the escape. So it turns out right at the end that Tom had known all along that Jim's owner had died and left Jim his freedom, otherwise, of course, Tom would not have helped smuggle Jim to freedom; he only entered on it as a game in the circumstances. And Huck learns this with relief, it frees him from the fear of having corrupted Tom. The irony, we see, was mordant.

Mark Twain had been brought up himself to assume negroes were merely property and had no rights or feelings, and his subsequent realization, on going out into the world, that this was not a universal truth but a horrifying evil filled him with disgust for the South and by extension, suspicion of his fellow-men and of organized society, and of religious institutions too, since the southerners were pious Baptists or similar, and he was filled with anger at every kind of cruelty. His novels and tales are essentially critical interpretations. Jim and Huck sample the various forms of Southern society such as lynch-law, family feuds shot to a finish, pride in a gentleman's code that is really contemptible and inhuman, and the pious farmers and their good wives, whose Christian conduct and feelings apply only to white people. Tom Sawyer, when he turns up, complements Huck as the product of this society, the kind of boy who, we can see, will grow up to be a smart business-man (seen clearly in the famous episode in the novel *Tom Sawyer* of the white-washing of Aunt Polly's fence). The structure and method of *Huckleberry Finn* are curiously like those of *The Confidence Man* of nearly thirty years earlier, though it is most unlikely Mark Twain ever saw Melville's novel. Melville also has made use of the boat going down the great American river, though his load of passengers are explicit representatives of the American public of his time, a society that Melville saw as morally fraudulent and spiritually dead, at the mercy of every form of con-man, whether literary moralist or medical quack, religious charlatan or financial speculator, all seen as avatars of the Devil who, by sweet-talking the passengers into subscribing money to some bogus cause, through playing on their weaknesses, show it to be a society bound for Hell.

Edith Wharton's subject was the American rich, and in her first successful novel, *The House of Mirth* (1905) and the maturer *The Custom of the Country* (1913), she analysed the New York society she was born into in order to expose what she personally had felt to be the worst features – 'the quality', she wrote, 'of making other standards [that is, any other than materialistic ones and social conventions] non-existent by ignoring them'. She saw it as a destructive society, 'underpinned by wasted human possibilities'. But her novels are carefully structured: each group or character is representative, in the American tradition, and each advances the ironies of the plot and of the American situation. In the later novel I have mentioned the theme is the destruction of the old static Society (society with a capital S) by the newly-rich barbarians, coming up from below or in from the raw Western states. The heroine Undine Spragg, daughter of a Melville-type speculator, hauls herself to the top of the ladder by a complete lack of moral sense, trampling underfoot husbands and son, family decencies and social codes, in a mounting irony. Edith Wharton's novels form a sequence, like Hawthorne's and Fenimore Cooper's, showing the progress, in the lifetime of each, of American deterioration from its original ideals. Edith Wharton shows its last stage, the disintegration of the family, which occurred in her later days.

Scott Fitzgerald's mythical character, the unfortunate Jay

Gatsby, is an irony in himself – the poor boy from the Middle West who had tried to form himself on the acclaimed American pattern for success, but had the misfortune to find himself in an America where there was no scope for honest enterprise except during the First World War when he *had* made good as a hero in the army. He remains naïve – he wants only love and friendship, but this now needs a lot of money, and he can make it only outside the law. The damage to respect for the law in the Prohibition Era was a new stage in American disintegration, for the corruption soon spread to every element in its society – even the great baseball competitions are now 'fixed' we learn from the novel, and the wealthy Americans who prey on Gatsby in his prosperity while despising him, and who eventually destroy him, make his essential innocence seem preferable to their brutal selfishness. The narrator of Gatsby's history ends it by noting the irony of the contrast between 'the fresh green breast of the new world' as it must have appeared to the first settlers, to whom, he says, it represented 'the last and greatest of all human dreams' and the inability to achieve that Utopian vision. 'The land of the future', which Henry James's father declared his country to be and which Melville too had at first anticipated, is, Fitzgerald says, 'a future that year by year recedes before us as we run ever faster and stretch out our arms farther in the vain hope of catching it'. This is a rather sentimental way of expressing what was for Americans a very unpleasant reality. Scott Fitzgerald's hero is idealized, even more than Henry James's self-made men, who of course had made their millions in at least legitimate business, whereas Jay Gatsby was a racketeer. We can see that not altogether consciously he stood in for the author: Scott Fitzgerald was himself the victim of the ideals of his age of American success, and prostituted his talent, wrecking himself as a writer and as a person too, in order to make a large income to gain and keep his beautiful wife and her life-style; this could only be done by writing for the American magazines, in a style and with romantic fictions acceptable to the media. This was the age of the corruption of the arts in America – tin-pan alley a substitute for music, the Hollywood cinema for drama, the glossy magazines for literature.

Fitzgerald's case is thus a good introduction to Randall Jarrell's novel, *Pictures from an Institution*, a generation after Scott

Fitzgerald. Sinyavsky, the Russian dissident and poet, wrote that all novelists have to find the model which suits them and enables them to interpret their reality. Jarrell chose the American progressive university, on the same principle, I imagine, that Trollope in Victorian England chose for his model the cathedral close and its hinterland. Trollope evidently felt that in a professedly Christian country, as Victorian England was, the genuineness of its religion could best be tested by examining a society endowed and ordained to practice that religion as a vocation. Jarrell, abandoning as hopeless the American city culture, says, in effect: in our universities at least we have a society of professional students, by definition, disinterested intellectuals, cultivated, endowed to support the life of the mind and inculcate in the young true values. Let us then look at what it does, in fact, to account for the absence in American life of what Europe has historically always been able to produce – creative geniuses in the arts and a society educated and trained to sustain them, peoples who, though not affluent, delighted in and cherished the arts and assisted the makers of art.

The resulting picture of Benton, the progressive post-Second World War American university, is rich in irony, and situations that though comedy, inspire serious, even despairing, reflections in the narrator. The critical eye through which we apprehend the reality is an American poet, who has an endowment at Benton for translating the poems of Rilke, and we have no doubt that *he* at least, like his author, has a genuine and informed passion for literature, music, art and ideas, but, we note, he is, in this, isolated. He is alerted to what is wrong with the education purveyed by this university by the presence of two Europeans, Dr Rosenbaum, an Austrian composer, and his Russian wife who had been an outstanding opera-singer, refugees from Hitler's Europe, who protect themselves from the American scene by ironic amusement, she as a spectator and he as Composer in Residence at the university. Literature was previously taught there by a Miss Batterson, a Southern real lady who represented the genteel American tradition then in its last stage of dissolution by its acceptance of democratic standards and progressive education – her attitude to the teaching of literature was, as currently, 'therapeutic' and her democratic beliefs precluded the applying of standards to her students' work. 'Aesthetic discrimination', Jarrell's narrator remarks, 'is not pleasanter, seems no more just and rational to those discriminated against, than racial discrimination.' But without standards and discrimination there cannot, of course, be literature and a public capable of distinguishing the good from the bad. Jarrell notes that the disaster originated in the democratic theory of equality – in the 'demand' American education could not meet – that it give a continent a college education! As these fallacies have spread to England and to Western Europe we all, as educators and ones, who are, moreover, engaged in teaching literature, must be deeply concerned. Miss Batterson's successor is the novelist, Gertrude Johnson, a brilliant writer and intellectual, whose talents in such a society have been characteristically directed to a warfare against humanity. We see not only why this is so but feel some sympathy with her, in her contempt for the President of the university who was so perfectly adjusted to his environment 'that sometimes you could not tell who was the environment and who was President Robbins', and, in a chapter near the end, in her disposal of Mr Daudier, a typical American man of letters, who 'made anthologies all the time' and was 'a director of a club that picked books for readers who didn't know what to read'. He is also a literary critic for the Press, a creative novelist, and a writer of one-act plays, and has published several insignificant volumes of poetry – as Gertrude tells him, with intent to insult, he is 'a really democratic writer'. We had previously, related to this, a significant little scene between Gertrude and the civic-minded wife of the professor of sociology, Flo Whittaker, which highlights the effects of the teaching of literature in American universities, and which is spreading here:

Gertrude was looking at Flo narrowly, like a hydrogen bomb staring at an Act of God. 'Have you ever read *Le Misanthrope*?' she asked Flo.
'I don't *think* so. No, I'm almost sure I haven't.'
'It's a play by Molière about –.'
'Oh, *that* one! Of course I've read it', said Flo. 'I read it in fourth year French.'
'Sometimes you – sometimes one of the characters reminds me of you. Do you remember a character named Alceste?'
'Oh, *no*', said Flo. 'I just read it in fourth year French.'

Remembering that George Eliot felt that *Le Misanthrope* is 'the finest, most complete production of *its* kind in the world', we may reflect that when literature is studied merely as a means to acquire credits towards an American university degree, the whole object of introducing the young to a great work of literature is frustrated, and literature itself will perish.

In such a society – for the students of art, drama and ballet, under the kind of instructors they have, are shown to be as possessed of no more understanding of these arts than Flo, or than Gertrude's students have of literature – in such a society Gertrude's novels are, as an Irishman had said of them, 'a Barmecide feast given by a fireworks company'. She is essentially uncreative. Her books, says the narrator, 'were a systematic, detailed and conclusive condemnation of mankind for being stupid and bad'. She, of course, uses her year's appointment at Benton to get material for writing one of her devastating novels about it and its staff. But she is incapacitated as a novelist, Jarrell argues, because she has no sympathy for humanity:

Gertrude pointed at the world and said, her voice clear and loud: 'You see! You see!' But as you looked along that stretched shaking finger, you didn't see, you saw through. Her vision was too penetrating. She showed that anything, anything at all, is not what it seems; and if anything is not anything, it is nothing. How Gertrude did like Swift!...She saw the worst: it was, indeed, her only principle of explanation.

This is a true insight into the state of the American novel since the last stage of the classical American novelists. Novelists without any belief in humanity and life are essentially uncreative. Gertrude, for all her wit, powers of observation, courage and independence, was disqualified as a novelist, Jarrell says, because 'she had one fault more radical than all the rest: she did not know – or rather, did not believe – what it was like to be a human being. Her hand was against every man's; she had not signed the human contract when the rest of us signed it.'

'So because of all of this – of all of this, and much more – even the best of Gertrude's books were habitat groups in a Museum of Natural History; topography, correct; meteorological information, correct; condition of skins, good; mounting of horns, correct...But inside there were old newspapers, papier mâché, clockwork.' Her characteristic emotion as a writer was anger. 'To her generosity, tenderness, good-humoured indifference were unaccountable except as fear or caution.' Gertrude, in fact, is a continuation of the typical contemporary American women writers, one of them being Mary McCarthy to whom this novel is dedicated.

After the comedy of the Art Night at Benton, and Gertrude's annihilation of the New England man of letters, there is the outstanding and corrective scene when the narrator goes home with Dr Rosenbaum to find his Russian wife reading Milton's *Comus*, which she has discovered for herself as 'almost better than Hölderlin'. She reads aloud Comus's account of the effects on him of singing – first of his mother Circe's and then of the Lady's – which ends 'such a sacred and home-felt delight. Such sober certainty of waking bliss, I never heard till now.' He himself then reads to the Rosenbaums Milton's account of a plant that, alas, does not flourish in America:

> But in another country, as he said,
> Bore a bright golden flower, but not in this soyl:
> Unknown, and like esteemed, and the dull swayn
> Treads on it daily with his clouted shoon,
> And yet more med'cinal is it than that *Moly*
> That *Hermes* once to wise *Ulysses* gave.

'All of us had, I think, the same rueful smile', he says. He now shares these European survivors' attitude to America.

We are reminded of a previous occasion, when the ageing Mrs Rosenbaum, looking back on *her* career in Europe and her husband's, said: 'We at least have the memory of having had a world that respected us.' And in their company the narrator says that 'Gertrude, and Mr Daudier, and Miss Rasmussen [the art teacher] were thousands of years away.' Dr Rosenbaum in the final chapter tells them a story, a parable of how the standards of music and learning that originally looked to courts for maintenance in Europe, were destroyed by democracy and industrialism, and which he calls 'a bedtime story from the Evening of the West'.

It is the experience of knowing the Rosenbaums and absorbing their reaction to the United States and its culture and assumptions that makes the narrator question his – for, as he says, 'you saw that they had brought along with them, when they had had to cross the Atlantic, Europe'. Nevertheless, Gottfried Rosenbaum 'always had a great deal of sympathy for the American past; he said that Americans had tried to do what had never before even been tried – "perhaps", he said, "they had failed because it could not be done"'. Thus the method of James in *The Europeans* was still the necessary one for the American novelist of the mid-1950s even though it led him to different conclusions. He reflects that when he thought of the Rosenbaums and himself 'in terms of the old American comparison of Europeans and Americans, something was wrong'. In those novels of Henry James, he remembers, an American is someone kept good by *naïveté*, which gives his country a moral victory over Europe. But Jarrell's narrator now has his doubts of this as a great truth: 'to believe this I would have had to be good and naïve', which he can't claim Americans to be, or believe, as the old American novels claimed, that the sophistication of Europeans (seen here in the persons of the Rosenbaums) made *them* bad. He feels that perhaps there *is* one superiority of his country, that the American mind is more open to experience than a European's.

Thus, the method of justifying the American democratic culture, invented by Fenimore Cooper and Hawthorne, and refined by their successors, the method of Henry James in *The Europeans*, was still the necessary technique for an outstanding American novelist and critic of post-Second World War America, even though it led him to question their conclusions.

Hawthorne as poet

I

For an English person to offer an opinion on Hawthorne, much more an evaluation of his *oeuvre*, must be felt in America to be an impertinence. But the excuse that would justify writing on Hawthorne in an English context – that he is, except as author of one 'Puritanical' novel, unread and unrecognized, will, it seems to me, serve here too if somewhat modified. To me, a tremendous admirer of long standing of much of Hawthorne's work, it appears that the essential nature of his achievement has not been isolated and established critically, in spite of the immense amount that has been published on Hawthorne the man, Hawthorne as material for the psychologist, the Hawthorne period and all the rest. I should like to present my own reading of his work, if only to get endorsement from others. In England one can never assume an intelligent knowledge of Hawthorne in the professional world of letters – witness the complacently stupid whole-page article in our august *Times Literary Supplement* two years ago when Mr Randall Stewart's book came up for review. And in the English academic world Hawthorne's existence as a considerable writer is not even acknowledged. But what is one to conclude when faced with the account of Hawthorne in that admirable American work *The American People* (1949) by Professor H. B. Parkes? Here Hawthorne is characterized as

a man of low emotional pressure who adopted throughout his life the role of an observer. Remaining always aloof from the world around him, he was able to record what he felt with a remarkable balance and detachment...But since he lacked the compulsive drive of the writer who is himself the victim of conflict and must find a way of salvation, his work lacked force and energy. Carefully and delicately constructed, it was devoid of color and drama and almost passionless. Hawthorne's obsessing personal problem was his sense of isolation. He came to regard isolation as almost the root of all evil, and made it the theme of many of his stories. But Hawthorne's treatment of the subject was always too conscious and deliberate; he expressed it allegorically and not in symbols; and consequently he was unable to say anything about it that enlarges our understanding either of human nature or of the society in which Hawthorne lived.

This is in effect the account of Hawthorne that has always been in currency – stated for instance with more authority and more persuasively by Mr Yvor Winters in the interesting essay 'Maule's Curse, or Hawthorne and the Problem of Allegory', where, though he claims that *The Scarlet Letter* is 'faultless, in scheme and detail; it is one of the chief masterpieces of English prose', yet he classifies it as 'pure allegory', and dismisses all 'Hawthorne's sketches and short stories [as] at best slight performances'. Even Henry James, whose monograph on Hawthorne is felt, and was clearly intended, to be the tribute of an artist to the predecessor from whom he inherits, even James demurs at what he calls 'allegory, quite one of the lighter exercises of the imagination'. But it is clear that James is deploring Hawthorne's merely fanciful pieces; he exempts the works 'redolent of a rich imagination'. The standard account relegates Hawthorne along with Bunyan to an inferior class of writer who depends for his effects on 'allegory', something mechanical and inferior, as Dr Johnson implied when he wrote 'allegory is perhaps one of the most pleasing vehicles of instruction'. But when James wrote 'Hawthorne is perpetually looking for images which shall place themselves in picturesque correspondence with the spiritual facts with which he is concerned, and of course the search is of the very essence of poetry', he admits, however inadequately, that Hawthorne's intention is a poetic one, nothing less. Similarly, in general acceptance Hawthorne is a 'delicate' writer, but when he is praised for his 'delicacy' it is intended to stamp his art as something minor. I should prefer to have the purity of his writing noted instead. Nor is the epithet 'charming', selected by Henry James, appropriate.

The account, as endorsed by Mr Parkes, contrives to be unjust to Hawthorne's object and to ignore the very nature of his art. Hawthorne's less interesting work bulks large, no doubt, but it is easily cut free from what is his essential contribution to American literature. The essential Hawthorne – and he seems to me a great genius, the creator of a literary tradition as well as a wonderfully original and accomplished artist – is the author of *Young Goodman Brown*, *The Maypole of Merry Mount*, *My Kinsman Major Molineux*, *The Snow-Image*, *The Blithedale Romance*, *The Scarlet Letter*, and of a number of sketches and less pregnant stories associated with these works such as *The Gray Champion*, *Main Street*, *Old News*, *Endicott of the Red Cross*, *The Artist of the Beautiful*. This work is not comparable with the productions of the eighteenth-century 'allegorical' essayists nor is it in the manner of Spenser, Milton, or Bunyan – whom of course it can be seen he has not merely studied but assimilated. The first batch of works I specified is essentially dramatic, its use of language is poetic, and it is symbolic, and richly so, as is the dramatic poet's. In fact I should suggest that Hawthorne can have gone to school with no one but Shakespeare for his inspiration and model.[1] Mr Wilson Knight's approach to Shakespeare's tragedies – each play an expanded metaphor – is a cue for the method of rightly apprehending these works of Hawthorne's, where the 'symbol' is the thing itself, with no separable paraphrasable meaning as in an allegory: the language is directly evocative. Rereading this work, one is certainly not conscious of a limited and devitalized talent employing a simple-minded pedestrian technique; one is constantly struck by fresh subtleties of organization, of intention, expression and feeling, of original psychological insight and a new minting of terms to convey it, as well as of a predominantly dramatic construction. Yet of the above-mentioned works, apart from *The Scarlet Letter* which has had a good deal of inadequate attention, I can't find any serious *literary* criticism, even in *The American Renaissance* where Hawthorne is evidently intended in some way to be a focus and key-figure. Mr Quentin Anderson at the end of his article 'Henry James and the New Jerusalem' (*Kenyon Review*, Autumn, 1946) offers a metaphysical account of both *The Snow-Image* and *Major Molineux* – but these seem to me subjective interpretations (the second misses Hawthorne's meaning entirely) and not literary criticism rooted in the texts. The recent spate of Hawthorne books has not yet reached England but I am told – though I should be glad to hear that I have been told wrongly – that they add nothing.

The aspect of Hawthorne that I want to stress as the important one, decisive for American literature, and to be found most convincingly in the works I specified, is this: that he was the critic and interpreter of American cultural history and thereby the finder and creator of a literary tradition from which sprang Henry James on the one hand and Melville on the other. I find it impossible to follow Mr Parkes's argument[2] that 'what is lacking in [Hawthorne's] framework of experience is any sense of society as a kind of organic whole to which the individual belongs and in which he has his appointed place. And lacking the notion of social continuity and tradition, [he] lacks also the corresponding metaphysical conception of the natural universe as an ordered unity which harmonizes with human ideals.'[3] It is precisely those problems, the relation of the individual to society, the way in which a distinctively American society developed and how it came to have a tradition of its own, the relation of the creative writer to the earlier nineteenth-century American community, and his function and how he could contrive to exercise it – the exploration of these questions and the communication in literary art of his findings – that are his claim to importance. It is true that he is most successful in treating pre-Revolutionary America, but that, after all, is, as he saw it, the decisive period, and *The Blithedale Romance* is the finest test of his dictum in *Old News* that 'All philosophy that would abstract mankind from the present is no more than words'. As I see it, Hawthorne's sense of being part of the contemporary America could be expressed only in concern for its evolution – he needed to see how it had come about, and by discovering what America had, culturally speaking, started from and with, to find what choices had faced his countrymen and what they had had to sacrifice in order to create that distinctive 'organic whole'. He was very conscious of the nature of his work; he asserted that to be the function of every great writer, as when in *The Old Manse* he wrote: 'A work of genius is but the newspaper of a century, or perchance of a hundred centuries'. (Indeed, in some sketches, such as *Old News*, we can see the half-way stage between the newspapers and the work of genius; these sketches have a function like that of the *Letters* of Jane Austen in the evolution of her novels.) And he prepared himself for the task by study, though Providence had furnished him with an eminently usable private Past, in the

history of his own family, which epitomized the earlier phases
of New England history; this vividly stylized the social history
of Colonial America, provided him with a personal mythology,
and gave him an emotional stake in the past, a private key to
tradition. We know that his first pieces which he later burnt
in despair of getting published were called *Seven Tales of My
Native Land*. Though he was the very opposite of a Dreiser
(whom Mr Parkes backs in contrast) yet I should choose to
describe Hawthorne as a sociological novelist in effect, employing
a poetic technique which communicates instead of stating his
findings. The just comparison with *The Scarlet Letter* is not *The
Pilgrim's Progress* but *Anna Karenina*, which in theme and
technique it seems to me astonishingly to resemble. This brings
up again the objection cited above that 'Remaining always
aloof from the world around him, he was able to record what
he felt with a remarkable balance and detachment, but lacked
the compulsive drive of the writer who is himself the victim of
conflict and must find a way of salvation.' There is disguised
here a romantic assumption about the Artist. We surely recognize, equally in the Shakespeare of the great tragedies and
Measure for Measure, in Henry James in his novels and *nouvelles*,
and in the Tolstoy of *Anna* (as opposed to the Tolstoy of
Resurrection) that 'remarkable balance and detachment' which
is indispensable to the greatest achievement of literary art. Like
these artists Hawthorne in his best work is offering in dramatic
form an analysis of a complex situation in which he sides with
no one party but is imaginatively present in each, having
created each to represent a facet of the total experience he is
concerned to communicate. The analysis and the synthesis help
us to find our own 'way of salvation' (not a form of words I
should have chosen). Tolstoy *was* in many respects Levin, as we
know, but *Anna Karenina* the novel is not presented through
Levin's eyes, and could not have been written by Levin. To
analyse the way in which Hawthorne actually works as a writer
is the only safe way to come at the nature of his creation, to
make sure we are taking what he has written and neither
overlooking it nor fathering on the author some misreading of
our own or of inert traditional acceptance. Until there is an
established reading of the texts it is impossible to evaluate an
author at all, and it is this, the very first business of the critic,
that seems never to have been done for Hawthorne.

The Maypole of Merry Mount is an early work bearing obvious
signs of immaturity but it also shows great originality, and it
is a root work, proving that Hawthorne had laid the foundations of much later successes, notably *The Scarlet Letter* and *The
Blithedale Romance*, in his beginnings almost. It proves also that
he decided in his youth on his characteristic technique. We
notice that it is essentially a poetic technique: the opening is
almost too deliberately poetic in rhythm and word-order. But
once the convention has been established in the first two
paragraphs, he relaxes and proceeds less artificially. We are,
or should be, struck in this early piece by the mastery
Hawthorne achieves in a new form of prose art, by the skill with
which he manages to convey ironic inflexions and to control
transitions from one layer of meaning to another, and by which
he turns, as it was to become his great distinction to do, history
into myth and anecdote into parable. The essential if not the
greatest Hawthorne had so soon found himself.

The tale originally had a sub-title: 'A Parable', and in a few
prefatory sentences Hawthorne wrote that 'the curious history
of the early settlement of Mount Wollaston, or Merry Mount'
furnishes 'an admirable foundation for a philosophic romance'
– we see his decision to take for his own from the start the
associations of 'romance' and not of 'novel' or some such term
suggesting a disingenuous connection between fiction and daily
life. He continued: 'In the slight sketch here attempted the
facts, recorded on the grave pages of our New England
annalists, have wrought themselves, almost spontaneously, into
a sort of allegory.' If an allegory (unfortunate word), it is a 'sort'
that no experience of *The Faerie Queen* and *The Pilgrim's Progress*
can prepare us for. Its distinctive quality is its use of symbols
to convey meaning, and a boldness of imagination and
stylization which while drawing on life does not hesitate to
rearrange facts and even violate history in that interest. The
outline of the historically insignificant Merry Mount affair,
whether as recorded by the Puritan historian Governor Bradford
or so very differently by the protagonist Thomas Merton in his
entertaining *New England Canaan*, was a godsend to Hawthorne,
who saw in it a means of precipitating his own reactions to his
forefathers' choice. While Hawthorne's imagination was
historical in a large sense, he was never an imaginative

recreator of the romantic past, a historical novelist: he had always from the first very clearly in view the *criticism* of the past. The past was his peculiar concern since it was the source of his present. He always works through the external forms of a society to its essence and its origin. He felt that the significance of early America lay in the conflict between the Puritans who became New England and thus America, and the non-Puritans who were, to him, merely the English in America and whom he partly with triumph but partly also with anguish sees as being cast out (here is a source of conflict). He saw this process as a symbolic recurring struggle, an endless drama that he recorded in a series of works – *The Maypole, My Kinsman Major Molineux, Endicott of the Red Cross, The Gray Champion, The Scarlet Letter, The Blithedale Romance*, among others – that together form something that it would not be fanciful to describe as a ritual drama reminding us of, for instance, the Norse Edda. If his artistic medium is primitive, his intention is not. It is a kind of spiritual and cultural casting-up of accounts: what was lost and what gained, what sacrificed to create what? he is perpetually asking, and showing.

Perhaps the American Puritans, who must if so have had none of the humane qualities of Bunyan and his class that make *Pilgrim's Progress* so pleasing – perhaps those who emigrated were more intensively intolerant than those who remained at home, or perhaps the persecuting aspect of their way of life was peculiarly present to Hawthorne because of the witch-hanging judge and the Quaker-whipping Major among his ancestors. But the essential truth Hawthorne rightly seized on, that the decisive minority set themselves in absolute hostility to the immemorial culture of the English folk with its Catholic and ultimately pagan roots, preserved in song and dance, festivals and superstitions, and especially the rites and dramatic practices of which the May-Day ceremonies were the key. Morton did rear a Maypole at Merry Mount and the fanatic Governor Endicott did indeed (but only after Morton had been seized and shipped home) visit the settlement and have the abominable tree cut down. Moreover the early theologians and historians had dramatized in their writings the elements of the scene in scriptural and theological terms. But this theological myth Hawthorne adapted to convey subtle and often ironic meanings, just as he freely adapts the historical facts. Morton was actually as well as ideally a High Churchman of good birth, a Royalist and deliberately anti-Puritan, but the object of his settlement was profitable trading with the Indians. Having none of the Puritans' conviction of the damned state of the savages, he made friends with them. Thus Hawthorne could make these settlers embody the old way of living as opposed to the new. He starts with the Maypole as the symbol of the pagan religion for 'what chiefly characterized the colonists of Merry Mount was their veneration for the Maypole. It has made their true history a poet's tale.' A living tree, 'venerated' for it is the centre of life and changes with the seasons, it is now on the festival of Midsummer's Eve hung with roses, 'some that had been gathered in the sunniest spots of the forest and others, of still richer blush, which the colonists had reared from English seed'. Here we have the earliest use of one of Hawthorne's chief symbols, the rose, and we notice that the native wild rose and the cultivated rose carried as seed from England (with generations of grafting and cultivation behind it) are in process of being mingled at Merry Mount. Round the tree the worshippers of the natural religion are figured with extraordinary vitality of imagination: 'Gothic monsters, though perhaps of Grecian ancestry', the animal-masked figures of mythology and primitive art (man as wolf, bear, stag and he-goat); 'And, almost as wondrous, stood a real bear of the dark forest, lending each of his fore-paws to the grasp of a human hand, and as ready for the dance as any in that circle. His inferior nature rose half-way to meet his companions as they stooped'; 'the Salvage Man, well known in heraldry, hairy as a baboon and girdled with green leaves'; Indians real and counterfeit. The harmony between man and beast and nature that was once recognized by a religious ritual could hardly be more poetically conjured up. Then the youth and maiden who represent the May Lord and Lady are shown; they are about to be permanently as well as ritually married, by an English priest who wears also 'a chaplet of the native vine-leaves'. Later on he is named by Endicott as 'Blackstone', though Hawthorne protects himself against the fact that the historic Blaxton had nothing to do with Merry Mount by an equivocal footnote: Blackstone here represents a poetic license which Hawthorne is perfectly justified in taking. Blackstone, who is similarly imported into *The Scarlet Letter* in a key passage, was actually not a High Churchman nor 'a clerk of Oxford' as he declares in *The Maypole*, but like most New England divines a Cambridge man and anti-Episcopalian. But he must be of Oxford because Hawthorne needs him to represent Catholicism and Royalism, to complete the culture-complex of Merry Mount, which has been shown in every other respect to be ancient, harmonious and traditional, a chain of life from the dim past, from the tree and animal upwards, all tolerated and respected as part of the natural and right order. The reader is expected to take the reference to the historical Blaxton, who like Endicott and Ann Hutchinson, among others, become in Hawthorne's art cultural heroes. How eminently adapted for Hawthorne's purpose he was is seen in this account by the historian of *The Colonial Period of American History*:

The Rev. William Blaxton, B.A., M.A., Emmanuel College, Cambridge...removed to the western slope of Shawmut peninsula [Beacon Hill] where...near an excellent spring, he built a house, planted an orchard, raised apples, and cultivated a vegetable garden....Leaving Boston in 1635, disillusioned because of the intolerance of the Puritan magistrates, he went southward...saying as he departed, 'I came from England because I did not like the Lord Bishops, but I cannot join with you because I would not be under the Lord Brethren.' He too wanted to worship God in his own way.

He represents, among other things, the crowning, the un-Puritan virtue of tolerance, one of Hawthorne's main positives. Without what he stands for the dance and drama round the Maypole and the whole pagan year-cycle of 'hereditary pastimes' would be negligible in comparison with the Christian culture even of the Puritans.

Meanwhile a band of Puritans in hiding are watching the scene. To them the masquers and their comrades are like 'those devils and ruined souls with whom their superstitions peopled the black wilderness'. For

Unfortunately there were men in the new world, of a sterner faith than these Maypole worshippers. Not far from Merry Mount was a settlement of Puritans, most dismal wretches, who said their prayers before daylight, and then wrought in the forest or the cornfield, till evening made it prayer time again.

This, to judge by the 'most dismal wretches', is to be discounted by the reader as probably the prejudiced view of the Maypole worshippers, just as to the Puritans the others appear to be 'the crew of Comus'. But if so persuaded, we are brought up short by a characteristic taut statement about the Puritans, shocking both in its literal and allegorical implications, that immediately follows: 'Their weapons were always at hand to shoot down the straggling savage.' At Merry Mount we have seen a life where the 'savage', without and within the human breast, is accepted as part of life. Hawthorne continues in the same tone:

When they met in conclave, it was never to keep up the old English mirth, but to hear sermons three hours long, or to proclaim bounties on the heads of wolves and the scalps of Indians. Their festivals were fast days, and their chief pastime the singing of psalms. Woe to the youth or maiden who did but dream of a dance! The selectman nodded to the constable; and there sat the light-heeled reprobate in the stock; or if he danced, it was round the whipping-post, which might be termed the Puritan Maypole.

The practices of the Puritan are described as being a horrible parody of those of the Maypole worshippers, a deliberate offence against the spirit of Life. The force of the cunning phrase 'to proclaim bounties on the heads of wolves and the scalps of Indians', charged with a sense of the inhumanity that levelled the Indian with the wolf, should not be overlooked.

I need not continue to analyse and quote in detail, I hope, to demonstrate the success of the kind of literary art Hawthorne has here created, but I want to note a few more of his total effects, by way of prelude to his later work. We have seen and felt what the religion of the old order was. We find ourselves then inescapably faced by Hawthorne with the question: And what did the Puritans worship? We are left in no doubt as to Hawthorne's answer: Force. Hawthorne had realized that religion is a matter of symbols, and his choice of appropriate symbols is not at all simple-minded. The Maypole worshippers are not, it turns out, to be accepted without qualification. They have another symbolic quality attached to them, they are 'silken' – 'Sworn triflers of a life-time, they would not venture among the sober truths of life, not even to be truly blest.' Everyone was 'gay' at Merry Mount, but what really was 'the quality of their mirth'? 'Once, it is said, they were seen following a flower-decked corpse, with merriment and festive music, to his grave. But did the dead man laugh?' We have been rounded on as in the passage about the Puritans. Hawthorne is preparing a more complex whole for us, and preparing us to receive it. The term for the Puritans corresponding to 'silken' for the settlers is 'iron'. We find it immediately after the passage quoted above where their practices are described as systematically inhumane. A party comes 'toiling through the difficult woods, each with a horse-load of iron armour to burden his footsteps'. A little later they are 'men of iron', and when they surround and overpower the Maypole worshippers their leader is revealed as iron all through: 'So stern was the energy of his aspect, that the whole man, visage, frame and soul, seemed wrought of iron, gifted with life and thought, yet all of one substance with his headpiece and breastplate. It was the Puritan of Puritans; it was Endicott himself.' He cuts down the Maypole with his sword, which he rests on while deciding the fate of the May Lord and Lady, and 'with his own gauntleted hand' he finally crowns them with the wreath of mingled roses from the ruin of the Maypole. The associations of iron are all brought into play, suggesting the rigid system which burdens life, the metal that makes man militant and ultimately inhuman, and it is spiritually the sign of heaviness and gloom, opposed in every way to the associations of lightness – silken, sunny, gay and mirthful, used for the followers of the old way of life. The iron imagery is finally concentrated in the doom brought on New England by the Puritans' victory at Merry Mount: 'It was a deed of prophecy. As the moral gloom of the world overpowers systematic gaiety...' The armour in *Endicott of the Red Cross* and *The Scarlet Letter* has more extensive meanings too.

The Puritans' religion is expressed in their rites – acts of persecution, oppression and cruelty. Endicott and his followers pass sentence on 'the heathen crew'. Their tame bear is to be shot – 'I suspect witchcraft in the beast', says the leader, and even the 'long glossy curls' on the May Lord's head must be cut. 'Crop it forthwith, and that in the true pumpkin-shell fashion' – the brutal denial of personal dignity and natural comeliness is indicated with striking economy. The language of Bunyan is made to sound very differently in these mouths; Hawthorne, a master of language, has many such resources at his command. But Hawthorne's total meaning is very complex and his last word is not by any means a simple condemnation.

While the Merry Mount way of life embodies something essential that is lacking in the Puritans', making theirs appear ugly and inhuman, yet Hawthorne's point is that in the New World the old way could be only an imported artifice; New England, he deeply felt, could never be a mere reproduction of the Old. The fairies, as John Wilson says in *The Scarlet Letter*, were left behind in old England with Catholicism. And Hawthorne implies that the outlook of Merry Mount is not consonant with the realities of life in the New World, or the new phase of the world anywhere perhaps. The Puritans may be odious but they have a secret which is a better thing than the religion of nature and humanity. The May Lord and Lady, at Endicott's command, leave their Paradise – the reference to Adam and Eve driven from the Garden is unmistakable, as others to Milton in this tale – and there is a general suggestion that the 'choice' imposed on New England is like that made by Adam and Eve, they sacrifice bliss for something more arduous and better worth having. Hawthorne has no doubt that the May Lord and Lady enter into a finer bond in Christian marriage than they could otherwise have known as symbolic figures in a fertility rite. Nevertheless though their future is 'blessed' it is not pleasant or gracious. Hawthorne felt acutely the wrong the Lord Brethren had done to the Blaxtons, typified by the doings of an Endicott. The close parallel between the Merry Mount drama and the corresponding conflict in Milton's poem between the Brothers and the followers of Comus must be intentional – there are explicit references – and intended by Hawthorne as a criticism of Milton's presentment of the case. Virtue and Vice are a simple-minded division in Milton's *Comus*, however his symbolism may be interpreted. In Hawthorne's view that contest was quite other than a matter of Right and Wrong; his Puritans are an ironic comment on Milton's cause and case. Hawthorne's rendering shows two partial truths or qualified goods set in regrettable opposition. What Hawthorne implies is that it was a disaster for New England that they could not be reconciled. Hawthorne is both subtler and wiser than Milton, and his poem, unlike Milton's, is really dramatic and embodies a genuine cultural and spiritual conflict. Milton is a Puritan and Hawthorne is not; to Hawthorne, Milton is a man of iron. Hawthorne is seen explicitly as the unwilling heir of the Puritans, and their indignant critic, in a fine passage in *Main Street* which ends 'Let us thank God for having given us such ancestors; and let each successive generation thank him not less fervently, for being one step further from them in the march of ages.'

Just as the rose, the flower that symbolizes human grace and whose beauty is essentially something cultivated, the product of long training – just as the rose is used from *The Maypole* onwards, so the concept of the iron man becomes basic thereafter. The meaning is expounded in a remarkable section of *Main Street* which concludes:

All was well, so long as their lamps were freshly kindled at the heavenly flame. After a while, however, whether in their time or their children's, these lamps began to burn more dimly, or with a less genuine lustre; and then it might seem how hard, cold and confined, was their system, – how like an iron cage was that which they called Liberty.

I believe the image was taken by Hawthorne, consciously or unconsciously, from Bunyan; it may be remembered that in the Interpreter's House Christian is shown a Man in an Iron Cage as an awful warning of what a true Christian should never be. Now Bunyan's Man in an Iron Cage exemplified Despair. I have mentioned also that 'Blackstone' recurs in *The Scarlet Letter* in an almost mystically poetic context. In fact, these writings of Hawthorne's, to yield all they offer, must be studied as a whole, as a poet's works are, each illuminating and strengthening the rest. This is not the case with the fictions of any English nineteenth-century novelist. Perhaps this makes my point that Hawthorne needs a quite other approach from the one we commonly make to a novelist. His recurrent drama is a poet's vision of the meaning of his world, and it is communicated by poetic means.

Young Goodman Brown, visibly a much later and more practised work than the last, is also more powerful and more closely knit than anything else of Hawthorne's with the possible exception of the very complex and ambitious *Major Molineux*. It lends itself to much the same kind of analysis, that is, demands the same approach, as has been already outlined, and is even more unmistakably a prose poem. If its content has reminded literary critics of *Macbeth* and the Walpurgisnacht of *Faust*, that is unfortunate, for the relevant point is that Young Goodman Brown is Everyman in seventeenth-century New England – the title as usual giving the clue. He is the son of the Old Goodman Brown, that is, the Old Adam (or Adam the First as he is called in Bunyan), and recently wedded to Faith. We must note that every word is significant in the opening sentence: 'Young Goodman Brown came forth at sunset into the street of Salem Village; but put his head back, after crossing the threshold, to exchange a parting kiss with his young wife.' She begs him to 'put off his journey until sunrise', but he declares he cannot: 'My journey, as thou callest it, forth and back again, must needs be done 'twixt now and sunrise.' It is a journey he takes under compulsion, and it should not escape us that she tries to stop him because she is under a similar compulsion to go on a 'journey' herself – 'She talks of dreams, too', Young Goodman Brown reflects as he leaves her. The journey each must take alone, in dread, at night, is the journey away from home and the community, from conscious, everyday social life, to the wilderness where the hidden self satisfies, or is forced to realize, its subconscious fears and promptings in sleep. We take that journey with him into the awful forest. We note the division, which is to be the basis of *The Scarlet Letter*, between the town (where the minister rules) and the forest (where the Black Man reigns). From his pious home and Faith Young Goodman Brown reluctantly wanders back into the desert, meeting as he expects one who 'bears a considerable resemblance to him. They might have been taken for father and son.' He resists as best he can until he is made to realize to his surprise and horror that his father had gone on that journey before him, and sees many repected neighbours indeed pass him to the trysting-place. At first, confident in the appearance of virtue in the daily life of his fellows, he retorts indignantly: 'My father never went into the woods on such an errand, nor his father before him. We have been a race of honest men and good Christians since the days of the martyrs.' 'We are a people of prayer, and good works to boot, and abide no such wickedness.' The sinister likeness of his grandfather is able to convince him otherwise, though 'the arguments seemed rather to spring up in the bosom of his auditor than to be suggested by' the Devil. We feel how an accumulation of unconscious doubts about the 'saints' precipitates Young Goodman Brown's conviction of universal sinfulness.

As he loses his belief in the reality of virtue in others the scene grows increasingly sinister until the road 'vanished at length, leaving him in the heart of the dark wilderness, still rushing onward with the instinct that guides mortal man to evil. The whole forest was peopled with frightful sounds – the creaking of the trees, the howling of the wild beasts, and the yell of Indians.' We see Hawthorne making timely use of the traditional Puritan association of trees, animals, and Indians as the hostile powers, allies of the fiend.

But he was himself the chief horror of the scene, and shrank not from its other horrors.

'Ha! ha! ha!' roared Goodman Brown when the wind laughed at him. 'Let us hear which will laugh loudest. Think not to frighten me with your deviltry. Come witch, come wizard, come Indian pow-wow, come devil himself, and here comes Goodman Brown. You may as well fear him as he fear you.' In truth, all through the haunted forest there could be nothing more frightful than the figure of Goodman Brown.

The nightmare poetry gathers volume and power as he approaches the flaming centre of the forest, but Hawthorne's poetic imagination is as different as possible from Poe's – there is no touch of the Gothic horrors one might anticipate. When Goodman Brown ends his journey he finds his whole world, even the elders and ministers, assembled to worship at the devil's altar; he and his Faith are only the latest to be received into the communion of the lost.

When Young Goodman Brown returns to Salem Village with the morning light, 'staring around him like a bewildered man', his eyes have been opened to the true nature of his fellow-men, that is, human nature; he inescapably knows that what he suspected of himself is true of all men. He must live with that knowledge, and he is thenceforward a man of gloom, the Man in the Iron Cage, a Calvinist indeed. What Hawthorne has given us is not an allegory, and not an ambiguous problem-story (we are not to ask: Was it an actual Satanic experience or only a dream?). Hawthorne has made a dramatic poem of the Calvinist experience in New England. The unfailing tact with which the experience is evoked subjectively, in the most impressive concrete terms, is a subordinate proof of genius. I should prefer to stress the wonderful control of local and total rhythm, which never falters or slackens, and rises from the quiet but impressive opening to its poetic climax in the superb and moving finale, which I should have liked to quote in full. It ends 'they carved no hopeful verse upon his tombstone; for his dying hour was gloom'.

Hawthorne has imaginatively recreated for the reader that Calvinist sense of sin, that theory which did in actuality shape the early social and spiritual history of New England. But in Hawthorne, by a wonderful feat of transmutation, it has no religious significance, it is as a psychological state that it is explored. Young Goodman Brown's Faith is not faith in Christ but faith in human beings, and losing it he is doomed to isolation forever. *Young Goodman Brown* seems to me very much more impressive than the Walpurgisnacht scene in Joyce's *Ulysses*, which smells of the case-book and the midnight oil. If anyone is inclined to question its claim to be a dramatic poem he might be asked to examine along with it Cowper's acknowledged masterpiece *The Castaway*, comparable in theme but in every other respect so inferior. And I am tempted to ask what advantage has *The Castaway* or even *The Ancient Mariner* over *Young Goodman Brown* by being in verse? In fact, the regularity of verse and stanzas is a disadvantage, imposing monotony and other limitations; either of these poems is less forceful, artistically serious and truly 'poetic' than Hawthorne's prose poem. The alleged superiority of poetic form may be specious and there is in fact no sharp distinction between prose and poetry.

In this tale Hawthorne achieved a considerable contribution toward the comprehensive masterpiece he was to produce in *The Scarlet Letter*, for the tale is partially taken up into the later romance.

In his introduction to a volume of tales brought out in 1851 but mostly written much earlier Hawthorne, then in his prime as an artist, with *The Scarlet Letter* a year behind him, confessed that he was 'disposed to quarrel with the earlier sketches', most of all 'because they come so nearly up to the standard of the best that I can achieve now'. As one of the earlier sketches in his collection was *My Kinsman Major Molineux* (1831), he might justly have felt that he was never to achieve anything better.

Ideally it should be preceded by a reading of the three studies collected under the title *Old News*, which give the historical background and are clearly the fruit of work preparatory for *Major Molineux*. This remarkable tale might have been less commonly overlooked or misunderstood if it had had a sub-title, such as Hawthorne often provided by way of a hint. It could do with some such explanatory sub-title as 'America Comes of Age'. But though if a naturalistic story is looked for the reader would be left merely puzzled, the tale lends itself readily to comprehension as a poetic parable in dramatic form, and the opening paragraph as usual clearly explains the situation and furnishes the required clue. We are in the age which was preparing the colonies for the War of Independence and we are made to take part in a dramatic precipitation of, or prophetic forecast of, the rejection of England that was to occur in fact much later.

The actual tale begins by describing a country-bred youth coming to town, starting with the significant sentence: 'It was near nine o'clock of a moonlight evening, when a boat crossed the ferry with a single passenger.' The sturdy pious youth Robin, the son of the typical farmer-clergyman, represents the young America; he has *left his home* in the village in the woods and crossing by the *ferry*, *alone*, *at nightfall*, reaches the little metropolis of a New England port – that is, the contemporary scene where the historic future will be decided. He arrives poor but hopeful, confidently anticipating help in making his fortune from 'my kinsman Major Molineux', the reiteration of the phrase being an important contribution to the total effect. The kinsman is Hawthorne's and ours (if we are Americans) as well as Robin's, and his name suggests both his military and aristocratic status. Robin explains much later in the tale that his father and the Major are brother's sons – that is, one brother had stayed in England and the other left to colonize New England. Their children, the next generation, represented by Robin's father and the Major, had kept on friendly terms and the rich Major, representative in New England of the British civil and military rule and keeping 'great pomp', was in a position to patronize his poor country cousin. We do not get this straightforward account in the tale, of course, we have to unravel it for ourselves, for the presentation of the theme is entirely dramatic and we have to identify our consciousness with the protagonist Robin. The essential information is revealed only when we have ourselves experienced for some time the

same bewilderment as poor Robin, who cannot understand why
his request to be directed to the house of his kinsman is met
by the various types of citizen with suspicion, with contempt,
with anger, with disgust, with sneers, or with laughter. In fact,
Robin has arrived at a critical moment in his kinsman's history.
The colonists – with considerable skill and economy Hawthorne
represents all ranks and classes of the states in this dream-
town – have secretly planned to throw off British rule, or at any
rate to rid themselves of Major Molineux, a symbolic action
which, performed in the street outside the church at midnight
and before the innocent eyes of the mystified youth, takes the
form of something between a pageant and a ritual drama,
disguised in the emotional logic of a dream. As a dream it has
a far greater emotional pull than actuality could have.
Hawthorne never anywhere surpassed this tale (written when
he was not more than twenty-seven) in dramatic power, in
control of tone, pace, and tension, and in something more
wonderful, the creation of a suspension between the fullest
consciousness of meaning and the emotional incoherence of
dreaming. How this is achieved and for what purpose can be
seen only by a careful examination of the last half of the tale,
but I will quote as sparingly as possible.

Until this point, precisely the middle of the work, no
departure from the everyday norm has been necessary,
though we have been wrought to a state of exasperation which
is ready for working on. And Hawthorne now introduces
another note:

He now roamed desperately, and at random, through the town, almost
ready to believe that a spell was on him, like that by which a wizard
of his country had once kept three pursuers wandering, a whole winter
night, within twenty paces of the cottage which they sought. The
streets lay before him, strange and desolate, and the lights were
extinguished in almost every house. Twice, however, little parties of
men, among whom Robin distinguished individuals in outlandish
attire, came hurrying along; but though on both occasions they
paused to address him, such intercourse did not at all enlighten his
perplexity. They did but utter a few words in some language of which
Robin knew nothing, and perceiving his inability to answer, bestowed
a curse upon him in plain English, and hastened away. Finally, the
lad determined to knock at the door of every mansion, trusting that
perseverance would overcome the fatality that had hitherto thwarted
him. Firm in this resolve, he was passing beneath the walls of a church,

which formed the corner of two streets, when, as he turned into the
shade of its steeple, he encountered a bulky stranger, muffled in a
cloak. The man was proceeding with the speed of earnest business,
but Robin planted himself full before him, holding the oak cudgel
with both hands across his body, as a bar to further passage.

'Halt, honest man, and answer me a question', said he, very
resolutely. 'Tell me, this instant, whereabouts is the dwelling of my
kinsman, Major Molineux!'

...The stranger, instead of attempting to force his passage, stepped
back into the moonlight, unmuffled his face, and stared full into that
of Robin.

'Watch here an hour, and Major Molineux will pass by', said he.

Robin gazed with dismay and astonishment on the unprecedented
physiognomy of the speaker. The forehead with its double prominence,
the broad hooked nose, the shaggy eyebrow, and fiery eyes, were those
which he had noticed at the inn, but the man's complexion had
undergone a singular, or, more properly, a two-fold change. One side
of the face blazed an intense red, while the other was black as
midnight, the division line being in the broad bridge of the nose; and
a mouth which seemed to extend from ear to ear was black or red,
in contrast to the color of the cheek. The effect was as if two individual
devils, a fiend of fire and a fiend of darkness, had united themselves
to form this infernal visage. The stranger grinned in Robin's face,
muffled his parti-coloured features, and was out of sight in a moment.

The stranger, whose unearthly appearance we were prepared
for by the 'individuals in outlandish attire' speaking in a code
– for as we realize later they were obviously conspirators
demanding from Robin a password he could not furnish, but
they help to increase the nightmare atmosphere – is shown by
his face to be something more than a man in disguise. The
tension is being screwed up to the pitch needed for the approaching climax of the drama: this is not a man like the others
but a Janus-like fiend of fire and darkness, that is, we presently
learn, 'War personified' in its dual aspects of Death and
Destruction. But it is not just a personification, it is a symbol
with emotional repercussions which passes through a series of
suggestive forms. The account of its features at first: 'The
forehead with its double prominence, the broad hooked nose'
etc. suggests Punch and so also the grotesque associations of
puppet-show farce. The division of the face into black and red
implies the conventional get-up of the jester, and indeed he
'grinned in Robin's face' before he 'muffled his parti-coloured

features'. At this point Robin, carrying the reader with him, having 'consumed a few moments in philosophical speculation upon the species of man who had just left him', is able to 'settle this point shrewdly, rationally and satisfactorily'. He and we are of course deceived in our complacency. He falls into a drowse by sending his thoughts 'to imagine how that evening of ambiguity and weariness had been spent in his father's household'. This actually completes his bewilderment – 'Am I here or there?' he cries, 'But still his mind kept vibrating between fancy and reality.'

Now, so prepared, we hear the murmur that becomes a confused medley of voices and shouts as it approaches, turning into 'frequent bursts from many instruments of discord, and a wild and confused laughter filled up the intervals'. 'The antipodes of music' heralds 'a mighty stream of people' led by a single horseman whom Robin recognizes as the eerie stranger in a fresh avatar. With the 'rough music' that in Old England was traditionally used to drive undesirable characters out of the community, by the red glare of torches and with 'War personified' as their leader, the citizens of America, with Indians in their train and cheered on by their women, are symbolically if proleptically casting out the English ruler. The nightmare impression reaches its climax: 'In his train were wild figures in the Indian dress, and many fantastic shapes without a model, giving the whole march a visionary air, as if a dream had broken forth from some feverish brain, and were sweeping visibly through the midnight streets... "The double-faced fellow has his eye upon me", muttered Robin, with an indefinite but uncomfortable idea that he was himself to bear a part in the pageantry.'

It seems indeed that the pageant has been brought to this place for Robin's benefit.

A moment more, and the leader thundered a command to halt: the trumpets vomited a horrid breath, and then held their peace; the shouts and laughter of the people died away, and there remained only a universal hum, allied to silence. Right before Robin's eyes was an uncovered cart. There the torches blazed the brightest, there the moon shone out like day, and there, in tar-and-feathery dignity, sat his kinsman Major Molineux!

He was an elderly man, of large and majestic person, and strong, square features, betokening a steady soul; but steady as it was, his enemies had found means to shake it. His face was pale as death, and far more ghastly; the broad forehead was contracted in his agony, so that his eyebrows formed one grizzled line; his eyes were red and wild, and the foam hung white upon his quivering lip. His whole frame was agitated by a quick and continual tremor, which his pride strove to quell, even in those circumstances of overwhelming humiliation. But perhaps the bitterest pang of all was when his eyes met those of Robin; for he evidently knew him on the instant, as the youth stood witnessing the foul disgrace of a head grown gray in honour. They stared at each other in silence, and Robin's knees shook, and his hair bristled, with a mixture of pity and terror.

The pageant is thus seen to represent a tragedy and is felt by us as such; it arouses in Robin the appropriate blend of emotions – the classical 'pity and terror'. But Hawthorne has by some inspiration – for how could he have known except intuitively of the origins of tragedy in ritual drama? – gone back to the type of action that fathered Tragedy. Just as the 'War personified' suggests an idol or a human representative of the god, so does the other terrible figure 'in tar-and-feathery dignity' in the cart. We seem to be spectators at the most primitive of all dramatic representations, the conquest of the old king by the new.

If the story had ended here, on this note, it would have been remarkable enough, but Hawthorne has an almost incredible consummation to follow. I mean incredible in being so subtly achieved with such mastery of tone. From being a spectator at a tragedy, Robin has to fulfil his premonitions of having 'to bear a part in the pageantry' himself. He is drawn into the emotional vortex and comes to share the reactions of the participants. He has felt intimately the dreadful degradation of his English kinsman, but now he is seized with the excitement of the victors, his fellow-countrymen, and sees their triumph as his own – 'a perception of tremendous ridicule in the whole scene affected him with a sort of mental inebriety'. Drunk with success the whole town roars in a frenzy of laughter, and Robin's shout joins theirs and is the loudest. Then in a sudden calm that follows this orgy 'the procession resumed its march. On they went, like fiends that throng in mockery around some dead potentate, mighty no more, but majestic still in his agony.' We are left in the silent street, brought back into the world of problems in which the tale opened. Robin still has to settle with reality and decide his future, the future of his generation. He asks to be shown the way back to the ferry: 'I begin to grow weary of a town life', he says to the townsman who has stayed behind to note his reactions. But his new friend replies: 'Some few days hence, if you wish it, I will speed you on your journey. Or, if you prefer to remain with us, perhaps, as you are a shrewd youth, you may rise in the world without the help of your kinsman, Major Molineux.'

Hawthorne has been blamed for failing to provide a 'solution' and for not being optimistic as a good American should be, but it seems to me that here, as in *The Maypole*, he ends in reasonable, sober hopefulness for the future of life. Provided we recognize the facts and fully comprehend the positions, we can cope with it, if not master it, he implies. Declining to be, perhaps incapable of being, a naturalistic novelist, he was true to his best perceptions of his genius when he did the work of a dramatic poet, the interpreter and radical critic of the society which had produced him and for whose benefit he expressed his insight in a unique literature.

II

The Scarlet Letter has an unfortunate title, catchpenny in fact, which has some responsibility for the common mistake that the novel is 'about adultery' or even about Sin. The stress falls where it always does in Hawthorne as can be seen in the lay-out, the dialogue, the characterization and a rather obtrusive 'message' in the novel itself, which, incidentally, is described by its author as a 'Romance'. This term is strictly correct for both *The Scarlet Letter* and *The Blithedale Romance*; as Lord Raglan points out in his anthropological study *The Hero*, 'romance is often myth in disguise'. It is Hawthorne's distinction to have given artistic validity to the term Romance which he makes a serious vehicle. The kernel of this romance, and I believe the first form of it, is the rather crude story *Endicott of the Red Cross* (1837), and to examine that is to rescue the skeleton of *The Scarlet Letter* from the sentimental and moralistic misreadings that have given it a false appearance.

Endicott comes in historical time after *The Maypole* (which begins with the first settlers) and is contemporary with *The Scarlet Letter*. They are both supposed to occur in the reign of

Charles I, the age when the colonists felt menaced by the threatened Romanization of England by Laud and the royal family. *Endicott* is followed by *The Gray Champion* which ends with the overthrow of James II and that in turn is followed by *Major Molineux*, the prophecy of the Revolution. Hawthorne completes his series with *The Blithedale Romance*, wherein the contemporary scene is typified. It will be noted that Hawthorne took upon himself, very suitably for the originator of a national literature, the work of the Edda-poets, of the makers of antique tragedy and of medieval drama; hence a good deal of his writings, his best creative work, is a dramatization of the same theme, or portions of it. It must be something of this kind that James had in mind when he wrote of Hawthorne: 'No one has had a literary form that more successfully expressed his vision. He was not a moralist, and he was not simply a poet.'

The tale opens with Endicott mustering the Salem trainband in full armour – we recall that *The Maypole* ended with the triumph of the armoured Puritans, and we are now to face the consequences of the victory over what Blackstone and Merry Mount stood for. The social-moral scene of the new order is described by the symbol of Endicott's breastplate; reflected in such a mirror the details are doubly suggestive – the wolf's head on the meeting-house door splashing 'the sacred edifice' with blood is immediately understood like an image in a poem of Blake's.

This piece of armor was so highly polished that the whole surrounding scene had its image in the glittering steel. The central object in the mirrored picture was an edifice of humble architecture with neither steeple nor bell to proclaim it the house of prayer. A token of the perils of the wilderness was seen in the grim head of a wolf, which had just been slain within the precincts of the town, and according to the regular mode of claiming bounty, was nailed on the porch of the meeting-house. The blood was still plashing on the doorstep. There happened to be visible, at the same noontide hour, so many other characteristics of the time and manners of the Puritans, that we must endeavour to represent them in a sketch, though far less vividly than they were reflected in the polished breastplate of John Endicott.

A neatly symmetrical setting is staged for us thus. The grim meeting-house with 'in close vicinity to the sacred edifice that important engine of Puritan authority, the whipping-post' and 'at one corner of the meeting-house the pillory, and at the other the stocks'. Now for the living wolves nailed to the meeting-house: in the pillory is a suspected Catholic, while a Royalist is confined in the stocks; on the meeting-house steps are exposed ignominiously a man and a woman who in different ways have voiced heterodox views, the man being labelled 'A Wanton Gospeller'. There are other victims of the harsh rule of the saints in the crowd, including most notably a beautiful young woman doomed to wear the 'A' for adulteress on her gown. She has defiantly embroidered it in gold on scarlet cloth, but we hear no more of her now. Except for the malefactors, all the men are in the trainband, 'iron-breasted'. Gazing at them, armed with their superseded flint-headed arrows, are the ousted natives, 'stately savages, in all the pomp and dignity of the primeval Indian'; they also have an ironic function. They suggest that their conquerors differ from them chiefly in having matchlocks and iron armour and that 'pomp and dignity' are not proofs of civilization. They will recur in *The Scarlet Letter* in a more powerful context – the chapter there called 'The New England Holiday' stresses the 'Puritanic gloom' and slyly goes on to describe the party of Indian onlookers 'with countenances of inflexible gravity, beyond what even the Puritan could attain', a comment on the theory that gravity is a sign of godliness.

This is the actual setting also of *The Scarlet Letter*, a simple, almost primitive, stage-setting to which the romance adds only scenes in the forest. We are reminded again of the childhood of the drama; it is a stage suitable for the enaction of a morality play or a mystery. The setting is inevitably typical of the moral action, but Hawthorne's stress is here seen to fall on the sociological and not the 'moral' in the popular sense at all, since he is clearly demanding sympathy for the anti-social members of the community, victims of a theocratic society where 'religion and law were almost identical'. The only other actor is Roger Williams the minister, who serves a similar function to Blackstone in *The Maypole*. 'His aspect was perfectly that of a pilgrim', he comes onto the stage out of the wilderness, and his first act is to 'drink at a bubbling fountain which gushed into the sunshine' near the corner of the meeting-house. Historically Williams was a Cambridge divine who emigrated in 1630 and became, in Cotton Mather's words, 'the first rebel against the divine church-order established in the wilderness'.

He stood for tolerance and was finally obliged to fly to the wilderness and take refuge with the Indians, founding a liberal state on Rhode Island.

In the story, Endicott voices a characteristic tyranny which Williams endeavours to check without success; the culprits in durance make sardonic comments. Incensed at the news from England, Endicott demands: Why had they emigrated except for liberty to worship according to their conscience? '"Call you this liberty of conscience?" interupted the Wanton Gospeller. A sad and quiet smile flitted across the mild visage of Roger Williams. But Endicott shook his sword wrathfully at the culprit.' Finally Endicott rends the Red Cross, as the symbol of Papacy and Royalty, from the ensign. '"Sacrilegious wretch!" cried the high-churchman in the pillory, able no longer to restrain himself, "thou hast rejected the symbol of our holy religion!"' It is difficult to see how the last paragraph of the little drama can be anything but ironically intended.

Though *The Scarlet Letter* was not published till thirteen years later, its essence is still that of this story which Hawthorne must have been brooding over in the interval. The meeting-house as before dominates the square, with the same accompaniments. The scaffold of the pillory is the scene of the three main parts of the drama – the opening, the final act, and the chapter exactly half-way. At the close Hester expresses for us the reason for its omnipresence: 'There was a sense within her – too ill-defined to be made a thought, but weighing heavily on her mind, – that her whole orb of life, both before and after, was connected with this spot, as with the one point that gave it unity.' The iron-breasted Puritan is in control, the Indians and the wilderness surround the town which is open only on one side, to the seashore, where in turn all the chief actors have come from England and which offers the only way of escape. The chief difference is that the scarlet-lettered young woman has been brought into the centre of the stage and her history used as a measure of the inhumanity of the society she is fixed in. Just as Tolstoy's novel is framed to evoke the response: This is the society that condemned Anna! so Hawthorne makes Hester the critic of the society that similarly rejects and victimizes her. And just as in *Anna* Tolstoy managed to find room for all his interests, experiences, and problems, so *The Scarlet Letter* has a richer life than any other of Hawthorne's works because it is the most inclusive. What he had worked on and crystallized out in *The Minister's Black Veil, Endicott and the Red Cross, Young Goodman Brown, Main Street, Rapaccini's Daughter*, and *The Maypole of Merry Mount* he swept into a finely organized whole, so that every portion is concentrated with meanings and associations and cross-references. Only something in the nature of a poetic *procédé* and technique could have coped with such an undertaking and that is what we have here as evidently as in such shorter pieces of work as *Young Goodman Brown*.

For example, instead of the briefly indicated lay-out of *Endicott and the Red Cross* there is to *The Scarlet Letter* an introductory chapter of two pages called 'The Prison-Door' and which may be compared, for it is a prose poem, with Crabbe's introductory vision of *The Village* where there is a very similar mobilizing of symbols ('Lo! where the heath, with withering brake grown o'er... There poppies nodding, mock the hope of toil...O'er the young shoot the charlock throws a shade, And clasping tares cling round the sickly blade' etc.). It wonderfully concentrates the theme of the book. Hawthorne describes in one pregnant sentence a Puritan throng waiting outside a prison door, and we realize that that is an index of the nature of their life. He continues, with that disturbing likeness to Swift that shows another formative influence in his literary heredity:

The founders of a new colony, whatever Utopia of human virtue and happiness they might officially project, have invariably recognized it among their earliest practical necessities to allot a portion of virgin soil as a cemetery, and another portion as the site of a prison.

The graveyard and the prison: the existence of Death and Sin as primary factors in that way of life, equally inescapable, have thus been indicated. To Hawthorne the Prison represents man's punishment for transgression by society, and that is one aspect of his theme. Between the prison and the street there is a grass-plot overgrown with noxious weeds (like Crabbe's)

which evidently found something congenial in the soil that had so early borne the black flower of civilized society, a prison. But on one side of the portal, and rooted almost at the threshold, was a wild rose-bush, covered, in this month of June, with its delicate gems, which might be imagined to offer their fragrance and fragile beauty to the prisoner as he went in, and to the condemned criminal as he came forth to his doom, in token that the deep heart of Nature could pity him.

We feel of course that the rose ought to be Divine Grace, but Hawthorne's use of this symbol is his own. It seems to stand for him for the indestructible humane impulse that survives somewhere in some people even in the most repressive social order, in the most unpromising natural conditions:

This rose-bush, by a strange chance, had been kept alive in history; but whether it had merely survived out of the stern old wilderness, so long after the fall of the gigantic pines and oaks that originally over-shadowed it, – or whether, as there is fair authority for believing, it had sprung up under the footsteps of the sainted Ann Hutchinson as she entered the prison-door, – we shall not take it upon us to determine.

If we are – as Hawthorne assumes – acquainted with the history of Ann Hutchinson, we at once ask ourselves: Why sainted? and realize that she was a saint only in struggling for liberty of conscience against an intolerant church.[4] We now have an inkling of what the wild rose stands for in Hawthorne's symbolic structure. We remember its occurrence in *The Maypole* mingled with 'others which the colonists had reared from English seed'. Blackstone, Roger Williams, Ann Hutchinson, and Eliot 'the holy Apostle of the Indians' (who figures in the same way in *The Blithedale Romance*) keep the rose alive, or tend and cultivate it to the finer flower of traditional humane civilization. Hawthorne ends his prologue by plucking one of the roses and presenting it to the reader.

Hawthorne's preoccupation with something that is at once the cultural and the psychological classes him with George Eliot and Tolstoy and Conrad. Hence probably the enigmatic final sentence of James's *Hawthorne*: 'Man's conscience was his theme, but he saw it in the light of a creative fancy which added, out of its own substance, an interest and, I may almost say, an importance.' His profound concern with the history of his local civilization and its importance for himself distinguishes him even among his kind there. Here is the point where Hawthorne, Henry James, and Melville meet. If James found in Hawthorne a pattern of the novelist as social critic of New England and the mother country, Melville saw the archetypal American poet in him, one of 'the masters of the great Art of Telling the Truth' like Shakespeare – in fact, the American Shakespeare, 'an unimitating and perhaps an inimitable man.'[5] What is commonly considered as characteristic of Melville's mode of communicating his vision is often only a technique imitated from Hawthorne.

The scaffold for instance in *The Scarlet Letter* is the scene first of Hester's martyrdom before the throng and the temporal and spiritual rulers (after which she undergoes 'a new birth' and so can be said to have symbolically died); then of Dimmesdale's Agony when in the central chapter he offers himself on the scaffold in a midnight vigil in expiation of his sin; finally of his death, after he has preached in the adjacent church the Election Sermon prophesying 'a high and glorious destiny' for the chosen people of New England. Roger Chillingworth, the wronged husband whose passion for revenge has 'transformed a wise and just man to a fiend', declares then: 'there was no place so secret – no high place nor lowly place, where thou couldst have escaped me, – save on this very scaffold!' On her first exposure there Hester with her baby in her arms is likened (with reservations) to the Madonna and Child.

From this daring parallel with the symbolism of Christianity, wherein Hawthorne's idea of the martyrdom of man at the hands of a theocratic society is pretty clearly hinted, Melville must have taken the scheme of deliberately suggesting the crucifixion of Billy Budd with which that tale ends, and the symbolic history of Billy too. In *Israel Potter*, which Hawthorne admired, there is a marked imitation of Hawthorne in the fine opening and the poignant close. Israel's upbringing and history are described in impressive detail as the symbolic making of a nation until thus 'unwittingly preparing himself for the Bunker Hill rifle' Israel takes up arms against the British and we realize that we have really been given a chart of 'the temper of the men of the revolutionary era'. But in between there is only an uneven picaresque eighteenth-century novel, and *Benito Cereno* is a worthier instance of Hawthorne's influence on the one side; James's early *nouvelle*, *The Europeans*, that masterly symbolic analysis of the New England mores in the Hawthorne age, is James's finest tribute on the other. Hawthorne's achievement is thus seen to have been decisive for the American novel.

What Hawthorne can do by concentration is best seen in the

chapter 'The Governor's Hall' which, with the next chapter 'The Elf-Child and the Minister', is central to the 'romance'. The garden (New England) is seen from within the Hall, the account of the Governor, his Hall and clerical advisers and the portraits of the Governor's 'lineage', forms the climax of the book on its sociological side as the last chapters do of the emotional interest. Endicott's *breastplate* has become a much more subtle and elaborately reflecting *suit of mail*.[6] Hester draws Pearl away from it to look out of the window at the garden saying 'It may be, we shall see flowers there; more beautiful than we find in the woods.' But apart from 'some rude and immature attempt at shrubbery', 'the proprietor appeared already to have relinquished, as hopeless, the effort to perpetuate on this side of the Atlantic, in a hard soil and amid the close struggle for subsistence, the native English taste for ornamental gardening'. The conditions of pioneering settlement favoured both literally and socially 'cabbages in plain sight' and no flowers – understandably; but Hawthorne continues:

There were a few rose-bushes, however, and a number of apple-trees, probably the descendants of those planted by the Reverend Mr Blackstone, the first settler of the peninsula; that half-mythological personage, who rides through our early annals, seated on the back of a bull.

The apple-trees, like the rose-bushes, represent the fruits of civilization. Blackstone brought them with him when he crossed the sea like Europa (hence 'on the back of a bull'), who, thus taken from ancient Phoenicia, founded the civilization of Crete. As mother of Minos she was also connected with the Labyrinth, which probably also connected her with *The Scarlet Letter* in Hawthorne's mind where the Labyrinth is a recurrent image as will be seen. Blackstone is half mythological because his real history, like the existence of Merry Mount, furnished 'facts [which] have wrought themselves almost spontaneously into a sort of allegory'. Then the Governor appears. 'The wide circumference of an elaborate ruff, beneath his gray beard, in the antiquated fashion of King James' reign, caused his head to look not a little like that of John the Baptist in a charger' – we have evoked the Puritan theory, put in practice as it were, of the opposition between soul and body in this description of a head cut off from the body by the ruff. This theory is hinted and next enlarged on, then it is explained that in practice the rejection of bodily comforts 'or even luxury' was not acted on as it should in consistency have,been; the deduction is that hypocrisy is the consequence of submitting to an inhuman theory – another underlining of the argument of *The Scarlet Letter*. The case of John Wilson is next opened, as proof of the inextinguishable humanity of man, in a passage of great beauty and which to me might have sooner been looked for in this form in T.F. Powys:

This creed was never taught, for instance, by the venerable pastor, John Wilson, whose beard, white as a snowdrift, was seen over Governor Bellingham's shoulder; while its wearer suggested that pears and peaches might yet be naturalized in the New England climate, and that purple grapes might possibly be compelled to flourish, against the sunny garden-wall. The old clergyman, nurtured at the rich bosom of the English Church, had a long-established and legitimate taste for all good and comfortable things; and however stern he might show himself in the pulpit, or in his public reproof of such transgressions as that of Hester Prynne, still, the genial benevolence of his private life had won him warmer affection than was accorded to any of his professional contemporaries.

The imagery of the wall-fruit takes us back to the wider symbolism of the Garden that represents the cultural life of New England. The genial character of the English Church is delightfully evoked, contrasting with the Puritan government in the previous paragraph: 'the impression made by his [Bellingham's] aspect, so rigid and severe, and frost-bitten with more than autumnal age'. It is appropriately Wilson who asks Pearl 'Art thou one of these naughty elfs or fairies, whom we thought to have left behind us, with other relics of Papistry, in merry old England?'

The veins represented by *The Minister's Black Veil* and *Young Goodman Brown* are united toward the end of the book. When Hester comes out of prison near the beginning, emerging from the grave (it is implied), she is Young Goodman Brown – she cannot escape recognizing the evil in the hearts of the townspeople who treat her as a leper ('such loss of faith is ever one of the saddest results of sin', Hawthorne ironically explains[7]). This is balanced by the chapter 'The Minister in a Maze' toward the end, where after meeting Hester in the forest and agreeing to her plan of elopement Dimmesdale on returning to

Boston has Young Goodman Brown's experience on returning
to Salem but with this difference, that the minister learns that
in himself are all the evil impulses of other men. 'Another man
had returned out of the forest; a wiser one.' 'Nothing short of
a total change of dynasty and moral code in that interior
kingdom would account for it.' As Hawthorne has just
described the forest as 'that wild, heathen Nature of the forest,
never subjugated by human law, nor illumined by higher
truth', it seems that he did not endorse the theological myth.
Though the Puritans alleged the forest to be the domain of the
Black Man, Hawthorne shows that in comparison with the
settlement the wilderness is a blissful place for the lovers. There
they are able to assure each other that 'What we did had a
consecration of its own', and we recognize that the relation
between them has been the only good human relation in the
book. A proof of its validity is that it produced the child Pearl,
who appears as the choice channel of Life and is contrasted with
the horrible offspring of the Pilgrims (just as is the outcast
Quaker child in *The Gentle Boy*). Pearl is created in terms that
one would have looked for in D. H. Lawrence rather than in
the Hawthorne of common esteem and she alone escapes the
Puritan ethos, not by dying but by escaping to a fuller life in
Europe. Hawthorne's undisguised 'message' is that the evil lay
in the concealment – 'Thou wast not bold, thou wast not
true', Pearl accuses her father. The tragedy consists in the
separation of the genuinely united couple by an inhuman
society and originated in the false relation imposed on a girl
by an unlovable husband (as in *Anna*); Tolstoy shows in addition
that even avoiding the evil of concealment and being bold and
true cannot prevent disaster when people carry the world they
were born into about with them. Hawthorne points his
unorthodox position by ending, it may seem incongruously,
with a regenerated Hester promising to other unhappy women
a brighter future 'when the world should have grown ripe for
it' and 'a new truth would be revealed' which will 'establish
the whole relation between man and woman on a surer ground
of mutual happiness'. Though prepared for by a good many
'liberal' notes throughout the book, this, landing us with a bang
in the era of Margaret Fuller, is a finally discordant note. But
it is quite in keeping with the discussion in *The Blithedale
Romance* between the emancipated Zenobia and Hawthorne's

mouthpiece Coverdale about Woman, Love, and Society. It is really a touching proof of Hawthorne's democratic optimism. Without it the drama would have been a water-tight tragedy like Anna Karenina's or those created by George Eliot for her Gwendolen Harleth and Mrs Transome. It is, like theirs, a perfect sociological tragedy – given this kind of society and this situation occurring in it, with principals of such a nature and so conditioned, only this can result, there is no escape but in death. And the theological disputation between Hester and her husband is genuinely distilled from the action and its religious environment, not, like Hardy's President of the Immortals finishing his sport with Tess, an imposed 'philosophy':

'Peace, Hester, peace' replied the old man, with gloomy sternness. 'It is not granted me to pardon. I have no such power as thou tellest me of. My old faith, long forgotten, comes back to me, and explains all that we do, and all we suffer. By thy first step awry, thou didst plant the germ of evil; but since that moment, it has all been a dark necessity. Ye that have wronged me are not sinful, save in a kind of typical illusion; neither am I fiend-like, who have snatched a fiend's office from his hands. It is our fate. Let the black flower blossom as it may!'

'The black flower' is meant to connect with 'the black flower of civilized society, a prison' in the prologue which there typifies the social condemnation of sin in contrast with the other flower, the rose. We may pause at the image in Hester's speech to him ('who are wandering here together in this gloomy maze of evil, and stumbling at every step, over the guilt wherewith we have strewn our path') which is picked up in a later chapter-title 'The Minister in a Maze', and connects with Hawthorne's frequent use in this work of 'labyrinth' – 'Hester wandered without a clue in the dark labyrinth of mind', Hester is in 'a dismal labyrinth of doubt', Chillingworth is the monster who prevents the elopement from the labyrinth, whose action affects Hester as a 'dark and grim countenance of an inevitable doom, which – at the moment when a passage seemed to open for the minister and herself out of their labyrinth of misery – showed itself, with an unrelenting smile, right in the midst of their path'. Hawthorne was undoubtedly fertilized by his early classical studies as much as by his seventeenth-century reading. The myth of the labyrinth had obviously struck root in him, and it is characteristic of his genius that the use he makes of

it is psychological and emotive. There is the remarkable
sustained account of the psychological warfare Chillingworth
wages on the unconscious – though intuitively self-protecting
– minister, 'working in the soil like a dark miner'. Hawthorne
can with justice declare of the resolution of his drama: 'some
deep life-matter was now to be laid open to them', when the
way out of the Labyrinth was to be found. He has the right
to such a vocabulary for he creates it in the concrete. His
discovery of the need for creating such an idiom, at once poetic
and psychological – and who beside Shakespeare could have
helped him? – is one of his claims to rank with the most serious
masters of the novel. He produced a very moderate number of
volumes; and if even in that his creation was sometimes uneven,
his experiments were not always successful and his search for
'images which shall place themselves in picturesque correspondence with the spiritual facts with which he is concerned'
sometimes ended in the trivial or the laboured, that ís to be
expected of such a distinctly pioneering artist. Greatly as I
admire *The Scarlet Letter* I cannot agree with Mr Winters that
it is 'faultless in detail', for the want of tact in handling the
scarlet 'A' and the brook in the forest, for instance, everyone
must feel as strongly as Henry James did. When trying for an
archaic diction he can be seen to write no language, though
he is never unplausible like Scott and he can use Bunyan's
speech-idiom, which his ear had thoroughly caught, with great
skill for poetic and ironic purposes.

If *The House of the Seven Gables* has been consistently over-rated
(it seems to me quite uninteresting, illogical in conception and
frequently trivial in execution, proof of the mischief of the
pressure that forced Hawthorne to try and write something like
the popular idea of a novel), *The Blithedale Romance* has never
as far as I can make out had justice done it. Its style is more
consistently distinguished than that of *The Scarlet Letter*, its tone
ranges with remarkable command from the drily critical to the
poetic. It is only apparently more personal than the other
creative works I have discussed because the theme, still
Hawthorne's great theme, is treated in the contemporary context
and founded very slightly in an experience of Hawthorne's of
ten years back, which he must have been adapting ever since
to the artistic use he could have for it (like Shakespeare in

Keats's letter, Hawthorne must have 'led a life of Allegory – his works are the comments on it'; Hawthorne similarly wrote: 'Nelson expressed his life in a kind of symbolic poetry.') In this romance Hawthorne features as a 'half-mythological personage' himself, appearing as Miles Coverdale, though Miles, apart from obviously being a poet-novelist, is shown as the representative of his age. Instead of the country-bred Robin we have the spoiled city-bred young man about town with private means, an amateur of the arts and good living; there, Hawthorne saw, was now the decisive battle-ground of the future of American culture. Blithedale resembles Brook Farm only as Hawthorne's Merry Mount did Morton's, and Hawthorne tried to stave off the inevitable misreading of his work as a *roman à clef* by a warning in the Preface where he announces that 'His whole treatment of the affair is altogether incidental to the main purpose of the romance.' Blithedale is then the contemporary Merry Mount, the symbol of a life superior in the theory on which it is based and in the possibilities it offers to the form of life forced on one by the society in which one finds oneself by birth. Its existence represents the possibility of a choice – there is none in *The Scarlet Letter*, hence the Labyrinth is the comprehensive image used in that.

As always, we must pay the closest attention to the construction, to the form in which the story or plot is exposed to the reader, and to the associations of the characters and their attributes in order to grasp what Hawthorne is at. There are no irrelevancies in Hawthorne's best works and when we seem to find one it should be read with particular care as it will undoubtedly turn out to be structural. A first reading leaves most people bewildered, asking questions about the unresolved mysteries of the drama (was Westervelt Zenobia's husband or lover? why all this fuss about Old Moodie? what is the point of the Veiled Lady?), complaining of the long pauses holding up the action, of the disquieting way the plot skips about and of the apparent discontinuity. The stress seems to fall in the oddest places. A truly inward reading however sees how everything is part of a whole and in its appropriate place; the book is uncanny because unconventional, not incompetent, original as *Women in Love* or *Nostromo* had to be. For lack of space my account of it cannot be adequate but I can at least outline what it seems to me about and for.

The book seems as though it should start with the second chapter, 'Blithedale', but like the brief first chapter of *The Scarlet Letter* the short first chapter called 'Old Moodie' is indispensable. It puts us in possession of the personae and hints their relation: the bachelor 'I' has just visited an exhibition of the Veiled Lady and tomorrow will go to join 'the Blithedale enterprise' where he is to find the philanthropist Hollingsworth and a literary woman Zenobia. He is having an encounter toward midnight in the street (we recall the opening of *Major Molineux*) with an old man with a patch over one eye (suggesting Odin, a prime mover, who wears the patch because he sold his eye for knowledge) who tries ineffectually to tell Coverdale of a service connected with Blithedale and Zenobia that he wishes done. But something Coverdale says, connecting Zenobia and the Veiled Lady, in a simile, appears to seal the old man's lips.

Next day Coverdale leaves his comforts and 'plunges into the pitiless snow-storm in quest of the better life'. What this meant to him is conveyed finely in detail in the imagery of the journey as he travels in dead winter from the City to the Farm. The experiment is founded on ideals such as agriculture as the basis for the good life, no class distinctions, the equality of the sexes and the brotherhood of man. Disillusionment as the ideals are tested by the reality begins for Coverdale at once. The absence of class-consciousness proves theoretical rather than actually attainable. The presence of Zenobia, rich, luxuriantly beautiful, with a hothouse flower in her hair, 'caused our heroic enterprise to show like an illusion, a masquerade, a counterfeit Arcadia. I tried to analyse this impression, but not with much success.' More particularly, he notices from the start and in the next paragraph 'that, as regarded society at large, we stood in the position of new hostility, rather than new brotherhood'. They could support themselves in a competitive society only by 'getting the advantage over the outside barbarians in their own field of labour'. The connection with Zenobia of this 'dawning idea, driven back into my inner consciousness by her entrance', is very real though not immediately apparent: Zenobia is a luxury product. Her beauty, which is a matter of 'bloom, health and vigour', of always having had all that money can buy, her self-confidence and freedom and cultivation, all depend on her being a wealthy woman. She always wears an exotic flower in

her hair, fresh daily; and on Coverdale's arrival at Blithedale
the costly flower, flung to the ground because it has withered,
affects him immediately, and so the reader: 'The action seemed
proper to her character. Nevertheless, it was a singular but
irresistible effect; the presence of Zenobia caused our heroic
enterprise to show like an illusion.' We have just registered this
when Hollingsworth breaks in carrying an unknown young girl.
She is revealed as the very opposite of Zenobia, poorly dressed,
physically blighted. She is the Little Dorrit of the New England
city, the working-girl of the industrial age, the seamstress or
mill-hand, and Hawthorne's concern for this typical product of
his civilization is touchingly conveyed:

...her face was of a wan, almost sickly hue, betokening habitual
seclusion from the sun and free atmosphere, like a flower-shrub that
has done its best to blossom in too scanty light...In short, there has
seldom been so depressed and sad a figure as this young girl's; and
it was hardly possible to help being angry with her, from mere despair
of doing anything for her comfort.

Later on he says Priscilla 'reminded me of plants that one
sometimes observes doing their best to vegetate among the
bricks of an enclosed court, where there is scanty soil, and never
any sunshine'.

Her presence and her behaviour there are equally mysterious.
'She stood near the door, fixing a pair of large, brown,
melancholy eyes upon Zenobia, – only upon Zenobia! – she
evidently saw nothing else in the room but that bright, fair,
rosy, beautiful woman. It was the strangest look I ever witnessed;
long a mystery to me, and forever a memory...I never thoroughly
forgave Zenobia for her conduct on this occasion.' She begs
Zenobia to shelter her and let her be always near her, but
Zenobia is unresponsive. The scene is precisely that of a
morality play and offers the clearest indications that it is to be
understood as such. Only in this ideal community, of course,
can the two sisters, one the daughter of Poverty and the other
of Wealth, live together (we learn later that Zenobia and
Priscilla are daughters of the same father by different mothers,
though only Priscilla is aware of it). Hollingsworth the
philanthropist makes a high-minded appeal to Zenobia and the
community to receive Priscilla, warning them: 'As we do by
this friendless girl, so shall we prosper.' But the right, unaffectedly

human note is struck only by the genuine farmer, their host Silas Foster. Silas's contribution to the whole theme should not be overlooked. He is a touchstone of reality, explicitly so in the later chapter 'The Masqueraders' where we are told:

But Silas Foster, who leaned against a tree near by, in his customary blue frock, and smoking a short pipe, did more to disenchant the scene, with his look of shrewd, acrid, Yankee observation, than twenty witches and necromancers could have done, in the way of rendering it weird and fantastic.

Hollingsworth can tell them only that Priscilla was handed over to him by an old man who begged him to convey her to Blithedale.

Thus a number of flaws in the actuality of Blithedale have been insinuated into our consciousness before Coverdale goes shivering to bed with ominous anticipations fulfilled in 'half-waking dreams' all night. The chapter ends: 'Starting up in bed at length I saw the moon was shining on the snowy landscape, which looked like a lifeless copy of the world in marble. How cold an Arcadia was this!'

It is natural that the next chapter finds Coverdale too ill to rise. He has a delirious fever in which he virtually dies, seeing his previous existence as worthless. While thus out of life, as it were, in a state of clairvoyance or morbid sensitiveness he has an intuitive knowledge of the relation between Priscilla and Zenobia, of what each is, and of the true character of the others at Blithedale. His sense of values has been refined. He can now perceive that Hollingsworth's philanthropy is a terrible form of egotism, his benevolence not human tenderness but a disguise for the need to dominate others. Hollingsworth was formerly a *blacksmith*, that is, as Westervelt observes later on, 'a man of iron in more senses than one' – he is the Endicott of Hawthorne's age.

When Coverdale gets up again it is May Day, he is reborn with the coming of Spring (the symbolism is conscious, for we are told it is not the calendar but the seasonal May Day, and we are to recall the year-cycle celebrated in *The Maypole*, for Zenobia is celebrating with Priscilla). I cannot omit singling out the remarkable passage in which he explains this experience, of his reconcilement with Nature 'whose laws I had broken in various artificial ways'.

I was now on my legs again. My fit of illness had been an avenue between two existences; the low-arched and darksome doorway, through which I had crept out of a life of old conventionalisms, on my hands and knees, as it were, and gained admittance into the freer region that lay beyond. In this respect, it was like death. And, as with death, too, it was good to have gone through it. No otherwise could I have rid myself of a thousand follies, fripperies, prejudices, habits, and other such worldly dust as inevitably settles upon the crowd along the broad highway, giving them all one sordid aspect, before noon-time, however freshly they may have begun their pilgrimage, in the dewy morning. The very substance upon my bones had not been fit to live with, in any better, truer, or more energetic mode than that to which I was accustomed. So it was taken off me and flung aside, like any other worn-out or unseasonable garment; and, after shivering a little while in my skeleton, I began to be clothed anew, and much more satisfactorily than in my previous suit. In literal and physical truth, I was quite another man. I had a lively sense of the exultation with which the spirit will enter on the next stage of its eternal progress, after leaving the heavy burthen of its mortality in an earthly grave, with as little concern for what may become of it, as now affected me for the flesh which I had lost.

In this chapter, ironically called 'A Modern Arcadia', the new Coverdale sees the reality of the society for which he has abandoned (in every sense) the city. He perceives that those attracted to Blithedale were inevitably social misfits: 'Our bond, it seems to me, was not affirmative, but negative' – that is, it could not be true community. What his fellow-members had joined Blithedale for is conveyed in a digression, reminiscent of Swift, on old clothes. But even in spite of themselves the idealists acquire a schooling in reality and Coverdale can still believe in Blithedale in a disenchanted way: 'My hope was, that, between theory and practice, a true and available mode of life might be struck out.' And one of the positives of the Blithedale life is that Priscilla benefits from it.

Now the scene is set, Old Moodie appears again, 'A Visitor from Town'. Unaccountably interesting to Coverdale, as he says, and mysteriously connected with both women, he has come to see whether Zenobia and Priscilla are really equals here. But he is not satisfied, seeing they are still as mistress and servant, and he leaves a curse on the farmhouse. The following chapter begins with a visitor from the opposite direction who comes to fulfil Old Moodie's prediction. Coverdale has sought

'The Wood-Path'; being the artist whose function is 'to distill in his long-brooding thought the whole morality of the performance' (a clue for the reader), he needs at times to retire from the settlement to renew his inner life in the solitude of the forest. But a sinister figure who haunts the woods unknown to him takes him by surprise. There is no poverty in the imagination of evil in Hawthorne, and the evocation of it in this chapter is one of the most astonishing feats in his works. To Young Goodman Brown the Devil came in the sober likeness of his grandfather, distinguishable only by his serpent staff, and to Miles Coverdale he appears in an equally appropriate form, as a finished man of the world though still with a serpent-headed cane and the aura of scepticism. The nineteenth-century Black Man is insufferably familiar in manner and still more insufferable to Coverdale because his tone and appearance are a caricature of what Coverdale was in his former city existence. 'I detested this kind of man; and all the more because a part of my own nature showed itself responsive to him.' Later his 'dislike for this man' is rendered in physical terms as 'nothing less than a creeping of the flesh, as when, feeling about in a dark place, one touches something cold and slimy, and questions what the secret hatefulness may be'. No quotation can convey the psychological subtlety of the scene between the two, which is excellent 'novel' as well, but it is notable that Westervelt is introduced by association with 'the salvage man of antiquity, hirsute and cinctured with a leafy girdle'. There is something underlying his good looks which gives him away: 'there was in his eyes (although they might have artifice enough of another sort) the naked exposure of something that ought not to be left prominent'; and when he laughs, he 'disclosed a gold band around the upper part of his teeth, thereby making it apparent that every one of his brilliant grinders and incisors was a sham. This discovery affected me very oddly. I felt as if the whole man were a moral and physical humbug; his wonderful beauty of face, for aught I knew, might be removable like a mask.'

He also it appears has come to look up Zenobia, Priscilla, and Hollingsworth, with whose affairs he is intimately acquainted. Asked for his credentials

He offered me a card, with 'Professor Westervelt' engraved on it. At the same time, as if to vindicate his claim to the professorial dignity, so often assumed on very questionable grounds, he put on a pair of spectacles, which so altered the character of his face that I hardly knew him again.

He is also the lecture-hall quack of Hawthorne's day, appropriately symbolized as a mesmerist (the name is a happy stroke). Coverdale in his reborn phase reacts against Westervelt's personality and refuses to assist him, so the Professor, ceremoniously raising his hat, departs. Coverdale then climbs up into his secret 'hermitage', a green eyrie in a mass of vine-foliage up a pine-tree; he looks forward in autumn to surprising the Community with the fruits of the vine. The imagery of the fruit is as always in Hawthorne cultural in significance, and toward the end of the romance he finds on his return from the city that the grapes in his hermitage have ripened:

In abundant clusters of the deepest purple, deliciously sweet to the taste, and, though wild, yet free from the ungentle flavor which distinguishes nearly all our native and uncultivated grapes. Methought a wine might be pressed out of them possessing a passionate zest, and endowed with a new kind of intoxicating quality, attended with such bacchanalian ecstasies as the tamer grapes of Madeira, France and the Rhine, are inadequate to produce.

He seems to have agreed with Melville that he had originated a literature and of a different kind than any Europe could show.

Coverdale is next found with his three associates spending Sunday afternoon by a rock in the forest known as Eliot's Pulpit. The passage describing its situation suggests a duality of significance, and Hollingsworth the professed philanthropist (but actually the modern Endicott) preaching there is implicitly contrasted with the real philanthropist 'the holy Apostle Eliot' who had traditionally preached there to the Indians two centuries earlier. There follows a considerable discussion about the position of women and their relation to men, enabling Coverdale to exercise some irony and psychological insight in making his point that 'the intensity of masculine egotism' represented by Hollingsworth was more acceptable than his own offer of equal fellowship, to both the poor girl and the pseudo-emancipated woman because both were 'the result of ages of compelled degradation'. Both women love Hollingsworth, now seen to be the Victorian dominant male. Then we have a painful psychological battle between the two men when

Hollingsworth is forced to admit that he will suffer no freedom of thought and allow no one individual rights; they are forever sundered.

Sickened by these revelations Coverdale is now as stifled by the farm as he was formerly by the city, he feels he must return to 'the settled system of things, to correct himself by a new observation from the old stand-point'. After taking leave of the socialists he has an impulse he cannot explain to take leave of the pigs. Their unselfconscious contentment is a satisfying contrast to the quarrelsome idealists. It is a touch of Hawthorne's genius which is as rightly executed as prompted. Only the inhabitants of the pig-sty have come to terms successfully with life – a criticism of the teaching that preached a return to nature.

The action takes a long pause in the next chapters, 'The Hotel' and 'The Boarding-House' which form the dead centre of the romance and repay close consideration. Here, passively gazing out of the hotel window, Coverdale takes stock of his experience of Blithedale and formulates his now maturer attitude to 'city' life. Slowly he identifies himself with the life of the city again, the general culture of his age. The passage beginning

Whatever had been my taste for solitude and natural scenery, yet the thick, foggy, stifled element of cities, the entangled life of many men together, sordid as it was, and empty of the beautiful, took quite as strenuous a hold upon my mind. I felt as if there could never be enough of it.

is endorsed in minute particulars and he concludes: 'All this was just as valuable, in its way, as the sighing of the breeze among the birch-trees that over-shadowed Eliot's Pulpit.' There is an unexpected wisdom in this part of the book. Hawthorne understood the shallowness of complaining of a 'general sameness' in the houses in city streets and of concluding 'It seemed hardly worth while for more than one of those families to be in existence.' On examining even the one establishment opposite his window he finds it to be a boarding-house with an intriguing variety of forms of life (the opposite in fact of the 'lifeless copy of the world in marble'). To complete the discomfiture of his old assumptions, it turns out also to house Priscilla, Zenobia, and Westervelt. When he calls on Zenobia there he finds her in her town aspect, fashionably gowned and

in her mid-nineteenth-century setting of dazzling chandeliers,
baroque furnishings, and all the vulgar opulence that Henry
James reproduced in *The Wings of the Dove* for Aunt Maud's
London drawing-room. Hawthorne expresses here a genuine
personal disgust for the social life of the rich and the interior
of the purse-proud; his integrity was more than artistic. In
return for his contempt Zenobia twits him, enabling him to note
the American class-consciousness based on money ('In society
indeed, a genuine American never dreams of stepping across
the inappreciable air-line which separates one class from another.
But what was rank to the colonists of Blithedale?'). It seems to
me that in spite of Mr Parkes's denial, in this book alone
Hawthorne enlarges our understanding of the society in which
he lived.

Coverdale then hunts up Old Moodie in a saloon, an aspect
of the city thoroughly brought into focus. He coaxes out at last
for us, as the most telling moment, as in *Major Molineux*, the
clue to the plot. It might be called The Parable of The
American. Originally Fauntleroy, he was princely in his wealth,
living in a 'palace' in New York (one thinks of Henry James's
millionaire-princes typifying America) and the daughter of his
first marriage is an American princess Zenobia (her name
suggesting Eastern opulence and royal state). Losing his wealth
and position he sets up in another incarnation as 'Old Moodie',
in New England, among the poverty-stricken inhabitants of 'a
squalid court' which originally was 'a stately habitation' built
by a colonial governor whose aristocratic residence had become
by the evolution of history a slum tenement. Here his second
marriage to Poverty in the person of 'a forlorn, mean-spirited,
feeble young woman, a seamstress' leaves him with Priscilla who
'like his elder one, might be considered as the true offspring
of both parents, and as the reflection of their state'. This is the
life of the masses, the Priscilla described earlier by Coverdale
as one 'whose impalpable grace lay so singularly between
disease and beauty', and of whom he added, 'if any mortal
really cares for her, it is myself, and not even I for her realities
– but for the fancy-work with which I have idly decked her out'.
Thus Hawthorne already in 1852 had anticipated Dos Passos'
discovery of the Two Nations, symbolized at the end of *U.S.A.*
in a neat parable but compared with Hawthorne's artistically
barbarous.

The last section of New England to be mapped is covered in the next chapter, 'A Village Hall' – an occasion for a 'sociological' note on village life not unrelated to the Blithedale venture. Coverdale observes the farmers, the black-coated workers, the women and girls, and finds all but the old farmers 'looking rather suburban than rural. In these days, there is absolutely no rusticity, except when the actual labor of the soil leaves its earth-mould on the person.' He tells us that Puritanism 'however diversified with later patchwork, still gives its prevailing tint to New England character'. And here he naturally finds Hollingsworth. Westervelt in his role of quack produces Priscilla, the Veiled Lady, as his medium; we are back where the romance began. She is rescued by Hollingsworth and the scene instantly shifts to Blithedale, where there is a Masquerade, similar in intention to the scene in *The Maypole* to suggest the artificiality of the Blithedale communal life. Escaping this, Coverdale comes on a movingly dramatic scene at Eliot's Pulpit between the other three, 'at some acme of their passion that puts them into a sphere of their own, where no other spirit can pretend to stand on equal ground with them'. It is evident that some vital decision has been taken: the iron man, rejecting Zenobia and thus rejecting vitality, intelligence and passion chooses instead in Priscilla the fate we see him subject to in the last chapter. We have in *Blithedale* even more than in the other works I have discussed the disproof of the fallacious current account of Hawthorne. The true artist, he has the indispensable genius for knowing, and communicating, where life flows and wherein lies its value and health. He has consistently shown Zenobia as a creature radiant with life, the splendid human animal, but the stress falls on 'human'; she is not only contrasted with the run of New England women who lacked sensual experience, she is also characterized by her 'noble and beautiful motion' and we are told of her then: 'Natural movement is the result and expression of the whole being, and cannot be well and nobly performed, unless responsive to something in the character.' Her death by drowning is the most poignant of all Hawthorne's writing. Even after she has left the scene for ever Coverdale feels 'It was as if the vivid coloring of her character had left a brilliant stain upon the air', and the memory of her loss blights Coverdale's life. The meditation by her grave is outstanding too.

Hawthorne's sense of the truly human included intellectual freedom, passion and tenderness and he can thus bring home to us in the concrete the tragedy for New England life of the Puritan's rejection of the human possibilities represented by Zenobia who is drowned, Hester who is starved and outlawed, and the Maypole which is cut down, all by the death-dealing Puritan judge (Hollingsworth rejecting Zenobia seemed to Coverdale 'the grim portrait of a Puritan magistrate holding inquest of life and death in a case of witchcraft'). Hawthorne, we see, required man to be humane, and his ideal opposite he represents by the image of the iron man, whether it takes the form of Endicott, or Governor Bellingham with his head separated from his body, or 'that steel engine of the devil's contrivance, a philanthropist'. The very antithesis of the better form of social life he tried to indicate in his writings is represented by the Shaker community, used by him in *The Canterbury Pilgrims* and *The Shaker Bridal*. In the latter the very title is an irony, for the relation imposed on the betrothed couple by the Shaker system is the antithesis of marriage – death in life, ending with the woman 'like a corpse in its burial clothes'. With his usual genius for imagery Hawthorne concentrates the sense of life-hatred in the castration image of the 'awful' old man, Father Ephraim, their dying leader; 'Tradition whispered, that Mother Ann had been compelled to sear his heart of flesh with a red-hot iron, before it could be purified from earthly passions.' Hester Prynne's nature in afflicted households 'showed itself warm and rich, a well-spring of tenderness'.

Hawthorne's moral sense is not something in conflict with these instinctive preferences, it is a corresponding form of sensitiveness. He believed – the proof is in his art – that human beings have no right to take up attitudes of rejection and condemnation toward life. The Prison is Hawthorne's symbol of the society that condemns and punishes, and his heroes and heroines are its victims. The eternal pattern that he saw behind all social life in his America from the beginning has in *Blithedale* been traced in the nineteenth century too: the ideal community is disintegrated for the Puritan and hence the Devil cannot be kept out; the separation of rich and poor is insuperable in this age; the Puritan always masters the scene, and as always he rejects Zenobia for Priscilla and what Zenobia stands for is destroyed and lost to society. Coverdale relapses again, having no choice, into a self-indulgent man-about-town, for life. The Blithedale experiment has failed. 'Alas, what faith is requisite to bear up against such results of generous effort!' Those are almost Coverdale's last words, but his actual last are a positive affirmation of faith.

Not unrelated to Hawthorne's recurrent theme, but more directly personal, is the class of stories to which *The Snow-Image* belongs, which includes *The Devil in Manuscript* and *The Artist of the Beautiful*, the equivalents of Henry James's stories about writers. Their theme is equally the problem of the artist in a society in which, as James wrote, 'the interest in literature is of the smallest'. James continued: 'Poor Hawthorne, beginning to write subtle short stories at Salem, was empirical enough.' The finest of these, *The Snow-Image* – significantly sub-titled 'A Childish Miracle' – at first sight might seem merely a translation into the New England idiom of a Hans Andersen story. But it is not playful nor a fairy-tale, it is an exposition of Hawthorne's predicament as an artist in an entirely bourgeois society such as he found himself doomed to write for. Though Poe and Melville wrote admiring reviews of his stories, they otherwise fell flat until *The Scarlet Letter* made him known at the age of forty-six. 'Snow-images' occurs in the introduction to *The Scarlet Letter* as symbolic of what the artist makes – 'the forms which fancy summons up' and which, if 'a heart and sensibilities of human tenderness' are communicated to them, are 'converted from snow-images into men and women'. Literature needs collaboration; the Snow-Image is the creation of the artist's imagination but it is only by sympathetic participation, by an imaginative sharing of the whole community (the father and mother in the story, as well as the children) that it can continue to be kept alive or valid. It is destroyed by the uncomprehending spirit that has no belief in anything but the materially profitable. *The Artist of the Beautiful* puts the same case rather differently. Hawthorne was then forty, and we find him concluding that 'It is requisite for the ideal artist to possess a force of character that seems hardly compatible with its delicacy; he must keep his faith in himself while the incredulous world assails him with its utter disbelief.' Hawthorne had a good deal of experience of that, as the Preface to the *Twice-Told Tales* shows. He is the classic case of the artist foiled by his

inability to find an intelligent public, and it is a proof of his
genius that he managed to carry on so long without co-operation
– like Blake, Melville, D. H. Lawrence, Conrad, Henry James,
with whom he is entitled to stand. There are few things more
impressive in the history of the novel than the determination
of the first great American novelists to find a non-naturalistic
form for their work and to reject the English novelists' tradition
of social comedy and melodrama, derived from the theatre.
Hawthorne was truly 'empirical'. He can be seen consciously
trying, or somehow discovering for himself, the various possible
techniques for his purpose: the märchen (*Young Goodman
Brown*), the allegory of Bunyan (*The Celestial Railroad*), of
Spenser and Milton, the romance, the morality play, the legend
(*The Gray Champion* follows the widespread Holgar the Dane
pattern), the myth, the masque, drama of various kinds in the
light of Shakespeare, the panorama (*Main Street*), the pageant,
the fable, the parable. As became a pioneer, Hawthorne
instinctively kept close to the sources of literature. His stage is
the platform stage of early drama, his settings of the traditional
sort such as are provided for by a tree, an archway, a street,
a public square, a forest clearing, the outside of a church, a
fountain or well or pool. His stage noticeably differs from his
equally dramatic successor's – in comparison, James's is seen to
be the modern three-sided box. James took Hawthorne's drama
indoors, or if not always into the drawing-room then onto the
lawn or terrace of the country-house. Though both are equally
concerned with the problems of a social life, they work at
different levels. Over against Hawthorne's symbol of Young
Goodman Brown James has, among many such, Pandora Day,
a name so happily symbolic as to need no commentary. His
American Artist is Roderick Hudson, his Old Moodie is
Christopher Newman, he turns Westervelt (as Mr Bewley has
shown in *Scrutiny*) into Selah Tarrant. Instead of the problem
of the Snow-Image we have to decide what is the Lesson of the
Master. In sum, James's symbols belong to a later stage of
civilization, but greater sophistication is not necessarily a proof
of superiority in literature. It would have been impossible for
James to create Hawthorne's rosebush and fruit and scaffold
symbols, or to seize on Hawthorne's Maypole as the appropriate
symbol for describing the conflict between the cultures of the
old world and the new. James's drama has become secular,

whereas Hawthorne's concern for his culture is positively religious and never gets out of touch with the sources of a religious drama. His folk-lore element is always notably more serious than Scott's, though he has nothing so picturesque as *Wandering Willie's Tale* and many of his attempts to write American folk-story are failures (like *Mr Higginbotham's Catastrophe*) from poverty of the raw material. The apparent oddities of his writings are not due to incompetence but are inherent in their nature; he is fragmentary as are Shakespeare's *Winter's Tale* and the old Ballads.

This is the case it seems to me to urge against the argument that genius must be bulky and that Hawthorne did not write enough to be a major novelist. Hawthorne's claim does rest on a small body of work, but even ignoring his importance as a trail-blazer, an infector and literary ancestor, that work is sufficient. It is slight only in being tense, sensitive, elegant as a mathematical proof, sinewy, concentrated as a poem and incorruptibly relevant. Economy in art is not only a means but a test, a condition of significance. *The Europeans* has been dismissed as 'slight', 'a water-colour' and insignificant because it is brief, but it is none the less demonstrably a major work of art and profoundly significant;[8] whereas the bulkiness of a Dreiser or a Thomas Wolfe is positively against him. As in *The Europeans* there is always in Hawthorne's best writings the sense of a deeply significant public drama being enacted behind the deceptively simple apparent story. Looking back on his work, one's eye is inevitably caught and held by *The Scarlet Letter* with its structural symbols of the Scaffold and the Labyrinth, the Rose and the Black Flower, and one recalls Mr C. N. Deedes's conclusion in his essay on that most ancient structure 'The Labyrinth':

The Labyrinth was the centre of all the strongest emotions of the people – joy, fear and grief were there given the most intense forms of expression. These emotions were directed into certain channels, producing ritual and the earliest forms of art. The Labyrinth, as tomb and temple, fostered the development of all art and literature, activities which in those days possessed a religious and life-giving significance.

Melville: the 1853–6 phase

> This Shakespeare is a queer man. At times... he does not always
> seem reliable. There appears to be a certain – what shall I call it?
> – hidden sun, say, about him, at once enlightening and mystifying.
>
> *The Confidence Man*

The Piazza Tales

Julian Hawthorne wrote in an otherwise percipient reminiscence
of Melville's character and disposition that 'His later writings
are incomprehensible.' This, from Hawthorne's son, who had
presumably been initiated into the meaning and method of his
father's work and so should have had some insight at least into
that art which derived from Hawthorne's, suggests how
inevitable it was that Melville could find no public for his
fiction after his early phase as a writer of adventure books about
voyages by sea. Even the incomparable *Benito Cereno* made no
real impact in America in Melville's long lifetime.

But to the modern English and American reader, well trained
in practical criticism and knowing with regard to myth,
symbol, allegory and imagery, the writings of the great 1853–6
phase are of more interest than the earlier novels, evidently
more accomplished as art, more varied – written in the short
space of three years and with desperate need of money, they
show an astonishing range of subject-matter, attitude, tone
and style – and are noticeably more condensed, controlled
and mature than either *Moby Dick* or *Pierre*, the two previous
major works; and this in spite of the discouraging fact that
even *Moby Dick* had not been a financial success while *Pierre*
had been and remained a dead loss. Yet Melville rallied from
the disappointment, though it seriously affected his health, and
triumphantly wound up this last phase of prose creativeness

with an ironic masterpiece, *The Confidence Man*. But in order
to understand this difficult and still highly controversial work
one must, it seems to me, have grasped the nature of the tales
written while he was gestating the novel. Published mostly in
magazines, they were reprinted as *The Piazza Tales* and reveal
his interests and preoccupations in these fertile years as well as
the kinds of technique he was inventing for these new purposes.

The Encantadas is simply a series of ten sketches which have
as unifying theme the horrors of a tropical waterless Nature
which sustains only equally infernal forms of animal and
human existence. They show how Melville's imagination at this
period was haunted by the memory of the histories of the
wretched castaways with their inhuman treatment by fellow-men
who exceed them in cruelty. This culminates in the history of
the poor half-breed woman Hunilla, treacherously deserted
with her family by the captain committed to returning for them
and, as sole survivor, raped by whaleboatmen to whom she
looked for rescue. A pious Catholic, Hunilla had the fortitude
to preserve her sanity and faith. Melville concludes her history
with Hunilla riding away Christ-like on an ass, eyeing 'the
beast's armorial cross', and 'Humanity, thou strong thing, I
worship thee, not in the laureled victor, but in this vanquished
one' – an affirmation of faith, in humanity at least and in spite
of its worst manifestations, which must not be overlooked in
any discussion of Melville's attitude to God and man at this
period.

The others really are integral tales. They fall into groups, for
instance three double tales each consisting of a contrasted pair,
a technique that is to be seen in use in *The Confidence Man*, and
these all spring from experiences in England and America that
aroused Melville's generous indignation at social conditions –
treatment of the poor, class snobbery extending even to
religious worship, and surprisingly, in view of the exclusion of
women from his previous novels except as ideas in *Pierre* and
Mardi, to the treatment of women, who are seen as victims of
Nature as well as of man and society. Thus in these years
Melville was manifesting a considerable degree of emotional
and moral involvement in social life on land, both in England
and America. In *The Piazza Tales* we are not living in 'The
World in a Man-of-War' as in *White Jacket* or in the world
in a whaling-ship as in *Moby Dick*, but are taken into the full

living world of the Anglo-American mid-nineteenth century, a very great step forward for Melville as an artist into the complexities of living, even into the difficulties of family life for the man and the artist. We remember that Melville was married in 1847 and by now had children, a family to support, and was living in a household that contained also his mother and three of his sisters, a concentration of women with claims on him that inevitably forced on his attention the woman's point of view, and which also obliged him to reconsider the man's role as individual (as in *I and My Chimney*), and as artist tormented by the rival claims of his work and the support of his family.

The tale of *Bartleby the Scrivener* (1853) has received plenty of critical attention and there is no disagreement as to its meaning and the nature of its techniques, which present no difficulty. But recognition has not been given to the fact that it is one of Melville's try-outs and not an adopted position, much less a personal admission of neurosis. This is the only tale of the batch that ends in limbo. Bartleby is posited as the man who adopts a consistently negative response to the demands of unsatisfactory living in the Wall Street society (copying while facing a blank wall). His unshakable 'I would prefer not to' which he persists in until it inevitably leaves him dead of starvation in prison, with 'peering out upon him the eyes of murderers and thieves', is yet felt, like Hunilla's tragedy, to be a triumph of the indomitable spirit: Bartleby, even the lawyer his employer feels, is at rest 'with kings and counselors'. Melville himself concludes with 'Ah, Bartleby! Ah, humanity!' which is unfathomably ambiguous, perhaps a sad recognition of the human condition. Bartleby's suicidal choice is not so much the centre of Melville's attention as the complex reaction to it of his employer, whose mixture of exasperation and pity in his efforts first to save Bartleby and failing this, to wash his hands of him – all too human – are examined not without sympathy. For what could be done for a Bartleby? Can one envisage a society composed of Bartlebies? – Melville examines this question in *The Confidence Man*. Bartleby's having been a clerk in the Dead Letter Office, and then a mere copyist of other people's compositions, are not very obscure references to the kind of literary non-life Melville saw he himself would be relegated to in all likelihood after the failure of *Pierre* and the

destruction by fire in 1853 of the plates of all his novels, and
with the increasing weakness of his eyesight (like Bartleby's).
Not surprisingly, several tales of this period are discussions of
the problem of the artist who has to earn a living in
mid-nineteenth-century America – *Cock-a-Doodle-Doo!*, *The
Fiddler*, *I and My Chimney*. Only two years before (1851) Melville
had praised Hawthorne for, as an artist, always 'saying No! in
thunder' – 'the Devil himself cannot make him say *yes*' – and
had since been inclined to castigate all those who do say *yes*,
an indication of the line Melville was to explore systematically
in *The Confidence Man*. Characteristically, Melville had proceeded
from his ardent endorsement of Hawthorne's apparent attitude
to testing its validity by actualizing it in the case of a consistent
practitioner, Bartleby, when he recognizes that however heroic
it is impracticable; Bartleby's employer, the average citizen,
had always been convinced, he says, that 'the easiest way of
life is the best', which though ignoble is a means of survival,
we see. And a year after *Bartleby* Melville tried out such an
alternative to Bartleby's in an odd short sketch *The Fiddler*.

This opens with the despair of the narrator, a poet named
Helmstone: 'So my poem is damned, and immortal fame is
not for me! Intolerable fate!' But he is 'instantly soothed' by
being introduced to the amiable and winning genius Hautboy
(presumably meaning 'a high-flier') whose fame has passed
and his fortune with it. But he is quite content to drudge for
a living by teaching the fiddle: '*With* genius and *without* fame,
he is happier than a king', his friend Standard (the average
man) assures Helmstone, who feels 'I wish I were Hautboy.'
So he tears up his manuscripts and follows this model's
example. The tale is merely an annotation of an idea and has
none of the convincing detail, the sensitive complexity and the
involved technical devices Melville found necessary for the
more substantial tales, showing he did not entertain this
alternative very seriously. I simply cite it as another proof that
his mind worked from theory to posited embodiments in
alternative forms of life (like Dickens). For these he drew
equally on incidents in his own experience, on documents and
historical facts, and on the lives of real people, thus doing his
best to keep his theorizing in touch with actuality and to direct
his abstract thinking on to the life of the individual and the
welfare of society.

Nearly a year before, Melville had published the very remarkable tale *Cock-a-Doodle-Doo!* In this case Melville took off from Wordsworth's poem *Resolution and Independence* which must have exasperated him since, starting from reflections of a kind relevant to Melville's own position, on the disastrous fate of poets who from beginning in gladness pass through despondency to madness owing to poverty, Wordsworth apparently found arguments in the fortitude of the Leech-gatherer for reassurance and trust in Providence. To Melville, in debt, and in fear of blindness and possibly also of the madness from which his father died, such optimism was superficial. Accordingly, his tone in this tale is harsh and jeering. He exhibits in refutation of Wordsworth the painful history of Merrymusk (that is, 'Merry Music', creative genius) and his family, the tale being for the most part a rude parody of the poem. The narrator, in financial trouble himself and not finding comfort in Nature like Wordsworth, is cheered by the 'prodigious exulting strains' of a cock which ring through the whole countryside and throw him into a rapturous, buoyant state. It turns out to be owned by a desperately poor but dignified wood-sawyer who proudly declares: 'I raised it.' He calls it Trumpet and it crows only at his command – evidently the voice of his art which, while it can't bring him an income, makes up to him and his sick wife and children for their deprivations in material things. The narrator watches them all die happy in hearing to the last the 'glorious and rejoicing crow' of their unique Trumpet. This part is not satiric: the uncomplaining wife is heroic in her 'long-loving sympathy' with her husband, and as for the four children – listening to the cock 'Their faces shone celestially through grime and dirt. They seemed children of emperors and kings, disguised.' Merrymusk himself insists as he dies that he and all of them are well, 'in a kind of wild ecstasy of triumph over ill'. Last of all Trumpet dies, and the narrator buries them all in one grave with on the gravestone 'a lusty cock in act of crowing' and the possibly unironic inscription 'O death, where is thy sting? O grave, where is thy victory?' and – reverting now to the original tone – ends: 'and never since then have I felt the doleful dumps'.

I have never encountered an explanation of why Merrymusk should have named his cock 'Trumpet'. My own conjecture is that Melville had several poems of Wordsworth's, besides

Resolution and Independence, in his mind when composing this tale, all of them having in common the theme of the poet's creative powers. So Wordsworth's sonnet on The Sonnet was brought in by naming Merrymusk's art after what Wordsworth tells us was the favourite poetic form of great poets, as of Wordsworth himself; and the account culminates in Milton's use of the sonnet, when

> In his hand
> The Thing became a trumpet; whence he blew
> Soul-animating strains – alas, too few!

So in this complex and subtly Wordsworthian tale, which is surprisingly like D. H. Lawrence in tone and content, Melville registers belief in the sustaining and revivifying power of art, and in support of my interpretation we note that the rustic humour and scoffing tone are abandoned whenever the narrator confronts the Merrymusk household. And he is genuinely disturbed by the mighty power of Trumpet: 'the cock frightened me, like some overpowering angel in the Apocalypse' – as well as sincerely humbled by the character of Merrymusk who denies he deserves pity, declaring with superb conviction:

Why call *me* poor? Don't the cock *I* own glorify this otherwise inglorious, lean lantern-jawed land? Didn't *my* cock encourage *you*? And *I* give you all this glorification away gratis. I am a great philanthropist. I am a rich man – a very rich man, and a very happy one. Crow, Trumpet.

The narrator admits he 'was not wholly at rest concerning the soundness of Merrymusk's views of things, though full of admiration for him. I was thinking on the matter before my door, when I heard the cock crow again. Enough. Merrymusk is right. Oh, noble cock! oh, noble man!'

Note that New England is envisaged here as a Puritan; that is to say, the land of Puritan settlers was ignorant of art though desperately in need of it. Also, it is unable to appreciate art – no one in the countryside but the narrator and the Merrymusk family is able to hear the cock, a sly touch. An 'inglorious land' indeed! An interpretation that, because the rest can't hear the cock, the voice is imaginary and Melville trying to come to terms with a neurosis; or alternatively, that

'cock' being a sex-term the tale must be understood as a sexual
double-entendre – are equally instances of perverse critical
sophistry. The identification of cocks with poets is made beyond
doubt by Melville's parody of Wordsworth's lines (at the end
of the seventh stanza of *Resolution and Independence*) on the sad
history of poets:

> Of fine mornings,
> We fine lusty cocks begin our crows in gladness;
> But when eve does come we don't crow quite so much,
> For then cometh despondency and madness.

And in his description of the cock's crow we see the characteristics
of his own literary voice: 'full of pluck, full of fire, full of fun,
full of glee. It plainly says – "*Never say die!*"'

Merrymusk then is Melville's idea of a more convincing
model for Wordsworth's Leech-gatherer and he is also, with
his inspiring voice Trumpet, Melville the artist (who thought
of himself as poet-novelist) – we are told Merrymusk had been
first a sailor, then a small farmer, and was now a hired drudge,
Melville's own history. The story of the family dying prematurely
as they do from harrowing poverty is surely an ironic comment
on Wordsworthian trust, carrying on the ridicule with which
the tale started. There is also satire in the reiterated fact that
the baseless self-confidence the cock's crowing gives the
narrator inspires him to reckless financial behaviour and
evidently future ruin. Yet there is no doubt that Trumpet is
'the cheerer', and when he perches on the sick children's bed
'All their wasted eyes gazed at him with a wild and spiritual
delight. They seemed to sun themselves in the radiant plumage
of the cock.' This is sincere and moving. Melville seems to be
trying to explain that though the dolours of the poet's life of
poverty that Wordsworth brushes aside are inescapable and
bear hardest on his family, *yet* they all, and everyone else in
the world too, have thereby the consolations of art which can
make life blissful and suffering negligible. The artist's support
therefore can only be looked for in his sense of achievement,
Melville argues.

Wordsworth's 1815 sonnet to the unfortunate painter
Haydon is another that Melville seems to me to have drawn
on as a help to expressing his theme in *Cock-a-Doodle-Doo!* It
is next but one to the 'Trumpet' sonnet in the 1849–50 edition

of Wordsworth's poems and is of such importance in elucidating
Melville's argument and the conclusion we should extract that
I will cite it in full:

> High is our calling, Friend! – Creative Art
> (Whether the instrument of words she use,
> Or pencil pregnant with ethereal hues,)
> Demands the service of a mind and heart,
> Though sensitive, yet, in their weakest part,
> Heroically fashioned – to infuse
> Faith in the whispers of the lonely Muse,
> While the whole world seems adverse to desert.
> And, oh! when Nature sinks, as oft she may,
> Through long-lived pressure of obscure distress,
> Still to be strenuous for the bright reward
> And in the soul admit of no decay,
> Brook no continuance of weak-mindedness –
> Great is the glory, for the strife is hard!

It is important to note that in these tales Melville shows he
is as much concerned as Henry James or Hawthorne with the
problems of the life of the artist and the necessity of art for
the life of the spirit, because we must also note that these
considerations are completely absent from the picture of life
in the America of the 1850s drawn for *The Confidence Man* shortly
after. Something he knew to be central and vital has there been
deliberately omitted. And these tales, particularly the complex
Cock-a-Doodle-Doo!, show the kind of difficulty we are faced
with in reading these later Melville works. The complexity does
not disguise the meaning but it shows that several meanings
are intended which, united, provide the means of arriving at
a just conclusion. He is in his creative activity exploring all the
possibilities in a given human problem, facing and considering
them in turn and playing one off against the other, the changes
of tone and direction giving us guide-lines. Thus in these tales
he developed the method he was to need for *The Confidence Man*,
and one may well feel that tales like *Bartleby*, *Benito Cereno*,
Cock-a-Doodle-Doo! and *The Tartarus of Maids* are almost
inexhaustible.

This last, two years later than the story of Merrymusk, takes
up the question of man's relation to woman by contrasting
the light-hearted conviviality of bachelors, as Melville had
gratefully experienced it in England in the Temple and a

London Club (*The Paradise of Bachelors*) with a visit to the
representative hell of women, a paper-mill in a New England
winter. Melville actually visited such a mill to buy paper for
his writings, in 1851, and the occasion, the uncannily
suggestive physical features of the landscape there, and some
of the actual names of these features, evidently gave Melville
the idea of combining the two aspects of women's hardships
– being condemned to drudgery by man and to additional
suffering as being designed by Nature for child-bearing.

The mill is owned and managed by a bachelor ('Old Bach')
and the only other male is his heartless boy assistant called
Cupid. Melville was recurrently foot-loose, and now tied to a
household of women and children no doubt looked to the
care-free bachelor state as paradisal. There is no need to deduce
that Melville was therefore homosexual in feeling. He seems
to have formed these associations from the time of *Moby Dick*,
where the ship 'The Bachelor' encountered by the *Pequod*
represents, Richard Chase thought, 'America sailing off evasively
towards an archaic utopia'; Captain Delano's very
masculine American ship is named 'The Bachelor's Delight';
and in *The Confidence Man* the 'Missouri bachelor' figures
ambiguously as a Melville mouthpiece, his bachelor status
being part of his refusal on principle to be committed to any
human relationship; the name of the paper-mill's boss is
therefore consonant with Melville's ideas about bachelorhood
after he had married. Before, women don't figure in the novels,
but if it is argued that these take place on ships, necessarily
a man's world only, it is pertinent to reply that, in Conrad's
similarly restricted world of shipboard, women always figure,
if not actually then by inhabiting the memories of the sailors
– e.g. in *Typhoon* both officers and men are always thinking what
their mothers and wives at home would feel, are writing letters
to them, or recalling memories of their homes and shore-leaves,
so that their women-folk seem vividly present. This is never
so in Melville's ship-worlds. What matrimony and fatherhood
did for Melville, it seems, was to give him, as one who then
saw bachelorhood as the natural state of man's desiring, a sense
of guilt and remorse towards his wife and family, and by
extension to the corresponding state to bachelor in women,
whose lot was comparatively unenviable whether as maid or
wife. The implication here is that the bachelor's way of life is

only possible because he is selfishly using women as wage-slaves and domestic drudges as well as sexually. And in addition, for Melville in his vocation as writer they toil in the mill to make his paper as well as his children. No wonder *The Tartarus of Maids* carries such weight.

Thus this tale needs, and gets, a dual symbolism, each employed with a devastating effect. The duality is combined in the person of the narrator, who is always of great importance in a Melville tale. He describes himself as a seedsman, one needing paper for his business of distributing seeds to the whole country, thus he represents Melville as both a man and a writer, creative in both aspects, a living pun. This conceit is given a very sombre exposition and we are left with extremely painful impressions: by 'inscrutable nature' woman has been badly treated physiologically compared with man, and by society forced to live by self-destroying and unremitting toil, as the bachelor manager callously and self-righteously explains. The narrator perceives that the physical life of the female is governed by 'unbudging fatality'; horrified, he is overcome with a deadly chill, first brought on by the alarming scenery leading to the mill whose features are described not as erotic but as awe-inspiring, and the women are all consumptive and half-frozen owing to their working conditions. Just as the natural scenery outside is suggestive of the female anatomy in its mechanical aspects, so the machine-tending inside the mill suggests the processes of gestation and parturition. There is neither sniggering nor disgust, but much compassion towards the women, who are described at work 'like so many mares haltered to the rack' ('rack' inevitably suggesting a pun, for they are racked with pain too), and gestation is seen as 'a mere machine, the essence of which is unvarying punctuality and precision' that 'strikes dread into the human heart'. The two levels at which this tale must be apprehended is a technique Melville developed in these tales and later uses consistently in *The Confidence Man*. To call it 'a game', a device for hood-winking the reader, is to slight the art of a serious and responsible creative mind.

There are two other tales of this group during which Melville must have been thinking out *The Confidence Man* which are relevant to it. One is the much-analysed *Benito Cereno*, whose point for this purpose is the ambiguity of the final resolution.

The sub-title of *Pierre* was: 'or, the Ambiguities', and this might apply at least as well to nearly all the 1853–6 works which finally, in *The Confidence Man*, culminate in layer upon layer of ambiguity which has become an all-embracing technique. Captain Delano's disabilities for apprehending the truth – that is, the true state of affairs on board the Spanish slave-ship – are due to his having been indoctrinated with the convenient American theory that the black man is a kind of 'Newfoundland dog', devoted to his master, sub-human in intelligence but amiable and docile. Though Delano has had enough experience as a captain to know the facts of life about white men, this theory prevents him from following up his intuitions of something wrong aboard the *San Dominick*, making him believe, for instance, that the maternal affection shown by the negresses is reassuring, so that there cannot be a conspiracy at work. [This is a preliminary study of the harm done by the Confidence Man, and that novel actually opens with a Negro cripple as the first incarnation of this modern Devil.] Even when the full facts come out in court at the end, the ambiguity of appearances is not resolved by a final manifestation of the truth, for there is still the question that is raised by the introspective Spaniard: Was not the stupidity and blindness of the American what saved him from being murdered by the Negroes? To have been without illusions would have been fatal. Thus Melville in *Benito Cereno* is not only enquiring why we don't make true judgments but tentatively asks also, Is it always desirable that we should? The grey sky and sea and the indeterminate horizon give way at the end to blue skies and sunshine and apparent security (the blacks have been subjugated again), but the Spaniard, unlike the American who is untroubled by the experience and has learnt nothing from it – and survives – the Spaniard pines away from the horror of having learnt of what the mind and heart of man are capable. Misjudgment of the Negro due to a belief 'that they were all tractable' was the tragedy of the Spaniards, but, we learn, the salvation of the Americans. White and black as symbols of good and evil, truth and falsehood, are used, but less unambiguously, in *The Confidence Man*. Delano is therefore cast for the role of an American Candide. His optimism about human nature in general, and black in particular, transcends reality until he sees Babo about to murder Don Benito, when he instantly reassesses the situation and immediately takes all necessary steps to set things right. Melville thus acknowledges the courage and practical virtues of the American extrovert, which he valued, even though he saw its complacency as dangerous.

Another appearance, in person this time, of the con-man in a tale, *The Lighting-Rod Man*, brings us even closer to the novel of the following year. Here he comes as salesman for authoritarian religion, one who 'travels in storm-time and drives a brave trade with the fears of man'. The householder addresses him as Jupiter Tonans, but he is a 'gloomy' figure with melodramatic eyes and a denunciatory style of speech. He claims to be able to protect against lightning by the power of his magic rod which Melville, saying No in thunder, refuses to buy since to do so would be acquiescing in the intruder's pretensions. He is revealed as a combination of witch-doctor, Calvinist minister, Catholic priest, Hell-fire religionist, missionary – in fact, he stands for all domineering advocates of the one-true-religion orthodoxy. Melville's householder's opposition is not atheism but rational and humanistic: he refuses to be afraid of the thunder-storm and when the 'pedlar of indulgences' threatens to stab him to the heart with his trinitarian lightning-rod the dauntless householder breaks it and flings 'the dark lightning-king' out of his house. He has just made to the priest an affirmation of a higher faith, and it is interesting that this comes out in biblical form:

The hairs of our heads are numbered, and the days of our lives. In thunder as in sunshine, I stand at ease in the hands of my God. False negotiator, away! See, the scroll of the storm is rolled back; the house is unharmed; and in the blue heavens I read in the rainbow, that the Deity will not, of purpose, make war on man's earth.

So Melville is not here merely rejecting fear-based religions; his mouthpiece is affirming faith in Renaissance Man and in something symbolized by Noah's covenant with the God of Genesis, that was sealed by the rainbow. Like Ahab in *Moby Dick*, Melville's householder refuses to be 'god-bullied'; but unlike Ahab he is not godless. [Nevertheless, the tale was refused magazine publication.]

In accordance with these views, Melville had in the manuscript dedicated *The Confidence Man* 'to victims of Auto da Fe'; but he removed this before publication, suggesting that the novel

had far transcended the implications of such a dedication, even
if he had meant it to be taken widely as referring to the victims
of all religious orthodoxies or even all sufferers for intransigence.
The earlier parts of the novel do feature religionists – an
Episcopal clergyman, a Methodist chaplain and a sanctimonious
man in grey, an Evangelical who has mass missionary projects
against the heathen to be carried out in 'the Wall Street spirit'
– as incarnations or allies of the Confidence Man, but then
mid-nineteenth-century Christianity, perhaps the original
target, drops out of sight until the last chapter as the writer's
intellectual high spirits and fertility of speculation roam over
further fields and prospects than Christianity provides.

In none of the tales of this period can I find any justification
for Hawthorne's opinion (*English Notebooks*, 20 November 1856)
that Melville's 'writings, for a long while past, have indicated
a morbid state of mind'. In *I and My Chimney* (published 1855)
there is reassuring good-humour in the narrator's recognition
that the women of his family suspect the soundness of his home's
exceptionally tall and finely-wrought chimney, resent its bulk
and mysterious foundations, which they fancy must contain
a secret chamber with hidden treasure, and believe that the
house would be safer and more comfortable without such a
chimney. They torment the old man by getting in 'a
master-mason' to test it and arrange if unsound for its removal,
but the narrator circumvents them all. He has explained that
the chimney 'is my backbone', 'the one grand permanence of
this abode' and that 'when all the house shall have crumbled
from it, this chimney will still survive'. The tale ends: 'I and
my chimney will never surrender.' Thus the chimney is a
composite symbol standing, apparently, for his morale, his
immortal soul (which he is determined to call his own), the
source of his creative power (the chimney's foundations are
buried in darkness, deep down), his intellect, his personality,
and his inherited traditions (a kinsman named Dacres – that
is, 'Sacred' – built the house); the chimney also seems to stand,
like the personal tree in European folk-tales, for his life-force,
for it is sinking into the ground and crumbling as he himself
grows old. This is one of Melville's most intimate and most
suggestive tales. It is surely also good proof of its author's mental
health. There is much wry amusement at the narrator's situation
and some sympathy for the wife, misguided though she is, who

has to put up with the disadvantages of living with an obstinately conservative and privacy-loving intellectual, one resigned to old age and death but not to interference with his essential self.

In short, it must be generally recognized that the tales of Melville are some of the finest *contes* and short stories in the language, as well as some of the most original, and that, like D. H. Lawrence and Hawthorne, his claim to stature as an artist is to be based on his tales at least as much as on his novels.

The Confidence Man

Immediately Melville had got his new novel off his hands he set off for the East, stopping at Liverpool to visit his friend Hawthorne who was consul there. Hawthorne recorded his impressions of Melville in his diary (*English Notebooks*, November 1856) and the passage is so valuable as evidence of Melville's character and preoccupations at the time of writing his last major prose work that I will start by citing it. He notes that Melville on arrival looked 'a little paler, a little sadder' and 'with his characteristic gravity and reserve of manner' 'is much over-shadowed since I saw him last', guessing that Melville 'no doubt suffered from too constant literary occupation, pursued without much success, latterly'. A couple of days later when they had had a long talk he wrote:

Melville, as he always does, began to reason of Providence and futurity, and of everything that lies beyond human ken, and informed me that he had 'pretty much made up his mind to be annihilated'; but he still does not seem to rest in that anticipation; and, I think, will never rest until he gets hold of a definite belief. It is strange how he persists...in wandering to-and-fro over these deserts... He can neither believe, nor be comfortable in his unbelief; and he is too honest and courageous not to try to do one or the other. If he were a religious man, he would be one of the most truly religious and reverential; he has a very high and noble nature, and better worth immortality than most of us.

Before leaving, Melville told Hawthorne that 'he already felt much better than in America'. So writing this group of tales and the novel, and leaving America behind him, had evidently been therapeutic, and the 'annihilation' refers not to suicidal intentions but to his inability to believe in an after-life. And his position as revealed to Hawthorne was not that of the 'village atheist' he has sometimes been labelled but that of a truth-seeker with an open mind. This is what we should have expected from these creative writings, as I've shown. And *The Confidence Man* itself is speculative, not dogmatic, and diversified by apparently endless, effortless improvisations on the theme he has chosen.

This novel, confidently dismissed by Julian Hawthorne, and declared by later English critics to be 'unreadable', seems to have been rediscovered by Richard Chase in his pioneer book *Herman Melville* (1949), and we now have a consensus of at any rate American literary criticism that it contains Melville's most mature prose writing and some of his most interesting thinking. However, this theoretical agreement has gone along with some ill-judged interpretations of the novel, such as, for instance, that it is entirely or mainly an anti-Christian exercise, or in sum no more than an April Fool jape of an esoteric kind whose object is to reveal God as a heartless joker and life a pointless deceit, one that even adopts for this trivial end an elaborate disguise, the avatars of Hindu mythology, and a Buddhist interpretation of the riddle of the Universe as being a masquerade, or that life is an illusion where black is indistinguishable from white. All these do Melville a considerable injustice for they imply that he was either irresponsible (which we know from his previous creative work and all other evidence of this period that he could not be) or a contemptible thimble-rigger. We know that this was not so, from Hawthorne's testimony at this date to his 'very high and noble nature', nor should any *literary* critic fail to see that Melville is at various points in *The Confidence Man* deeply involved. We can point to the pugnacious style and strongly presented moral values implicit and explicit. Elizabeth S. Foster who made a careful study of the versions and earlier draft says that 'We see him in his revisions moving always...from the loose structure, open clarity, and directness of his earliest versions of passages' into a 'complexity that looks like simplicity', for which he evolved a style that 'desiderates under-statement, under-emphasis, litotes'; and she shows him 'pruning' and 'groping for the exact word' and 'toning down' – proof surely of a serious intention.

In fact, readers may well complain of considerable difficulties that Melville makes by having put excessive ingenuity into cross-references in the text and into concealing clues, especially quotations. These are generally from the Bible (a source no longer commanded by most highbrow readers) but which are essential for interpreting his meanings. The book therefore requires – and repays – repeated reading. The main difficulty is to decide how the multiple ironies, both local and total, which are generally doubled-faced anyway, are to be taken. An inordinate amount of misplaced ingenuity has been devoted to discussion of exactly who the 'avatars' of the Confidence Man are, and to assigning them to some mythological or theological system, and to tracking down possible clues to their significance. But for purposes of literary criticism they do not much matter; the 'avatars', really disguises of the Devil in contemporary forms of humbug or cant or dishonesty, serve Melville as excuses for attacks on aspects of mid-nineteenth-century America, for provoking reactions by the different types of passengers (the public), and for allowing Melville to activate his sociological and metaphysical ideas and arguments. A list of the Confidence Man's appearances may save the reader time and confusion. The first is Black Guinea the negro cripple. There is disagreement whether the Episcopal clergyman and the Methodist chaplain are either or both con-men, but as they seem to be present at the same time as Black Guinea (perhaps only the former is, though) they may be confederates but can hardly also be 'avatars'. The man with the mourning weed in his hat called John Ringman (a name taken from thieves' cant); the man with a grey coat who is agent for the Seminole (a Red Indian tribe of particular malignancy) Widow and Orphan Asylum, who is also an American Evangelical; the proprietor of the Black Rapids Coal Company keeping 'transfer accounts' of speculators thereby destined for Hell; the dishonest agent of the Philosophical Intelligence Office; the (Catholic) quack healer who as herb-doctor also propagands the Romantics' belief in Nature as a cure-all; and finally the Cosmopolitan calling himself Frank Goodman – all these are obvious shape-shiftings of the Confidence Man himself. But the boat-operator Charles Arnold Noble (another inherently suspicious name like John Truman) is less certain, and may be understood to be an unconscious agent of the Devil, while the boy accomplice of the Cosmopolitan in the last chapter is decidedly an imp of darkness. It has even been suggested that the Cosmopolitan who dominates the second half of the book with his sweet-talking and his ironic line in casuistry is the true Saviour; against this we must remember that he calls himself 'a philanthropist' (a suspect term) and 'ambassador of the human race', is described by the author as 'the mature man of the world, a character the opposite [of] the sincere Christian's, bilks the barber, and finally misleads the pious and confiding old man by stripping him of all sources of belief before quenching the light of the last lamp. Moreover, his sophistry is sardonically criticized by a Melville voice (that of the wide-awake man in the cabin). Melville has only himself to blame for these uncertainties. Another critical controversy centres on the 'lamb-like' non-resistant deaf mute, friendless and without any worldly goods, ironically described as the 'mysterious impostor supposed to have arrived recently from the East; quite an original genius in his vocation' for whose capture a reward is offered, who is clearly Christ – but is he a false or the true Christ? This depends on whether the placard offering the reward is taken straight or as irony, though it seems to me evident that the description of 'impostor' is ironic, since the stranger is vilified by the crowd which consists largely of pickpockets and sharks, the scene suggesting the original Crucifixion. Another theory is that Melville thus implies that the Gospel message is itself a device of the Confidence Man since if followed it leaves its practitioner defenceless against the con-men of this world. No doubt Melville had this last in mind at times, for it is debated in the book. In consequence, it has been alleged that the deaf-mute is the first avatar of the Confidence Man, but this cannot be Melville's intention for the reasons I have already stated.

An edited text with critical appendices and elucidatory footnotes is available in the Norton Critical Edition, edited by Hershel Parker (1971). Melville was a voracious but random reader, and had a better appetite than digestion for some of his reading matter, one feels.

The intellectual fare may be found indigestibly rich; alternatively, the absence of life in the round and of sensuous life may lead some readers to class the book with those characteristic modern American novels by and for the intelligentsia which Randall Jarrell has a character in his *Pictures from an Institution* describe as 'a Barmecide feast given by a fireworks company';

and by many the repetitiveness of the structure is felt to be monotonous.

This is due to the limitations of the *genre*, the novel of philosophic speculation, a neo-Classical art form with which Melville was evidently familiar and found congenial and to which *Rasselas, Candide, Gulliver's Travels* and *The Tale of a Tub*, as well as Peacock's novels, belong, and which type of novel Melville's chapter-titles deliberately recall. [We find the same characteristics in modern versions of the *genre*, e.g. Camus's *L'Étranger* and Kafka's *The Trial*.] It superseded the romance of spiritual pilgrimage or quest, with the satisfying progress towards a solution in a happy ending, that had been nourished by medieval faith and produced eventually Bunyan's *The Pilgrim's Progress*. Hawthorne had written an ironical translation into contemporary terms of this last, a tale called *The Celestial Railroad*, where the nineteenth-century pilgrims, on a quick trip by steam-train over the now safely modernized country of Bunyan's pilgrims' ordeals, are being driven unawares by devils to the opposite goal from the Heavenly City. No doubt this was one source of stimulus for Melville – he makes an allusion to the tale in *The Confidence Man* – but its influence is merely marginal, for Hawthorne's tale is straightforward and single-minded while Melville's offers evidence only for the difficulty (but not, as some critics allege, the impossibility) of deciding what *is* right conduct in such a world as this or how the truth as to evidence of good and evil can be arrived at. For Melville is enquiring what alternatives are available which allow one to combine some kind of social life with self-respect once one has perceived – as is essential – how fraudulent all relations and institutions generally are. And though the scenes devised for exhibiting the type situation are largely dramatic and varied in the novels of this kind, their method is inevitably repetitive, the progress of plot and increasing tension in the conventional novel being replaced by a circular movement that ends with a question-mark or merely breaks off when sufficient demonstrations seem to have made the argument carry conviction and exhausted the author's interest – in fact, Melville's seems to have slackened after the middle of his novel.

But these demonstrations need not be abstract, moralistic and didactic, as in *Rasselas*. Melville's lively discussions, like Peacock's, are carried on with versatility of character and language; he deploys rustic idiom as well as polished sentences; like Peacock, he is a master, of sardonic humour and makes his points with wit, as in the brilliant dialogues between the Missourian and the miser and the former and the herb-doctor in chapter 21. As Melville says, he passes 'from the comedy of thought to that of action'. The happenings and debates are not predictable, in fact the ironies provide a series of moral and intellectual shocks, the play of ideas is so stimulating as to make a 'plot' unnecessary.

The clue to the book is that, as will be noticed, great use is made of the words 'confidence', 'trust', 'suspicion', 'doubt', and 'belief', which the author examines systematically in dialogue and action. For purposes of the investigation he himself adopts the position of a critically regarded version of himself in an extreme form, who when asked: 'Pray, sir, who or what may you have confidence in?' replies: 'I have confidence in distrust.' But, Melville enquires, where will this apparently safe guide take us? The book applies this test to every aspect of life and ends by showing that a state of perpetual distrust is also impracticable; yet the only alternative is to be deceived to *some* extent, and to be deceived at all is liable to be fatal. Nothing will persuade me that Melville was not familiar with, and impressed by, Swift's 'Digression Concerning Madness in a Commonwealth' in *The Tale of a Tub* – Melville is using Swiftian arguments and wit constantly in *The Confidence Man* – where Swift argues that happiness 'is a perpetual possession of being well-deceived' and that 'In the proportion that credulity' is preferable to 'that pretended philosophy which enters into the depths of things and then comes gravely back with informations and discoveries, that in the inside they are good for nothing', 'the sublime and refined point of felicity' is 'called the possession of being well-deceived, the serene peaceful state of being a fool among knaves'. Melville shows likewise that the choice is between being a conscious dupe or a misanthrope, for he cannot be content with 'a state of being well-deceived' and accepting that as happiness.

Melville examines the soundness of such solutions as have been advanced to the problem in the form of the realistic scepticism promulgated in the seventeenth and eighteenth centuries by La Rochefoucauld and Chesterfield and Bacon; the theory of Original Sin as held by St Augustine and

Calvinists; the views of Greek philosophers and of such contemporary American ones as Emerson and Thoreau (postulated as Mark Winsome and his disciple Egbert in chapters 36–8); and numerous other possible strategies of living. One of the leading antagonists of the Confidence Man is described by another character as 'deuced analytical', while the former complains: 'Somehow I meet with the most extraordinary metaphysical scamps today. Some sort of visitation of them'; and the token figure of Emerson is introduced as 'more a metaphysical merman than a feeling man'. One of the disguises of the Confidence Man is an agent of the Philosophical Intelligence Office. One chapter is called: 'The Metaphysics of Indian-Hating', and the metaphysics of misanthropy are likewise examined as also the relation between goodness and righteousness (chapter 7) where the idea is raised that a good man is one lucky in being born well off enough to get his dirty work done by others (satire on slave-owners, Emerson's innocence, and upper-class gentry). There is a characteristic discussion on how we are to take Shakespeare's Autolycus because the playwright shows him as both 'wicked and happy', and such practitioners as Talleyrand and Machiavelli come up for reference. Though the action takes place on All Fools Day and the steamer is referred to as a Ship of Fools, this is from association with Pope's *Dunciad*, it seems to me, for the ending shows a 'great anarch's hand' bringing about 'universal darkness' as one light after another, as in Pope's finale, has been quenched, by doubt, that 'uncreating word'. In fact, in view of Melville's 'metaphysical' preoccupation here, *The Confidence Man* would merit the attentions of a professional philosopher. But the main fertiliser after all seems to be Shakespeare. The tragedies of Lear, Timon and Coriolanus are constantly invoked as of types of men who were victims of false confidence (in children, friends, fellow-countrymen and beneficiaries). The deployment of animal imagery is also Shakespearian, especially of the predatory class such as wolf, hyena, fox, rat, leopard; and of course the snake figures constantly as the sign of the con-man, these all being enemies of the Lamb. We know that just before Melville first met Hawthorne, in 1850, he had started on an intensive study of Shakespeare, who provided, it seems to me, a corrective to Melville's intellectualizing tendencies in composition.

I learn from an unpublished piece of research[1] by the Professor
of Italian at Belfast University (Professor G. Singh) that it
seems that Melville owed some of his disillusioned insights into
'the times and nature of the human soul' to Leopardi: Melville
had probably read, for it appeared four years before he
published *The Confidence Man*, the American critic Henry F.
Tucker's essay on Leopardi ('The Sceptical Genius') and
possibly he knew also of the previous studies of Leopardi by
Sainte-Beuve and, in English reviews, by G. H. Lewes and
Gladstone, for Melville refers more than once to Leopardi by
name in his poem *Clarel*. Professor Singh argues that not only
was Leopardi's thought and philosophy, and their expression,
of use to Melville in the undertaking represented by *The
Confidence Man* ('some Melvillian themes...have an unmistakably Leopardian ring about them') but that Leopardi's prose
works, *Operette morali* and *Pensieri*, provided an example of
'moral irony and satire used as instruments of exposition'.
These would associate conveniently with the Swiftian satiric
modes which Melville, as I've shown, employs in *The Confidence
Man*, but it seems to me that the novel also contains a satiric
strain of thought and mode of expression not present in any
previous work of Melville's and not to be found in English
eighteenth-century literature, and that Professor Singh's
identification of Leopardi as a visible influence accounts for this
very satisfactorily.

In the then recently recognized and named 'confidence man'
at work in America, operating on society at large, as well as
in the Mississippi boats (in addition to the card-sharper),
Melville saw a key to and symbol of the corruption he
diagnosed in institutions religious, mercantile, financial and
charitable, in social life and all personal relations, in the Press,
in the claims of quacks of all kinds, in the sentimental cant
of Romantic poets, American philosophers, Abolitionists and
other instruments of democracy, enlightenment and progress.
He saw all these as being operated by or in the interests of the
Devil who beguiled our first parents. The Devil in various
shapes fleeces the public (the *Fidèle*'s passengers, described as
the modern equivalents of Chaucer's Canterbury pilgrims) by
appealing insidiously to their weaknesses, greed and selfishness
to part with money as a sign of acquiescence in the diabolical
system. Thus the opposite of such a way of life, Charity, a

Christian key-word, comes in for scrutiny in all sorts of connections, after the bitter ironic drama of the opening chapter. Melville makes plain his disgust for a commercially-minded society whose charity is typified by the passengers throwing coins to the Negro cripple to catch in his mouth for their amusement, making him wince as these hit his teeth 'when certain coins, tossed by more playful almoners...proved buttons'. The unpleasantness of this 'game of charity' is increased by his being 'bound to appear cheerfully grateful' and his difficulty in avoiding swallowing the coppers (and pseudo-coins).

Allegory is the inevitable mode of this *genre* which works through a series of parables that culminate in one all-inclusive parable in a key position, generally towards the end, as Kafka's pregnant parable of the man outside the door of the Law Courts is set into the penultimate chapter of *The Trial*. Melville's is placed in the very centre of the book, in the three chapters devoted to considering the case of the Indian-Hater, a parable developed from the exemplary history of a real Colonel Moredock. In this parable Melville is able to bring together several different basic conflicts of American social history: the irreconcilable claims of the original owners of the land, a hunting people, and of the colonizing white settlers who must exterminate the Redskins to survive as farmers (and conversely); the unremitting warfare of the Calvinist against Original Sin, the Red Indians being children of the Devil in the mythology of the Founding Fathers of New England; and the impossibility of living by the code of Charity in a society composed of Cains, Iagos, children like Lear's, wives like Goneril, friends like Timon's, etc., who reveal the malignancy of human nature, the eternal Red Indian in everyone.

To cope with this situation of agonizing problems, which Christianity has not been able to change (and so, alas, Christianity must therefore be written off), Melville proposes a technique for self-protection and moral and emotional survival. It might well be called the Philosophy of As If, if that title had not been pre-empted for something different. Melville knows that all wives are not Gonerils, all children not like Lear's, all friends not broken reeds or potential enemies, and so on, but since, he argues, History and Literature and our own experience tell us that they so often and indeed characteristically *are*, it is safer to assume that they *always* are, as in the Greek philosopher's paradox: 'My friends, there are no friends!' We can thus take precautions as a form of insurance against the worst. Shakespeare has told us that 'Most friendship is feigning, most loving mere folly': Melville says, For practical purposes we had better behave as if *all* are. For not to recognize that the treacherous Red Indian is always potentially active in others is suicidal folly.

But this, he admits, is the ideal. Is it practicable as a mode of existence? This is where the tests of the theory cease to be a matter of the intellect and make the book a novel. Numerous tests are carried out to prove to us that we can trust no one and nothing, certainly not Nature as the Romantic poets and the Transcendentalists allege, or Man living in a state of nature as imagined by Rousseau. The backwoodsman complains that all the boys he has tried as servants are idle and dishonest and compares them unfavourably with machines in a very amusing speech (chapter 22), but he still can't manage his life without them as he hasn't succeeded in inventing a machine that would replace servants; he is persuaded, against all his experience, to believe the agent who argues he can supply a boy who is an exception to the rule, and thus weakening, is of course cheated of his fee. He weakens because, as Melville shows, unfortunately we are dependent on each other. So even the convinced Indian-Hater, devoting his life to exterminating single-handed the Red Indian 'in the forest primeval', will sooner or later feel an overpowering need to trust and love *someone* – just as the Missourian who protects himself by a bachelor and backwoods life and by keeping his 'misanthropic rifle' always at the ready, allowed the con-man 'insensibly to persuade him to waive, in his exceptional case, that general law of distrust systematically applied to the race'. Therefore the Indian-Hater

after some months' lonely scoutings...is suddenly seized with a sort of calenture; hurries openly towards the first smoke, though he knows it is an Indian's, announces himself as a lost hunter, gives the savage his rifle, throws himself upon his charity, embraces him with much affection, imploring the privilege of living a while in his sweet companionship.

This is a touching recognition of the pathos and tragedy of the need for human relationships, for the passage immediately concludes: 'What is too often the sequel of so distempered a procedure may be best known by those who best know the Indian' – for of course the now defenceless ex-Indian-Hater is invariably scalped. 'No Trust' is a hateful motto, but the barber when talked into suspending it is cheated by the Confidence Man.

The ideal of a wholly consistent Indian-Hater in real life, as Melville thus admits, is impracticable; the best that can be expected is 'the diluted Indian-Hater'. The status of this brilliant parable is indicated by the chapter-title 'The Metaphysics of Indian-Hating'. The parable is then novelized in several dramatic scenes with dialogues illustrating bogus friendship and sham conviviality: 'The Boon Companions', 'The Hypothetical Friends' and the tale of China Aster, ruined through officious 'friendship'. But along with these there is an important appendix representing an alternative to reacting to Timon's situation either by vindictive bitterness and mis-anthropy, or blindness to being deceived. This is shown in the history of Charlemont, 'a kindly man' but 'not deficient in mind' (that is, though a nice man he is a realist) who, when he falls from prosperity through business losses, cuts dead all his friends in order not to put them to the shame of cold-shouldering him, and disappears, to reappear nine years later having made another fortune abroad. He then reassumes without explanation his convivial habits in his former society but is the prey of a secret melancholy which is at last revealed to an old acquaintance who questions him. Charlemont says only:

If ever, in days to come, you shall see ruin at hand, and, thinking you understand mankind, shall tremble for your friendships, and tremble for your pride; and, partly through love for the one and fear for the other, shall resolve to be beforehand with the world, and save it from a sin by prospectively taking that sin to yourself, then you will do as one I now dream of once did, and like him will you suffer.

'Save it from a sin, by prospectively taking that sin to yourself' is surely a Christ-like procedure. But the tale is ironically labelled: 'The Story of the Gentleman-Madman' – 'mad' in the eyes of the average American who could not be expected to appreciate such sensitive forbearance, and who was not a gentleman. This is reinforced by the Cosmopolitan's admission that he invented the story – 'it is what contrasts with real life' he says, ironically challenging his auditor (a hypothetical friend) to say whether in real life friends, himself for instance, would behave as Charlemont assumed his would on hearing he had gone bankrupt. The need to have associates, even such as he knew his friends to be, put Charlemont in the position of the man

accounting wine so fine a thing, that even the sham article is better than none at all... It is a fable...it illustrated, as in a parable, how that a man of disposition ungovernably good-natured might still familiarly associate with men, though, at the same time, he believed the greater part of men false-hearted... And if the Rochefoucaultites urge that, by this course, he will sooner or later be undermined in security, he answers, 'And do you think I don't know that? But security without society I hold a bore; and society, even of the spurious sort, has its price, which I am willing to pay.'

In this way only can one avoid the dilemma of being, as Swift puts it, a fool among knaves or else going mad. But Melville never accepts Swift's brutal alternative, for he implies that there is a sensitive and high-minded man to be considered, who is for Melville the norm. We noted that his objection to Emersonian Man was that that was not 'a feeling man' and was therefore inhuman.

Melville discusses also the alternative to Charity, uncompromising Truth. The wooden-legged man declares: 'Charity is one thing, and truth is another' – being 'charitable' ('Charity thinketh no evil') is easy, but being truthful means exposing dishonesty and false confidence: all the passengers turn on him, especially the Methodist, for declaring the Negro cripple to be a fraud though he is right in his suspicions. Yet truth, Melville also sees, is destructive: 'Truth is like a threshing-machine; tender sensibilities must keep out of the way', says the Missourian, who tells the truth with the relentless incivility that is necessary. He, also, is unpopular, and the Methodist urges him to 'Be not such a Canada thistle', to which he replies, as he broadcasts the seeds of doubt: 'Now, when with my thistles your farms shall be well stocked, why then – you may abandon 'em!', a recognition by Melville of the sterility of perpetual distrust.

The Confidence Man characterizes the wooden-legged man as 'a scoffer who, even were truth on his tongue, his way of speaking it would make truth almost offensive as falsehood', a little joke against Melville himself, for there are other ironic references that identify this scoffer with the author. And this is the point at which one must consider Melville's difference from Swift. Melville had also considered it, since he has taken care to dissociate himself from what was for him a morally unacceptable attitude to his fellows, whom Swift in all his writings treats with disgust and contempt. Melville, a morally sensitive man, is unlike him in not being arrogant and in being continuously self-critical. He shows that the Missourian bachelor, who like Swift denigrates the human race in general but objects to being disrespectfully considered himself, is disconcerted when the Cosmopolitan retorts: 'And what race may *you* belong to? Now don't you see in what inconsistencies one involves himself by affecting disesteem for men?' And of the wooden-legged man when he denounces the Negro cripple, the author himself remarks: 'These suspicions came from one who himself on a wooden leg went halt' and that 'cripples, above all men, should at least refrain from picking a fellow-limper to pieces', a rephrasing of the axiom that we are all miserable sinners. Melville also declares his possible bias as a satirist: the wooden-legged man is 'a limping, gimlet-eyed, sour-faced person' suffering under a grievance against 'government and humanity' and like 'a criminal judge with a mustard-plaster on his back' – 'In the present case the mustard-plaster might have been the memory of certain recent biting rebuffs and mortifications.' Government had recently failed to give Melville a remunerative consulship and humanity had rebuffed and mortified him as a novelist. Hence he sees that he is liable to take, like the wooden-legged man, a 'one-sided view of humanity'. Humour directed against himself and self-awareness of this kind are unusual in satirical writers, a proof of candour; Melville's irony is not self-protective like that of the Bloomsbury school; on the contrary, his art is profound and courageous.

Melville therefore seems closer to Conrad than to Swift or Samuel Butler, the Conrad who devoted a novel to considering one brought up to be an Indian-Hater – Axel Heyst, warned by his father, the 'destroyer of systems of hopes, of beliefs', to be scornful of mankind and believe in nothing, and never to become involved with flesh and blood. But Heyst finds a life of moral and physical isolation impracticable, and involvement proves to be both his undoing and his salvation. Melville does not say like Conrad: 'Woe to the man whose heart has not learned while young to hope, to love – and to put its trust in life!' but the constant irony and the sub-title of 'Masquerade', the outbursts of jocosity and jeering, should not mislead us into assuming that there is no depth of feeling in Melville's novel, no *parti pris* or involvement. There is real moral feeling and demand for moral courage in social life visible in Melville's attack on the cowardly who protect themselves by deploring this as 'aggressiveness', when the Missourian condemns the herb-doctor's cant of this kind with: 'Picked and prudent sentiments. You are the moderate man, the invaluable under-strapper of the wicked man. You, the moderate man, may be used for wrong, but are useless for right.' Melville is not therefore imprisoned in a moral void like the author of *L'Étranger*, or in contempt and disgust like Swift, or in a neurosis like Kafka, or even in the joylessness of *Rasselas*. He attempts to work out some satisfactory strategy for living because he subscribes to the insight Kafka recorded in his *Reflections*: 'No one should say that we lack faith. The mere fact of our living implies a degree of faith which is inexhaustible' – in spite of Melville's ever-present exasperation at the human dilemma. This he constantly comes back to in different forms, as in making a character say: 'The suspicious man kicks himself with his own foot.' He shows in the novel, though it seems a tissue of ironies, that he thirsts for honesty, courage, honourable conduct, love, integrity, true friendship, true charity, social justice, and that he is agonized because these necessities of life seemed to be victims of the spirit of his age, or even of social life in any age. Thus the Methodist's rant against the 'mad' unbeliever is only partly ironic, for the description of 'the end of suspicion' in a madhouse looks to me to have been taken from the terrifying last plate of Hogarth's 'The Rake's Progress'.

Besides the satiric emanations of himself as the wooden-legged man and the bachelor backwoodsman, there is a much more startling and profoundly serious Melville representative, that of his past self as artist. This is the 'kind of invalid Titan in homespun' who seems to have stepped inexplicably on board the *Fidèle* out of some earlier Melville novel, 'his countenance tawny and shadowy as an iron-ore country in a clouded day', his 'child', of true native American breed, in one hand and a heavy club of swamp-oak in the other; he is a melancholy giant bowed down with suffering and his child (his creative work) is 'a little Cassandra', that is, a prophet of doom; his voice is like 'a great clock bell', it is 'a stunning admonisher'; but though sad and ill and 'bowed over' he is indomitable. Rejecting the salvation cure-all and declaring the healer to be a 'Profane fiddler on heart-strings', a 'Snake', he fells the quack with a blow of his staff and disappears from the book. Melville's self-directed irony again appears in ascribing to his Titan the bias of which he himself was suspected by reviewers – a 'countenance lividly epileptic with hypochondriac mania', and the herb-doctor in the same spirit dismisses him as 'Regardless of decency and lost to humanity!' But these sardonic jokes don't deprive the 'invalid Titan' of his impressiveness. While invoking thus the author of *Moby Dick* Melville seems to be recognizing that he is defeated and remote: his 'voice deep and lonesome enough to have come from the bottom of an abandoned coal-shaft', he is offered as a tragic figure.

Again, though there is sardonic treatment of the *organization* and current *practice* of Christianity, of Christianity as repre- sented by churches, priests, the claims of dogmatists and the behaviour of so-called Christians, there is manifest regret at his own inability to accept the religious inheritance of the Bible (which we can see he read closely). Christian practice is examined in the parable of the Indian-Hater, where Melville notes the self-righteous attitude of the New England settler whose devout religious practices did not prevent him from treating the Indians as diabolical enemies. Melville says: '... in which the charitable may think he does them some injustice. Certain it is, the Indians themselves think so... The Indians, indeed, protest against the backwoodsman's view of them', etc. And 'the instinct of antipathy against an Indian grows in the backwoodsman with the sense of good and bad, right and wrong. In one breath he learns that a brother is to be loved, and an Indian to be hated.' This is also a satiric parable on the doctrine of Calvinism and Original Sin, the natural man being unregenerate and the stronghold of the Old Adam, therefore conveniently identifiable with the Redskin.

But the final chapter seems to admit the need for religion with its account of the passengers' cabin which is lit by 'a solar lamp' that 'the commands of the captain required to be kept burning till the natural light of day should come to relieve it' – though whether this natural light is Reason, or Eternity (when Truth will make all things plain), is not explained. This lamp, we are told by Melville, is the only light left to see by, for the 'other lamps, barren planets, had either gone out from exhaustion, or been extinguished by such occupants of berths as the light annoyed, or who wanted to sleep, not see'. This is straight-forward – the extinct lamps are dead religions, and the passengers who had extinguished the lamps are deplored; the 'perverse man, in a berth not remote' who now wanted the last lamp put out is again Melville himself, seen from this point of view as misguided, as no doubt he sometimes feared – for from this berth comes presently the voice of the wide-awake man jeering at the Cosmopolitan.

The Cosmopolitan wins the confidence of the pious old man ('one of those...untainted by the world, because ignorant of it') and by sophistry deprives him of *all* his beliefs, so bewildering him that he gives himself over to the guidance of this false Saviour and agrees to let him put out the lamp, leaving them in darkness and with a bad smell on the premises. This last is a Swiftian joke unworthy of the novel, but it does not disguise Melville's recognition of the despair and danger of the outcome which is thus intentionally pictured as degrada-tion. The lamp had on its shade a horned altar (a traditional symbol for the Old Testament) and a robed figure with a halo (representing the New); with the quenching of the light these disappear from view. No doubt Melville, interested like other American writers and academics of his time in Oriental religions, knew that Nirvana means 'to quench the light', not his idea of what humanity should strive for. Thus the book ends on a note of despair. Note that we never see the captain or otherwise hear of him, and his commands are conveyed to the passengers only by a placard outside his office or more directly by the steward; a Kafkaesque situation. Christ is also, as a deaf mute, in keeping with this implied criticism of deity as incommunicado.

Yet Solzhenitsyn's much more dreadful account in *The First Circle* of an evil society (evil beyond Melville's conception and yet an actuality, not a satirist's caricature) does not end in despair, and we must ask why Melville's novel should. We have seen how, shortly before *The Confidence Man*, Melville had written tales which acknowledged the place of art in the life of mankind and emphasized, and examined, the role of the artist. Why then does he leave out of this book the whole question of the function of the arts, which no primitive society has ever been found without? This omission gives a sense of a hole in the middle of his argument, endorsing the belief of Blake and Hogarth that 'The whole world without Art would be one great wilderness.' If this hole had been filled by representations of the nature of creativeness, which is collaborative, and of its life-enhancing function, the book would not have been open to the charges of aridity and one-sidedness. All that Melville provides in recognition of man's creative achievements as a social being is the racy idiom, rich in exaggeration, picturesque in imagery and delighting in grotesque humour, of the backwoodsman from Missouri, representing the pioneer achievement which Melville backed as the valuable strain in American life – Western as opposed to New England – full of energy and originality because free of restraints and conventions. But the limitations of such a culture are obvious both intellectually and spiritually; the arts were the first loss in a pioneer life. We think of what *The First Circle* would have been if Solzhenitsyn had left out of that novel the representative artist Kondrashov and the account of his work and ideas, and left out too the parts of the novel that testify that literature and music, even the mere remembrance of them, as also of their religious traditions, together with their inherited code of professional ethics, are what combined to sustain the morale of the prisoners as self-respecting human beings capable of disinterestedness, even in an environment designed to reduce them to subordination as starving animals fighting for survival.

But then Solzhenitsyn had Tolstoy as forbear, and alerted by him he asks Melville's questions in a different form. Melville in *The Confidence Man* asks repeatedly: How can one believe in anything or anyone? Solzhenitsyn proceeds to ask, as Tolstoy had done: What then do men live by? – even in a society that is a cancer ward or the first circle of the Inferno. Thus *The Confidence Man* seems to take place in something like a prison without the aeration provided by the factors that Solzhenitsyn shows social life provided in the Old World and that George Eliot, writing at the same date as Melville, showed, in *Silas*

Marner, English village life had provided. Therefore her discussion of the problem of reintegration into social life of a man who had lost his beliefs is optimistic in conclusion. Poetic in character, it is also witty and full of humour, providing a useful comparison with Melville's satiric, philosophic and negative approach to the same situation. Both use the moral fable and the parable as their art-form [see my critical introduction and notes to the Penguin English Library edition of *Silas Marner*]. But of course there was in Russia a great, undying tradition of a literature in general possession and of the poet's importance, which a pioneer society lacked. Melville clearly felt that he and Hawthorne had created great and truly American novels and tales, in defiance of the imitative colonial tradition that they considered was not American but pseudo-English and merely genteel; yet they had been defeated by the indifference of the American public to spiritual values and literary art. So in this last novel the artist and creative thinker appears only as a decrepit Titan. Hence we should not be surprised that *The Piazza Tales* and *The Confidence Man* are predominantly ironic and painful. What is surprising is that Melville retained his control over satiric impulses and that these works display so much humour, humility, sensitiveness and even, as in *I and My Chimney*, show him accepting without ill-will the odium and misunderstanding that must be incurred by an artist and intellectual in such a society. It is natural that, in his discouragement after the failure of his tremendous expenditure in creative writing between 1853 and 1856, and of the failure to secure a reading public for *Moby Dick* and *Pierre*, that he should direct his talents in *The Confidence Man* to isolating the sources of blight and corruption in his age, and write more as a satirical philosopher than as an artist. His death soon after his subsequent twenty years of drudgery as an outdoor Inspector of Customs on the waterfront brought no recognition; he died unknown, and as a prophet unhonoured in his own country, the final irony that confirms the justice of the view of his America expressed in *The Confidence Man*.

ℰHenry James and the disabilities of the American novelist in the nineteenth century

> If a writer puts all of himself in his writings (and what else can he
> put into it?) his work inevitably forms a single book.
>
> Silone, *The Story of a Humble Christian* (1968)

If you have any interest at all in English literature you will have given some thought to the conditions required to produce a great national literature. But I wonder whether you've ever considered the difficulties of a creative writer who, unlike a French or English writer, was born into a dependent culture, or into a disparate one in a country which has never been unified. As for instance, a culture which started as colonial, as did the American, or as the New Zealand and Australian till recently essentially were; or a country which was artificially engendered like Belgium, consisting of two individual and hostile peoples each with a different language and religion and traditions of which the higher culture is the inferior numerically and neither large enough to support financially a separate literature in its own tongue. Or a country like Norway, so divided geographically (as indeed England was in Caxton's time) that it had no standard language, only three very distinct dialects of practically equal status, a country which, unlike Italy, didn't produce early on a genius at once critical and creative like Dante who, by writing great poetry in his own Tuscan vernacular, made that for all his countrymen the language of literature, instead of the academic *lingua franca* Latin. Or a country like Finland which till recently always lived under an alien and resented government of foreigners with a governing-class, in turn Swedish or Russian, whose language was unrelated to that of the natives so that they had only an oral folk-literature in their own tongue till they achieved independence and which are still hampered, like Iceland, by a population so small and a language that no one else learns, that its writers have to be subsidized to get published. Or a country like Ireland which for historical and religious reasons was even more violently stratified, consisting till late in the nineteenth century of a Gaelic-speaking Catholic peasantry and small-farmer class, largely illiterate but possessed of a richly poetic oral literature, while an English-speaking intensely Protestant Ascendancy and an Anglo-Irish-speaking largely Catholic middle class together formed the only public for a printed English literature, but, even so, a public divided by religion and traditions. Or a country like Russia which developed a wealth of all kinds of folk-literature because till the end of the eighteenth century the Orthodox Church permitted nothing but religious works to be printed, and where the educated class did not really speak Russian and so depended entirely on German, French and English literature for its reading until Pushkin and his circle decided to alter that humiliating state of affairs by developing a national literature out of the poetic language of the peasants as current in their ballads, oral epics, folk-tales and in their lively talk, in which Pushkin was followed by Turgenev and Tolstoy.

In contrast, a people may develop a richly individual national literature, even if this language has only been developed on the magpie principle by borrowings from different sources – this was the case with Yiddish, a splendidly expressive and adaptable *lingua franca* which was the only tongue that the Jews of North America, England, Northern and Central Europe and the Slav countries had in common, but which they developed through conversation in ghetto conditions and thus produced a very distinctive literature of poetry, fiction, drama and newsprint.

Bearing all these cases in mind, you may now reflect that England and France have such long-established and glorious literature because they were each a settled and independent folk, and unlike Germany and Italy, were unified early in their history as regards language and culture. American novelists born in the early nineteenth century offer us a good field for investigating the problems of the evolution of a national

literature because, though only a generation after their country
had ceased to be a mere colony, when such writings as it
produced were parasitic, imitating the imported works of the
eighteenth-century English essayists, poets and novelists – yet,
once independent, they did, surprisingly, manage to produce
even before the Russians a distinctive body of fiction in tale and
novel. New Zealand, even a century and a half later than the
United States, was still a colonial people and so without a
literature of their own because they had no confidence in the
possibility of being independent culturally of the mother-
country. And so New Zealand poets, for instance, till World
War II wrote imitations of the poems in English anthologies
that were used in their schools, poems in which they neglected
their own highly individual flora and landscape and instead
worked up imaginary feelings about the English birds and
flowers and countryside that they had mostly never met except
in print, but spoke and thought of as 'Home'. Katherine
Mansfield caused a great sensation, in fact started a literary
revolution in New Zealand, merely by writing quite unsensa-
tional short stories about New Zealand life and themes, not
till then considered suitable subject-matter for literature by New
Zealanders.

The American history in this field is the exact opposite of New
Zealand's, for they had as far back as 1776 an American
Revolution, which was a defiance and rejection of the
mother-country and therefore valuable in throwing off such
crippling literary parasitism as New Zealand's. But this made
its creative minds turn quite deliberately to the problem of how
to create from nothing a specifically American novel, a novel
which, while ranking, as national pride now demanded, with
the art of the masters of fiction of the Old World, should be
written as seemed essential to them, not in educated English
but in native American idiom, drawing on American dialects
wherever possible, as Mark Twain is seen to do in *Huckleberry
Finn*, choosing, like Twain and Fenimore Cooper and
Hawthorne, American subjects in American settings and, for
characters, uniquely American people. This at least was the
theory. The trouble in implementing this programme was that
if you are going to use the language of pioneers you are limited
to expressing only the feelings and experiences of such people
who are leading a basically simple life with a restricted and

coarsened vocabulary, unlike the dialects of settled peasantries in countries with a class system and oral traditions – peasantries like those of Scotland, Ireland and England which, as proved by the novels of Scott, the nineteenth-century Anglo-Irish novelists and George Eliot, for instance, and in their folk-songs and ballads, were not crude, unsophisticated or impoverished.

It is a truism that just as all music originates from folk-music, so a national literature developed from the nation's folk-literature, that is, its long-evolved oral traditions of poetry and tale. But it is this natural, slow-growing literary process that North America lacked, settled so recently by pioneers of mixed races who had doubtlessly some remembered ballads and folk-tales of their English or European ancestors, but even when these survived Puritan censorship, they were no use for the self-consciously American writer, while the abundant native American – that is, Red Indian – folk-lore and mythology, which really belonged to the land, were hopelessly alien and inaccessible. Longfellow's attempted epic, *Hiawatha*, a pious attempt to feed the American Indian mythology and folk-lore into nineteenth-century white American poetic equipment, was merely an academic hybrid concocted in the study out of books and translations and rendered in the alien verse-movement of the Finnish national epic.

Hawthorne was the true pathfinder here. He saw that the undertaking to produce an American fiction demanded a critical effort, in fact a revaluation of the American past since and including the first New England settlements. This he initiated in the group of tales that preceded, and were amal-gamated to culminate in, his remarkable novel *The Scarlet Letter*. For this he drew on the historical documents of the first settlers and his own, usefully representative, family traditions, and could therefore use the English of the seventeenth century. Melville, coming later to the literary scene, drew the conclusion from Hawthorne's work that here at last was the great, truly American writer he desiderated – not, he wrote, one of 'these smooth, pleasing writers' who 'but furnish an appendix to English authors'. 'We want no American Goldsmiths', he continued; 'nay, we want no American Miltons...no American writer should write like an Englishman...away with this literary flunkeyism towards England...' and he concluded: 'This matter of a national literature has come to such a pass

with us that in some sense we must turn bullies.' Yet nearly
half a century later, in 1889, Henry James, in a dialogue-piece
he wrote called 'An Animated Conversation' supposed to take
place in London between English and American writers and
readers made an American man of letters complain:

It has grown up roughly, and we haven't had time to cultivate it...
Our great writers have written in English. That's what I mean by
American having been neglected.

And the same speaker gives the explanation of how the original
English settlers and their descendants developed English into
something different, the American language:

A body of English people crossed the Atlantic and sat down in a new
climate on a new soil, amid new circumstances. It was a new heaven
and a new earth. They invented new institutions, they encountered
different needs... They went in for democracy, and that alone would
affect – it *has* affected – the tone immensely...[for he argues] a
language is a very sensitive organism... It serves, it obeys, it
accommodates itself.

This 'Animated Conversation' registers James's understanding
as a creative writer of the complexity of the subject and of being
an American novelist, even after he had been living in England
for so many years. His characters discuss in their 'Animated
Conversation' the opportunity, as James saw it in his optimistic
moments, no doubt, 'for two great peoples to accept, to
cultivate with talent, common destiny, to unite in the arts of
peace. It will make life larger and the arts finer for each of them.'
But one of the characters, presumably English, points out that
there's a little difficulty: is there a common language? An
American answers passionately: 'Haven't we a right to have
a language of our own?' Then follows the reply 'It was
inevitable', etc. and gives the historical explanation that I have
just cited. But the real crunch comes in the subsequent exchange.
To the American critic who has complained that as to the
American language 'its divergence was inevitable' – 'But it
has grown up roughly, and we haven't had time to cultivate
it', one of the English replies kindly: 'New signs are crude, and
you, in this matter, are in the crude, the vulgar stage' and
another American argues 'But we have always the resource of
English. We have lots of opportunity to practice it.' 'As a
foreign tongue, yes' is the retort – 'To speak it as the Russians

speak French.' Someone notes that 'The Russians are giving up French' and the American replies, that they're able to do so because *they've* got the language of Tolstoy. 'Our great writers have written in English. That's what I mean by American having been neglected.'

This debate seems to be important in revealing James's uneasy conscience that in not having cultivated the American language but developing a literary English instead he was not doing his duty either as an American or an artist, that he was a Tolstoy who had chosen to write in French instead of working in and therefore improving in fact Russian – a form of artistic treachery. Indeed, we can see the striking difference between the living speech of James's American characters (until his late phase when he had lost touch) and the undifferentiated English spoken by his educated English characters which contrasts so notably with the conversation of English men and women of the same class and type in novels of George Eliot or Trollope, where they are given convincing personal idioms. James did indeed in this respect pay the penalty as an artist of expatriation and of opting out of his native idiom in favour of a higher form of the same language. James compensated for this disability as regards spoken English by inventing a stylization of English speech which takes it out of the vulgar or colloquial actuality and compensates for the consequent lack of flavour by brilliance of wit. This does give a kind of life to his English dialogue, but gives also the impression of its being a perpetual *tour-de-force*, and when his wit flags, as in his last phase (e.g. in *The Ambassadors* or *The Wings of The Dove* or *The Sacred Fount*), the effect is wearisome.

And of course, as James recognized in his 'Animated Conversation', speech isn't only words, it is an index of character, of social life, of a whole civilization. Ralph Touchett in *The Portrait of a Lady* remarks to his father, the unalterably American banker: 'You've lived with the English for thirty years, and you've picked up a good many of the things they say. But you've never learned the things they don't say.' This is a good point, that picking up the kind of things that English people were likely to say is not a substitute for a native sensitiveness to the implications of English speech – English silences. Thus, for instance, though James had noted that educated English people did not give any satisfaction to the personal questions fired off at them by Americans, he never understood, it seems from his fiction, that this was the reaction of a people who respected and demanded privacy – a right felt by Americans to be undemocratic, as our Victorian novelists and travellers noted. Like his cultivated Boston heroines Bessie Alden and Isabel Archer, James never seemed to realize that the hesitancies, the embarrassed laughs and evasive little jokes with which the English gentleman (in his novels as in Trollope's) replied to the American demands for inside information – were polite rebuffs, not evidence of intellectual deficiency. They were, as Trollope knew, the defences of a social code of a people to whom good manners implied diffidence and reticence. Moreover they were the expression of a real intelligence that recognized that there are no simple answers to such questions as Americans asked, or no answers that these American girls could understand. Trollope gets a good deal of humour from such situations in his novel *The American Senator*, and James registers this last point in his tale *A London Life*.

I think we may now account for James's sympathy with Robert Louis Stevenson, a minor novelist whom he overrated so surprisingly, perhaps because he saw in Stevenson a parallel case to his own. In an essay devoted to Stevenson, collected in his early book *Partial Portraits*, James describes him as 'a Scotchman of the world', saying,

If it be a good fortune for a genius to have had such a country as Scotland for its primary stuff, this is doubly the case when there has been a certain process of detachment, of extreme secularisation. Mr Stevenson has been emancipated: he is, as we may say, a Scotchman of the world.

But the emancipation did not enable Stevenson – rather it prevented him – from creating anything at all in the class of such massive if insufficiently artistic successes as Scott's *Old Mortality* and *Heart of Midlothian* and Galt's *The Entail*, for all Stevenson's superior sophistication and knowledge of 'the art of the novel'. Stevenson's 'emancipation' seems to have had the effect of making him self-conscious in his use of things Scottish so that his native characters always seem theatrical and are rendered romantically.

So we see that it is not so easy, as James witnesses, to fulfil the positive demand for an Instant Great National Literature, especially when the nation speaks a crude idiom, the vehicle of a society, lacking nearly everything that a European country provided as materials and traditions for sophisticated writers. High art literature had developed over the ages in the Old World in societies centred in courts, castles and great houses, but originally from the oral literature of the organic society of village life where exchange of song and story, legend and folk-lore had traditionally taken place round the fire in winter and at work outdoors at all seasons. Henry James, in his well-known listing in his book on Hawthorne (in 1897) of what Hawthorne and all other American artists had to do without, was in fact only extending a list already made by Hawthorne to account for his handicaps. James begins:

One might enumerate the items of high civilization, as it exists in other countries, which are absent from the texture of American life, until it should become a wonder to know what was left

– and he enumerates, among many other things I haven't time to cite, 'No state in the European sense of the word' and 'No Sovereign, no court, no aristocracy, no church, no clergy' and then the architectural category (which is also social): 'no palaces, no castles nor manors nor old country houses, nor parsonages, nor thatched cottages...no cathedrals or abbeys' and then the absence of what more directly affects the writer: 'no great Universities nor Public Schools, no literature, no novels, no museums, no pictures', and so on to a great extent. The senior American man of letters at the time, W. D. Howells, took this up and wrote to James indignantly that *everything* was left that constituted America, the rest being 'dreary and worn out paraphernalia'. James disagreed, and retorted that all that remained was American humour, which it seems he did not think much of though (or perhaps because) it provided the whole or at least the main stock-in-trade of many other and more popular American writers. In so far as American humour had resulted in the tall story and Western and Yankee myths, the American substitute for a folk-literature, it could not have seemed to James a basis for a great national literature; nor was it. We may not want to accept James's dictum to Howells that 'It takes an old civilization to set a novelist in motion', but the fact is that the novel is an art form that does not appear except in a sophisticated society. The American novelist's deprivations that James and Hawthorne had listed were what led James to wander in Europe seeking a fruitful habitat for his art, finally settling in England for life. Hawthorne and Melville, who though travellers abroad remained faithful to their native land, soon dried up once back there while others like Poe died of America. At that time America simply couldn't provide a sufficiently large reading-public to support avant-garde writers financially, nor, equally important, enough cultivated people to give them the appreciation and recognition creative writers need which have always enabled artists in England and Europe to persevere in spite of poverty. Howells late in his life said that America had treated James badly; it had treated Melville even worse.

And yet the writers who visited, or lived for spells in, or even settled in England, like Henry Adams, Hawthorne and James, encountered a psychological problem that made their situation as creative writers more difficult on other grounds even than lack of sales or appreciation. Intelligent European observers like Tocqueville and Talleyrand when in America had noted how touchy the ex-colonials were regarding what they suspected was the English reaction to them and their manners and attitudes, and Trollope when travelling widely in America, noted it still in 1860 after nearly a century of emancipation from colonial status. And the American in England could not bear to admit even to himself the inevitable superiority of a long-settled country in aesthetic charm, or the superior cultivation of an aristocratic (and therefore morally reprehensible) society. Even Henry Adams, a member of a privileged Presidential family, who joined his brother at the American Legation in London when a young man, wrote revealing letters home on these lines, complaining of imaginary slights and social insults and, like William James whenever he visited England, hating the Englishman and still more the Englishwoman (for qualities Americans didn't have). Hawthorne's complicated and ambivalent reactions are set down in his *English Notebooks* as are Adams's own directly in his letters home and indirectly in his tales and novels. Though William James was a professional philosopher and psychologist, he is an unconscious example in the most ludicrous form of one combining a ferocious emotional and a theoretically based hostility to the English and England

with resentment at having to recognize that in some respects
England had many advantages over America. He wrote to
Henry after such a visit expressing an adverse view of England
and denying its value to the world even compared with France
or Germany, to which his brother replied, combining tact with
honesty:

Of course you know, true as it all is, it is only part of the statement.
There is more besides, and it is this *more besides* that I have been living
on in London.

And he gave as his reason for settling there: 'I felt it was the
right place' – that is, for a novelist. This statement is amplified
in the essay 'London' he wrote in 1888 and reprinted in his
book *Essays in London*, where he says:

It is a real stroke of luck for a particular country that the capital of
the human race happens to be British... For after all if the sense of
life is greatest there, it is a sense of the life of people of our
incomparable English speech... London... is the single place in which
most readers, most possible lovers are gathered together; it is the most
inclusive public and the largest social incarnation of the language,
of the tradition.

He also said of London that 'The human race is better
represented there than anywhere else.' In 1869, when he was
in his mid-twenties, he had written revealingly to his mother
from England:

The truth is that the face of things here throws a sensitive American
back on himself – back on his prejudices and national passions, and
benumbs for a while the faculty of appreciation and the sense of
justice.

But the sense of justice cannot be numbed for more than a while
in a serious creative writer, and in the main James is seen to
strive in his fictions for impartiality and discernment in his
dealings with the Anglo-American confrontations that, directly
or indirectly, provided so much of his best work. (It is surely
significant that it did absorb his attention as a creative writer.)
Consider the tale called *The Point of View*, written in his fortieth
year; it consists of a number of letters from characters of various
nationalities and both sexes, foreigners from Europe or England
and Americans returning there from trips abroad. The epistolary
technique is one which absolves the author from backing any

one character or even adjudicating between them, and it
enabled James to assemble all the conflicting positions in the
debate going on inside himself in his efforts to integrate his
attitude to his native land.

The buoyant Mr Cockerell, after three years of touring the
world, says he hasn't written a book about Europe because,
as another letter-writer reports him: 'Europe isn't worth
writing about...he wants America to behave as if Europe didn't
exist... He describes America as complete in herself.' This was
of course the patriotic view, and that of all the James family
except the novelist. Henry James Senior had actually written,
when Henry was 13,

The English are an intensely vulgar race, high and low... They are
not worth studying. The prejudices one has about them, even when
they are unjust, are scarcely worth correcting. They belong, all their
good and evil, to the past of humanity, to the infantile development
of the mind, and they don't deserve, more than any other European
nation, the least reverence from a denizen of the new world.

And when Henry Junior was 26 and had written home from
Rome how deeply aroused he was by that city, his father
warned him that

The historical consciousness rules to such distorted excess in Europe
that I have always been restless there, and ended by pining for the
land of the future exclusively.

The son dutifully, though hardly, one suspects, sincerely, wrote
back to endorse this attitude, alleging that

I conceived at Naples a tenfold deeper loathing than ever of the
hideous heritage of the past, and felt for a moment as if I should like
to devote my life to laying railroads, and erecting blocks of stores
on the most classic and romantic sites. The age has a long row to
hoe.

But of course though he was the son and brother of Europe-
spurning Americans, the novelist could not be satisfied by the
crudely patriotic stance. He not only offers it for criticism in
Mr Cockerell in *The Point of View*, as I've noted, but he does
not hesitate to endow the disagreeable Olive Chancellor with
it in *The Bostonians*. Though she is a cultivated woman and
a member of one of the old, rich, Boston families, her sister
summarizes her attitude to the Old World as 'She hates it; she

would like to abolish it.' We know from Henry James himself that his friend the American Minister in London, also of a great Boston family, James Russell Lowell, was a complete anglophobe. To Melville's credit – he clearly was an exceptionally intelligent and open-minded man – there are no traces in his writings of discomfort in his relations with English people, though he was more thoroughly American than James or Hawthorne were.

The Frenchman writes home to report of America that 'A Frenchman couldn't live here.' But the American traveller has decided he couldn't live anywhere else – by travelling about the Old World, he says, 'I've got Europe off my back' and thanks God for the truly American type of his own western states who has, he declares, 'the Future in his vitals'. This placing of hope in the Westerner as the archetype of the American of the future and the justification of the American form of society was common, and even Hawthorne, having been disappointed in New England, looked to the West on principle, telling Howells when as a young aspirant to the literary life he came East and met Hawthorne, that he himself would like to visit the West, saying with surprising vehemence that he would like to see 'some part of America on which the damned shadow of Europe had not fallen' – Hawthorne died four years later without having seen what the West was in practice. Melville also idealized the Westerner, though Trollope when travelling across America in 1860 excepted the Westerners from any of the virtues he found, often with difficulty, in the inhabitants of the Eastern and Mid-Western states; *he* found the Westerners dirty, uncivil and wholly unimpressive.

In such a sketch – for it is hardly a tale – as *The Point of View*, James records and balances all positions impartially (though the critical American spinster's is the one that echoes much that he has expressed as his own sentiments in his letters). But in his finer tales and novels we see him subsequently trying to *examine* all possible positions by dramatizing them and acting them out, either separately or in combination, working them out to their logical conclusion with painful honesty, and thus arriving at insights that were not simple-minded, or patriotic at the expense of truth, or unrealistically optimistic. Through reading these works we can understand why Stendhal wrote in his copy of *Le Rouge et le Noir* 'M. de Tracy told me that truth can only be achieved by means of the novel.' There James shows that he could not be contented with emotional confusion in his attitude to England, or with uncritical acceptance of American achievement; he leaves the reader to draw possible conclusions from the data he has so courageously furnished. This must have been the more difficult for him owing to the preponderance among Americans of his own family's attitudes to England and the English then; because it laid him open to charges of being a traitor as well as an *émigré*; and because there was already an American tradition of popular fiction pandering to patriotic tastes in the first post-colonial phase, described in 1826 by an Anglo-Irish novelist, Gerald Griffin, as 'American novelists who take care to construct their narratives so that they may be enabled to Jonathanize all the virtues, while all the villains of the tale shall be either Indian or Englishmen', a 'plan' which he says he attributes to 'narrow-minded national conceit, which cannot relish a strong truth'. (This was well put, one guesses that it was because Griffin had a similar temptation to resist in his work of exploring the Anglo-Irish confrontation in his own country's history and present state. And we also learn from Griffin's illustration of the American bad example that by 1826, when he wrote this, in a preface to some of his tales, seventeen years before Henry James was born, there had already been established an anti-British American school of fiction; though when Hawthorne and Melville were working on the conception of a serious and truly American use of the novel subsequently they did not mean this.)

A woman reporting the New Peace Movement for Ireland in one of our weeklies recently remarked with surprise that 'The Irish are forever sitting around and saying: "What is it to be Irish? What does it mean?"', and she gives examples of what she rightly calls their 'obsessive sense of history'. Indeed, one can't read nineteenth-century fiction written by Irishmen without noticing that it was produced by an irritated need to justify themselves through their history and to find themselves as a nation in spite of their multiple divisions. Correspondingly doubts not as to their place in history but whether they had achieved a culture corresponding to their pretentions is what obliged American novelists to ask themselves: 'What is it to be an American?' as no French or English novelists ever needed to ask similar questions for themselves.

So James as an American had a number of handicaps to his task of becoming a master of the art of the novel. I will list some more. He was inevitably if unconsciously influenced by popular literary projections of the national conflict with the English as thrown up by the theatre of his youth. Constance Rourke in her classic work *American Humour* pointed out long ago that Henry James when a boy 'frequented Barnum's, where the Yankee farces were often performed, in which the whole American legend was racily sketched'. These popular plays typically featured an uncouth New England rustic or an unsophisticated Westerner, called first Brother Jonathan and later Uncle Sam, defeating by his native wit and shrewdness the Briton, who was shown as nefarious or complacent. One sees this in a refined form sometimes cropping up in James's fiction (though more often in reverse, the innocent American suffering at the hands of the corrupt European or English, and gaining only a moral victory). But the most usable and psychologically truthful form of the legend was actually the work of an *English* playwright, Tom Taylor, a London barrister, whose play, *Our American Cousin*, written about 1850 for the American market, was first produced in New York in 1858, when James was 15. It was one of the greatest American successes of the nineteenth-century theatre and played all over the United States for generations, owing, it was thought, to the success of a character-actor, Sothern, in creating, largely by gagging, the famous part of Lord Dundreary, though one feels that the true appeal of the play in America evidently lay in its mythical basis. The plot is that a crude but smart Yankee comes to England to claim an inheritance – the stately home, estates, title and fortune of his English relative, a baronet. The Yankee, in melodramatic circumstances, behaves heroically and with initiative and thus succeeds in regaining the inheritance. Tom Taylor, one sees, was artfully cashing in on an already existing American day-dream that represented a national psychosis. Hawthorne published in 1863 under the revealing title *Our Old Home* a selection from his *English Notebooks* kept when he was American consul in Liverpool and on his travels about England, a book acutely characterized by Matthew Arnold as 'the work of a man chagrined'. In it Hawthorne gives some examples of what he actually encountered as consul and calls it the 'diseased American appetite for English soil' – the fantasy that apparently many Americans then cherished of being the rightful claimants to English estates and titles, either by supposed descent, or by allegedly having been changed at birth, or even merely because they resembled the family portraits in a great house they had visited. Hawthorne christened it 'this Anglo-American myth'. James of course well knew Hawthorne's book and from there and *Our American Cousin*, or his own inner consciousness, concocted the symbolic plot of his first characteristic story, *A Passionate Pilgrim*, published in 1875 but no doubt written earlier; a story so sentimental and so crudely melodramatic, improbable and self-pitying that one could hardly credit that its author, who published it when 32, could ever develop into a good novelist. Moreover, it is a myth that even Hawthorne himself had partly succumbed to. He admitted identifying with his English ancestor who left for New England in 1635 and says he often felt the *déjà-vu* sensation in English scenes, explaining that 'perhaps the image of them, impressed into the mind of my long-ago forefather, was so deep that I have inherited it and it answers to the reality'. Less fanciful Americans, though their country had cut the tie with what they still felt to be their 'Old Home', compensated for the deprivation by persuading themselves that they were the true heirs of the English achievement and therefore entitled in one way or another to return and displace the present owners. The consequences of this were not only passionate pilgrims but cheque-book collectors, and this activity was idealized for literary purposes by James. Thus the opening of *The Portrait of a Lady* shows an Elizabethan mansion by the Thames, Gardencourt, whose pedigree we are given as symbolic of English history. But now, with all its pictures and furnishings from its storied past, Gardencourt is in the possession of an American banker, one who has, however, 'no intention of disamericanising', we are told. The idea incarnated in this early novel is steadily maintained on and into a late one, *The Golden Bowl*, where the fabulously rich American Adam·Verver owns the most enviable of English great houses and is buying up the art treasures not only of England but of all Europe, with the object of transferring them to a museum intended to elevate the culture of his native town, the symbolically named American City; in the same spirit he has also bought an Italian prince for his daughter to marry. But these fantasies became representative facts of American nineteenth century social history, and isn't it sad that a great novelist like James should underwrite such tendencies instead of giving them the hard, critical look they needed? Constance Rourke mentions incidentally that 'Even in the early 1850s American travellers had begun to announce their judgement on the European scene...A considerable number began a private "pillage of the past", bringing home copies of the masterpieces, marbles, tapestries. By the end of the 60s, the long and serious quest for European culture was well under way.' This was when James, born 1843, was only a boy. Only in the disillusioned few chapters he wrote called *The Ivory Tower* after his last visit to New York in the Gold Age did he at last recognize, too late, the acquisitiveness of the American rich as what it was, a form of national egotism, greed and envy. But in neither phase did he recognize the pathetic and comic elements in it, of which a novelist might have made so much, that a country without living art and as business-men contemptuous of artists, should feel that artifacts are necessary for a successful society to have, and should be satisfied to acquire them by purchase from their impoverished owners in the Old World, who had of course inherited them from the original patrons of artists. Behrman's witty book *Duveen* gives us a priceless insight into the mentality of the American millionaire class which made a Duveen's career possible. Only in his first novel *Roderick Hudson* did James attempt to tackle this question, of the need for America to grow its own artists; he seems to have given up the idea as hopeless thereafter.

A literary offshoot of the myth of the socially and culturally innocent American who gets the better of the effete or depraved Briton was the innocent and virtuous self-made American, though in fact this class were more likely to be robber barons or sweaters of chain-store employees unless they had had the luck and merit to strike oil or a gold-mine or, like one of Howells's millionaire characters, owned a farm found to cover natural gas-wells. Howells liked to show that such crude wealthy Americans were really worthy and estimable in spite of appearances. James admired Howells's novels excessively – Howells was his senior and an encouraging friend who edited a magazine which published James once, but even apart from these factors it was natural that James should be tempted to take up this idealization and work it intensively in spite of his ability at times to see this unrealism ironically. As when the Frenchman in *The Point of View* writes home from America

They've a novelist with pretensions to literature who writes about the adventures of rich Americans in our old corrupt Europe, where their candour puts the Europeans to shame. It's *proprement écrit*, but it's terribly pale.

This no doubt refers to James's own early novel, *The American* (1879). We find him using this conventional figure consistently and almost till the end, suggesting how necessary such moral support was to the expatriate. It seems to me that it was the myths, the inheritance from American popular historical legend and from the psychologically-based American fantasies that were responsible for the weaknesses and elements of unreality in James's representations of Anglo-American confrontation, and that it was his family's typical hostility to an undemocratic society which produces the spiteful elements in James's representation of English people of the upper classes. And this is the place to emphasize that there is an essential difference between his and other American writers' relations with English people and with French, German or Italian people. The Europeans, as distinct from the English, did not entail any psychological problems; they had not been their rulers or betters as the English had. Trollope recognized that this distinction needed explaining, and in his novel *The American Senator* opines that it is because of the nearness of the two peoples 'each speaking the same language, governed by the same laws', etc. so that 'the differences which present themselves', he says, are the more unacceptable, and 'In this spirit we Americans and Englishmen go on writing books about each other.'

James gave as his reason for not settling in Paris that there he would have been 'an eternal outsider', but he seems not to have realized that he was similarly an outsider in England, and moreover conditioned against a real understanding of England and the English by the American's compulsive antipathies and ambivalence towards the whole English subject. We know what his ambitions and intentions were, for he wrote to his brother William in 1888 that he saw the English and Americans 'as a big Anglo-Saxon total destined to such an amount of melting together that an insistence on their

differences becomes more and more idle and pedantic; and
that melting together will come the faster the more one takes it
for granted... Literature, fiction in particular, affords a magnifi-
cent arm for such taking for granted, and one may so do an
excellent work with it.' But this is not what James is in fact seen
to do in his fiction, where he concentrates on the differences
and induces an extreme pessimism about any melting together.

In later years Hamlin Garland visited James at Rye and
James made this confidence to him (*Roadside Meetings*), that he
ought to have stayed in America, because 'The mixture of
Europe and America which you see in me has proved
disastrous. It has made of me a man who is neither American
nor European. I have lost touch with my own people, and live
here alone.' But we should check this against William James's
observation in a letter to his sister in 1889, when visiting his
brother in England, 'beneath all the accretions of years and
the world, (Harry) is still the same dear, innocent old Harry
of our youth. His anglicisms are but "protective resemblances"
– he's really, I won't say a Yankee, but a native of the James
family, and has no other country' (the fate of the alien
resident). Henry James continues: 'I have not the least hesitation
in saying that I aspire to write in such a way that it would be
impossible to an outsider to say whether I am at a given
moment an American writing about England or an Englishman
writing about America (dealing as I do with both countries),
and so far from being ashamed of such an ambiguity I should
be exceedingly proud of it, for it would be highly civilized.'

James, Trollope and the American–English confrontation theme

James had a very great handicap in coming to grips with reality in England, which was that as an American he suffered from a similar disability to the New Zealanders'. His knowledge of England, like that of most educated Americans then, was first acquired in early life through English literature, notably the visual pictures of English life he obtained from Hogarth, and from the pages of *Punch* (and its illustrations by Leech, Keene, Du Maurier in particular) and from the novels of George Eliot, Dickens, Thackeray and Trollope, as he tells us in his autobiography, and which we may see endorsed by the evidence in his fiction of this practice. Thus he could never really form truthfully first-hand impressions of English people and scenes because other writers' and artists' had intervened. He tells us in his autobiographical book *The Middle Years* on his first arrival, in Liverpool in 1869, of his 'immediate intensities of appreciation' but they come down to such things as his delight in what he calls 'the incomparable truth to type of the waiter, truth to history, to literature, to poetry, to Dickens, to Thackeray, positively to Smollett and to Hogarth, to every connection that could help me to appropriate him and his setting, an arrangement of things hanging together with a romantic rightness that had the force of a revelation'. He was, we see, simply checking approvingly what literature and art had taught him to look for and expect. Thus, either he saw only what he was looking for and seeing that as he had been trained by his reading to do, or else he was resentful when pronounced divergences from the cherished patterns forced themselves on him. He projects himself thus as the American narrator of 'The Author of *Beltraffio*' who, visiting the English novelist he so much admires, as a matter of course sees his country home as a Pre-Raphaelite picture, his sister as a

Rossetti lady, his wife as a Gainsborough painting and so on.
'That was the way things struck me at that time, in England
– as reproduction of something that existed primarily in art
or literature. It was not the picture, the poem, the fictive page,
that seemed to me a copy; these things were the originals, and
the life of happy and distinguished people was fashioned in their
image.'

It seems to me due to this dependence on literature and art,
which acted as a pair of coloured spectacles between him and
a total apprehension of things English, that he habitually used
patterns and situations that were congenial to him, or struck
him as fine, in the English fiction of his formative period, for
renditions of American society; and he drew on French novelists
in the same way. This was a more legitimate artistic activity
since he adapted the themes as well as the settings with a free
hand. Thus *Washington Square* is patently an American *Eugénie
Grandet*, and I imagine the debt of one of his more interesting
early tales, *Madame de Mauves*, was only a rather more oblique
translation in terms of Flaubert's idea of a moral study of his
society in *Madame Bovary*; while the desire to show what an
American Dorothea Casaubon would be, do and feel, produced
The Portrait of a Lady, with its very images as well as situations
and some actual scenes taken over from George Eliot's *Middlemarch*. But there was another English novelist to whom James
was indebted for a good deal more (though no one seems to have
noticed it) and a much more valuable service, in forcing an
American critic of the English to reconsider his own American
hostilities and prejudices and assumptions because the English
novelist had first depicted all these in his novels with wit,
humour and a disconcerting critical insight that could not be
faulted as English prejudice, still less ignorance. James's use
of *him* was mainly a reaction of mincing acceptance or
attempted refutation.

This was Anthony Trollope, most of whose novels James had
read and about whom he wrote a good deal, reviewing some
of his novels, on the whole adversely, though admitting
admiration for the tragic figures of Trollope's clergymen Mr
Crawley and Louis Trevelyan, the modern Othello of *He Knew
He Was Right*, and for Trollope's brilliant idea of his bringing
the Italianized Stanhope family back to scandalize Barchester
Close and the country. With more though still inadequate

recognition, James wrote an obituary critique (he had even met Trollope once on board ship). Trollope had visited America five times and had travelled extensively right across and also up and down the States, and James admitted that Trollope's knowledge of America was 'excellent'. He also stated that it was Trollope who had launched the American girl in fiction (Howells mistakenly credited James himself with this) and James might well have added that it was Trollope who launched in fiction the Anglo-American marriage in High Life, and in terms that evidently stung James, since *his* heroines, who reject English noblemen as not good enough for an American girl, are evidently reactions against Trollope's galling assumption (in at least three of his novels) that superior American girls would accept titled English suitors with rapture mitigated only by fear of not being equal to the position or of not being acceptable to the aristocratic relatives. This was the more intolerable to American feeling since, as James admitted, Trollope's dealing with Americans in those novels and tales he devoted largely to them was 'friendly'. Trollope's way of offering criticism of Americans' ideas and character was candid and disarming, and his points were made without exaggeration, though indeed, as quotations from Henry James Senior and William James show, American political rhetoric and contempt and hostility to England parodied itself. Trollope's American characters and themes occur in novels written before James had established himself as a writer of fiction at all. In these novels – *He Knew He Was Right*, *The American Senator*, *The Duke's Children*, and such a short story as *Miss Ophelia Gledd* (1867), and repeated in other novels, Trollope fixed for the future American novelist a number of American types and a diversity of Anglo-American situations comic, matrimonial, and sociopolitical; he also improved, by making realistic instead of farcical, Dickens's dealings with American rhetoric (in *Martin Chuzzlewit*) of the anti-British, self-congratulatory kind. Trollope showed his open-mindedness by incarnating as equally ridiculous the blindly anti-American English squire, as in one of his best novels, *Mr. Scarborough's Family*; and in another, *The American Senator*, he makes the exceptionally impartial effort to do the American point of view justice by employing as candid eye and critical intelligence an American Western politician who is visiting England on an invitation from an English landowner, a professional diplomat he had met at Washington, but who finds the senator a social embarrassment in England. The Western senator is shown as dignified and courageous and a man of principle, though he inevitably makes errors of judgment which he later has to admit. Trollope allows him to score a good many points at the dinner-table, in the drawing-room and on the hunting field against the illogicality of English institutions and even the demerits of some. Therefore when Trollope intermittently shows the Senator airing his American prejudices or making absurd claims of the kind usual then, for the achievements of American democracy, these criticisms can't be written off as those of an anti-American writer. Trollope exactly hits off the American assurance of being an improvement on the English combined with the resentful feeling of inferiority to the actual English product. Trollope had also noted that 'it is the unconscious self-assurance of the Englishman which irritates the American', rightly seeing the hostility as basically psychological. He has many other such insights.

It will be thus seen from such novels as *The American Senator*, *The Duke's Children* and *He Knew He Was Right*, to go no further, that James was not giving an adequate account of Trollope in his various dismissals of him as a coarse, hearty, etc. type of Englishman. It is true Trollope had no sense of form and little respect for technique in his use of the novel, but the contents of parts of many are certainly not dismissable, nor did Henry James in fact dismiss them. They were very useful to him in the way that irritants are to the pearl-oyster (at any rate, from the point of view of a collector of pearls). And they must have given him food for thought in his chosen field, if indeed he didn't choose that field because of the provocation given him by Trollope. The patronizing attitude he adopted in his critical references to Trollope and in his reviews of some of Trollope's novels, was probably a self-deceiving reaction, implying a greater degree of immunity to Trollope's shrewd criticisms of Americans and their reactions to the English than James really had.

James must have been dependent on Trollope not only for his very usable knowledge of English *mœurs* but for a quite painful knowledge of how a shrewd and travelled Victorian saw Americans, even educated Americans of superior social standing. Trollope preceded James in his handling of the Anglo-American subject and must have been important in deciding the nature of James's treatment where it is neither mythical nor romantic, that is, where James faces realistically the problems inherent in it. Trollope seems to me to have forced upon James insights that were a challenge that James rose to, and the results are of greater interest than most of his work. Take the American parts of Trollope's novel *He Knew He Was Right*, forming one of the sub-plots. It takes place in Italy where the American Minister's niece, a charming, clever and sprightly girl like Isabel Archer, captures a future peer and is not prevented from accepting him by the indignation of her American bosom friend, an extremely vocal, anti-British poetess and journalist, though this friend and the rhetoric-charged American uncle, have almost deterred the English lover from proposing; and they are shown after the marriage in their great country-house with the American bride enjoying her position and her sister hoping for a similar position. This was intolerable to the Americans and we see James rewrote Trollope's sub-plot into the main stream of *The Portrait of a Lady* in order to counteract it. James has the notable suitor rejected by his American heroine in spite of ancestral homes and wealth and title; Trollope's Miss Wallachia Petrie becomes Miss Henrietta Stackpole softened by good looks but otherwise unmistakable; Trollope's off-putting American uncle becomes a likeable American uncle, Mr Touchett. One feature James must have welcomed, for he retained it; Trollope's heroine defends her American bosom friend against her lover's criticism in an outburst of American feelings, in much the same terms that Isabel Archer so surprisingly defends Henrietta against Ralph Touchett's view of her, that is, in each case claims for her virtues which only an American can value, as 'a kind of emanation of the great democracy – of the continent, the nation'. Yet James was surely obliged to admit to himself that *he* couldn't live in a society in resonance with a Wallachia Petrie and the Honourable Mr Spalding; he must have derived self-knowledge from Trollope as well as characters and forms in which to cast fictions. James seems to have been an American novelist peculiarly dependent on Old World novelists for techniques, themes and patterns, and one sees

why, for he was not original in the sense that Hawthorne and
Melville were and much more a sufferer from Colonialism.

If, then, one half of the life in *The Portrait of a Lady* derives
from translating George Eliot (Dorothea Brooke and Dorothea
Casaubon even more than *Deronda*'s Gwendolen Harleth), the
other half of its life derives from Trollope, that is, both as a
reaction against and an acceptance of different parts of
Trollope's extensive treatment in his novels of the theme
of the American–English conflict, social, psychological and
linguistic.

As regards language, the novelist's essential medium, we can
see (as James apparently never did) that instead of having an
advantage in having two closely related languages at his
disposal he hadn't a really sensitive mastery of spoken English,
while his native ear for American, at first so fine and sharp,
gradually dulled, so that later American heroines like Maggie
and Milly speak insipidly, while in *The Ivory Tower*, his
unfinished last work set in America, he has no longer anything
recognizable as an American speech at his command. Of course,
even the greatest genius in his position would not be able to
rival George Eliot, for instance, who in *Adam Bede* and *Silas
Marner* is seen to have the complete range of spoken English
from the several dialects she grew up among through town and
country, vulgar and educated usages. Yet this is something that
even minor talent can command too, if the writer lives fully
in his own country. Let me recommend in this connection the
novels of Somerville and Ross, two nineteenth-century Anglo-
Irishwomen who in two outstanding novels, *The Big House at
Inver* and *The Real Charlotte*, not to mention a string of lesser
novels and many volumes of stories, did use the Anglo-Irish
dialects and the educated idiom of their countrymen of all
classes with power and wit and a sensitive understanding of
the relation between speech and nationality. In maximum
contrast are Henry James's latest novels and tales, the characters
speak a literary or non-language and even his American
characters have lost their native and individual speech. When
Henry James returned to his native shores – in *The Ivory Tower*
– he reacted realistically to the American millionaire class
whose tables he then dined at and had to abandon the myth
of the good rich American he had so long cherished. But *The*

Ivory Tower, while registering Henry James's state of horror and disgust at that, does not do anything else – the novel was unfinished and one cannot believe it could have been finished or would have been anything more concrete than *The Sacred Fount*.

Thus, in general, as regards England, and his 'immediate intensities of appreciation' on his first arrival in his late twenties, which he records in *The Middle Years*, it was not always fresh perception but checking off 'the incomparable truth to type of the waiter, truth to history, to literature, to poetry, to Dickens, to Thackeray, positively to Smollett and to Hogarth, an arrangement of things hanging together with a romantic rightness that had the force of a revelation', so that he was seeing only what literature had taught him to expect and look for, and taught him also how to feel about it. James turned a blind eye to pronounced divergencies from the cherished pattern and ignored any perplexing complexities. We note his words 'a romantic rightness'. I conclude that it was owing to this formation of a romantic literary imagination that his sense of the past was so unhistorical and imprecise – everything tended for him in England to amalgamate into a timeless Past with a capital P. That was a real handicap in an undertaking such as his unfinished (and clearly unfinishable) novel *The Sense of the Past*: he was there committed to conveying and establishing exactly what he hadn't the power, the sensibility, the effective knowledge, to conceive, and it remains one of James's mere bright ideas.

It is true Dickens, for instance, seems not to have possessed much historic sense, and as a hearty Radical had little interest in or respect for much of the past anyway, but deplore Sir Leicester Dedlock and Foodles and Doodles (in *Bleak House*) as he might, he registers that baronet's typical fully human relation with his housekeeper and his obligations to his estate, as something lacking in the new Victorian class of self-made rich men like Mr Rouncewell, the iron-master, who knows his workmen only as 'hands' and has no feeling for the class he rose from and which has made him rich; and in the penultimate chapter of *Bleak House* Dickens writes an effective and moving elegy to the passing from power and cultural influence of Chesney Wold, the Dedlock estates and the dwindling light of its drawing-room, that focus of great expectations – 'passion and pride' – the aristocratic heritage being driven out by the dull conventions of the new dominant bourgeoisie. It is true that English country-houses, to which James was personally highly susceptible on aesthetic as well as romantic grounds, do figure in many of his works, but he either dislikes them, seeing house and grounds as embodiments of the conservative politics and rigid attitudes that he always attributes to the English owners, or he sees them as beautifully desirable but in degenerate or unworthy hands. This is what makes it all right for them to be taken over by American money.

In one tale, *Miss Ophelia Gledd*, Trollope actually anticipated the characteristic James *conte* in style, method, characters and theme, though one might also deduce that *An International Episode* derives from it and takes place entirely on Boston soil. The tale is narrated, after James's fashion, by an Englishman, the friend of the protagonist, the latter being the younger brother of a baronet and a literary man of some merit. They have made the acquaintance of a Boston girl who is, in her independence of chaperons and her freedom of speech and manner, unlike anything they are used to in England, and they can't decide whether she is a lady or not. She determines to marry the cultured and well-connected Englishman, in spite of his friend's (the narrator's) disapproval, because she admires England and wants to live there; but after he has been got to propose and she has accepted she has doubts as to whether his aristocratic family will accept her, and she makes her lover promise that in the event of her not liking them, or conversely, he will settle with her in Boston. The story ends at this point, with a question-mark as to what will happen, otherwise we might have had James's tale of *Lady Barbarina* in reverse. The style, and the wit, are remarkably like those of James in *Roderick Hudson* and *Daisy Miller*. Trollope was much struck by the relation of American girls to their mothers, who were too helpless to take charge of their daughters who saw the situation as a source of comedy. James accepted this insight and treats this feature of the democracy of the New World in the same spirit. Perhaps one way to make the point of Trollope's irresistible influence for James is to quote a passage that has so many of the qualities of the James novel of the period of *The Bostonians* and where one sees how he got his style for *The*

Portrait of a Lady; it comes from *The American Senator*, written in 1877, only a while after *A Passionate Pilgrim*:

It was very hard to put Mr Gotobed down; or it might be more correctly said, – as there was no effort to put him down, – that it was not often that he failed in coming to the surface. He took Lady Penwether out to dinner and was soon explaining to her that this little experiment of his in regard to Goarly was being tried simply with the view of examining the institutions of the country. 'We don't mind it from you', said Lady Penwether, 'because you are in a certain degree a foreigner.' The Senator declared himself flattered by being regarded as a foreigner only 'in a certain degree'. 'You see you speak our language, Mr Gotobed, and we can't help thinking you are half-English.' 'We are two-thirds English, my lady', said Mr Gotobed; 'but then we think the other third is an improvement.'

Trollope makes the Senator the vehicle for his understanding of the dilemma of the American of principle faced with a society he must disapprove of but which he finds in practice seductive. The Senator writes home with the characteristic American ambivalence:

And yet there is a pleasure in associating with those here of the highest rank which I find it hard to describe, and which perhaps I ought to regard as a pernicious temptation to useless luxury. Their principles are no doubt very bad.

This is hardly a parody, more an accurate spot-lighting of a sentiment that occurs in a less naked form in letters and journals of many nineteenth-century Americans, including William and Henry James. But Trollope expands the situation with a thorough realization of its comic implications, as in the unconscious confusion of the American Minister in Florence whose principles are aggressively democratic but who is highly gratified by his niece's marriage to an English aristocrat. Trollope's treatment of the most sensitive areas of American feeling in the peculiarly realistic forms of his fiction and mainly in connection with love and marriage must have made James take up seriously the question of Anglo-American confrontation in its most testing and dramatic form, that of inter-marriage. This subject produced some of James's best fiction, especially in the form of a whole batch of short stories, and it is the most striking of these I want to stress for this purpose. They are *An*

International Episode (because it was the forerunner of *The Portrait of a Lady*), *Lady Barbarina, The Modern Warning, A London Life*, which associates with the brilliant later novel *What Maisie Knew, The Real Thing*, which associates with the fine later novel, *The Tragic Muse*. In these, which reveal his difficulties, and his successes in dealing with the difficulties, he is to be seen transmuting a personal problem, his feelings towards the English, into an impersonal work of accomplished literary art. I should expect *An International Episode*, which, though charming in its American first half, is thereafter a very simple story of James's first period, simply to make the point, later repeated in Isabel Archer's rejection of the young nobleman she really likes because he isn't intellectual, doesn't take his position as a member of the House of Lords seriously enough for her, and because his family show hostility to her. This, in contrast to the complexity of the later tales, is purely a fiction for American gratification. Like *Daisy Miller*, which was a defence of the kind commonly made by W. D. Howells of the American girl – finding saving virtues in her in spite of her apparently insufferable limitations – the tale was bound to be popular for the American public. But as early as his second novel *The American*, James had seen the possibilities of a dramatic treatment of the inter-marriage subject if taken realistically. His defence of the unpopular treatment in this novel is a pointer to his later development towards a psychological realism in this field, which of course enables him to sound real instead of invented feelings. For James wrote to Howells in 1876, with regard to his novel *The American*, whose painful ending Howells, as magazine-editior, had objected to:

I am sorry that as a private reader you are not struck with the inevitability for the American dénouement...they would have been an impossible couple, with an impossible problem before them. For instance, where could they have lived?...Mme de Cintré couldn't have lived in New York, depend upon it, and Newman, after his marriage (or rather *she*, after it) couldn't have dwelt in France. There would have been nothing left but a farm out West.[1] No, the interest of the subject was, for me, (without being at all a pessimist) its exemplification of one of those insuperable difficulties which present themselves in people's lives and from which the only issue is by forfeiture... We are each the products of circumstances and there are tall stone walls which fatally divide us.

This is profoundly wise compared with the folly of 'narrow-minded national conceit', a folly which Hawthorne exemplified in his plan for an Anglo-American confrontation story, in his last phase (when he couldn't finish anything he started), where he wrote, in his *American Notebooks*:

It must be shown, I think, throughout that there is an essential difference between English and American character, and the former must assimilate itself to the latter, if there is to be any union.

But why, except to satisfy 'narrow-minded national conceit', was English assimilation to America the inevitable conclusion of there being 'an essential difference between English and American character'? Why not face the reality, as James did, that no union had better be attempted in such circumstances? James's is a just insight and he was courageous in refusing to make the happy ending to *The American* that Howells wanted, and which James's more intelligent English friends feared he might have in mind, he wrote. But Mme de Cintré was French and James could admire the French aristocracy. When he came to write *Lady Barbarina*, though he seems to show, almost unwillingly, good reasons why the English wife too 'couldn't have lived in New York', his hostility to the English aristocracy manifested itself in somehow finding this blamable in her, while her American husband is shown sympathetically as a victim in being made to settle in England by his wife, though he has been seen choosing to live in England before marriage the life of the idle rich, quite happily, without even having the duties of an English landowner and Member of Parliament. We learn he has had, owing to his marriage, to sacrifice his vocation as a doctor (though he hardly seems to have practised before) and his patriotic desire to do something to improve his country by establishing a *salon* in New York under the inspiration of a high-bred English wife – an unrealistic ambition, for, as James shows, Lady Barbarina was as hopelessly unfitted to undertake such an enterprise as New York Society to collaborate in it. James holds her deficiency against the Englishwoman but does not seem to acknowledge that New York Society of the time is also to blame (as Howells showed in *A Husband of New Fortunes*). No sympathy is shown in *The Siege of London* for the inevitable misery of Sir Arthur Demesne's married life with Mrs Headway, a woman who, unlike Lady Barbarina, does not bear children, is not amiable and well-bred, not even young and chaste. But she is American, a much-divorced Western beauty with several living husbands but now a rich widow of thirty-seven and anxious to marry a young baronet she has picked up, a Tory M.P. Sir Arthur Demesne, simply in order to get into English society, to the distress of the dowager, the baronet's mother, who begs in turn each of the Americans who knew Mrs Headway to tell her the truth about the Lady's past (which she suspects) so as to prevent Sir Arthur engaging himself. Two Americans (one Littlemore, a Westerner, the other a diplomat) are in London to discuss Mrs Headway's character together and their own course of conduct about her, mainly in order to underline their separate but similar reactions to the Demesnes as Americans confronting English upper-class symbols. Both the Americans refuse in turn to tell, partly out of loyalty to a compatriot, but quite as much from irritation at what the Englishman and his mother represent (class patronage, a stately home, good breeding, high standards of conduct), but most of all from a feeling that no Englishman can be too good for any American woman, even a Mrs Headway whom both the Americans actually find embarrassing to themselves. The detailing of the story is finely realized and the technical devices quite subtle such as the tale's opening in the Paris theatre where the men come across Mrs Headway with her baronet, while on the stage a drama of the same theme as the story's is enacted but resolved in terms of French theatrical conditions (such as all-round lying and calculation) which disgust the Americans. The interesting thing is that James has constructed all the characters in their extreme forms so as to test the attitudes to the problem – the Demesnes are worthy people and quite inoffensive by any civilized standards, while Mrs Headway has nothing to be said for her except that she is pretty and expensively dressed: she is pushing, vulgar, ignorant, besides having a dubious past. She admits she cares nothing for Sir Arthur personally (he bores her), so the marriage will clearly be disastrous for him. The American diplomat when invited to stay at the Demesnes's West Country mansion registers hostility to the whole place, both the stately home and gardens and its guests, though not on any rational grounds; while the other American refuses his sister's plea to save English society from such an undesirable American specimen as Mrs Headway, saying 'If she can succeed, she's welcome. It's a splendid sight in its way' and he tells his friend 'Some of these Western women are wonderful. Like her, they only want a chance.' There is a kind of defiance in the novelist's refusal to make Mrs Headway more acceptable and the Demesne's people less admirable, which would have made it easier for him to justify the two Americans' refusal to intervene when implored both by Lady Demense and also Littlemore's sister who, having married an English squire, has become – to her brother's annoyance – completely English. This tale is amusing and good as well as interesting because it explores American feelings honestly and in all their complexity. It is in close touch with reality and undercuts myth.

James's uncertain and sometimes unmanageable anti-British drives took a much more useful and convincing form when expressed as the creative artist's rejection of English Philistinism, as shown by bourgeois values, by the absence of any intellectual life (as he thought) in the upper class, and the widespread fear of Art on moral grounds – all points made already by Matthew Arnold and George Eliot of course, but James illustrated them with gusto and virtuosity.

In *A London Life* James uses two sisters, the younger, Laura, an unspoilt American girl, the elder, long since married to an Englishman with a town- and country-house, has become a depraved London socialite; but the theme is the disparity between the beauty and charm of the great house and its unworthy English owner stated as typical of the age, a theme repeated in the later and more elaborate *conte The Spoils of Poynton*. Thus, while James had written in his *Notebook* in 1878 that 'the British country-house is one of the ripest fruits of time and here in Scotland of the highest results of civilization', he also recorded a few years later, as to the class that inhabited the country-house, that 'The condition of that body seems to me to be in many ways very much the same rotten and *collapsible* one as that of the French aristocracy before the revolution – minus cleverness and conversation.' Thus, in *A London Life* Laura 'marvelled at the waste involved in some human institutions' – the English landed gentry, for instance – where she noted 'how much it had taken to produce so little' which gives her 'the sense of some curious duplicity'. Here James is seen expressing resentment at a disparity between the romantic illusions he had made for himself from his frequentation of English literature and art of the past, and the therefore no doubt disappointing reality. 'The view of the garden...reminded her of scenes in Shakespeare's comedies while of course what took place in that garden now were Edwardian comedies – dramas by Pinero and Traherne.' It's not only the upper-class that are degenerate: when the young diplomat in *The Siege of London* visits Longlands he feels that in England Nature has been corrupted too; 'the trees had an air of conscious importance, as if Nature herself had been bribed somehow to take the side of country families' while in the hedges he sees 'the first trees in England, springing out of them with a regularity which suggested conservative principles'. Thus a vein of spiteful hostility constantly rises to the surface of James's fiction, but the charged feeling provided unforgettable scenes, such as that in *The Tragic Muse* where the hero, staying at his cousin's Palladian mansion, has rowed over an artificial lake to an artificial island on which stands an elegant eighteenth-century imitation of the Temple of Vesta, so that he may there make an obligatory proposal of marriage in a suitable place. Sitting inside the temple Julia nervously opens her parasol on receiving the proposal from the man she loves and sits under its unnecessary shelter, presumably in an instinctive movement to protect herself from a condition of which she is afraid (James interpreted the reserve of well-bred English people as fear of showing feeling) and it is also a mechanical social gesture in a situation demanding a personal response. James does not comment on the scene, he doesn't need to, for it communicates what is intended of itself. James's accounts of the English gentry, while becoming increasingly confident, are always hostile and external, and they are used for propaganda. His English lords and gentlemen are satisfyingly cut down to less than American size.

    In *The Modern Warning* James embodies the tragedy of another 'impossible couple', a sensitive American girl and her English husband who, though united by love, are divided against their will and even through their marriage, by patriotism and conflicting traditions. James set out the problem as impersonally and fully as possible; it appears from his *Notebooks* that he originally planned more violent treatment of the subject than he thought fit eventually to produce. The American girl, now

alone in the world except for a brother described as 'an
anglophobist' but who is deeply attached to his sister, has
therefore to make a choice between her nationality and family
feelings on the one hand and her love for her English suitor,
an agreeable but obtuse baronet and Tory M.P., on the other.
She marries him, hoping to win him over to an admiration of
her country. But a post-matrimonial tour with her of the States
fills him with horror of America, and he writes a book warning
England against becoming Americanized. To the brother,
Agatha's marriage was 'a kind of moral treachery', for he
considers the British Empire and the English class system
unrighteous and these views are embittered by his having had
an Irish grandmother (as the James family had) through whom
hereditary hostility to the English had been transmitted.
Agatha perceives that her brother's objection to the alleged
British 'denial of equality' was unfair since he was deceiving
himself in supposing that he was 'a passionate democrat and
an unshrinking radical', though like him she is herself 'a
passionate American'. Gradually in her married life she realizes
that she has had to sacrifice all her early associations and
natural pieties, but that then, after living in London for years,
she would never be able to live in America again even if she
were ever widowed, so she sanctions the publication of her
husband's book which he has hitherto abandoned in deference
to her feelings. She thinks she has now 'achieved the solution'
of her problems. But then her brother for the first time comes to
London to visit her, just as the book is published. Unable to
stand the strain of the position she will find herself in, she
impulsively poisons herself just as the two men arrive at her
home together. Neither is able to answer the question each puts
to himself across the dead body of the woman they both love:
'Why, why just now?' But the startling conclusion has been
prepared for by the psychological study of Agatha and an
analysis of all the factors that produce an inevitable tragedy.
We are made to see that the suicide would not have been
necessary if the brother had not precipitated it by his
uncompromising attitude over the years or if Sir Rufus
Chasemore had not been so completely English as to be
unaware of his wife's American sympathies and point of view.
This is manifested with sensitive insight on the novelist's part
– Agatha has a secret wound that she has married 'a man who

could feel no tenderness for the order of things which had encompassed her early years and had been intimately mixed with her growth which was a part of her conscience, the piety of many who had been most dear to her and whose memory would be dear to her always'. James recorded in his *Notebook* of his idea for this tale that 'Of course internationalism etc. may be found overdone, threadbare' – after all, he had written a great deal on it by now – but, he adds: 'It is always enough if the *author* sees substance in it.' He thus recognizes the fascination and importance of the subject to himself at any rate. Agatha's feelings are thereby his own, and he wanted to explore them. The tale is pessimistic to the last degree, but if we think of it we see that so are all the others in this series and this story, in which there is no superfluous word or ambiguous sentence, the tone is throughout profoundly serious, nothing is shirked or undervalued, and complete impartiality is maintained throughout. It seems to me to be the finest expression of the deepest realization of the insoluble difficulties of the member of the James family who was in spite of his disabilities a major novelist, making his art out of those difficulties and knowing any solution of them must be illusory or dishonest. It is interesting that in this tale the American brother is shown set (involuntarily, it is made clear) in attitudes of hostility and rejection to England, while the English gentleman has a good-natured, friendly attitude to the American family, until a tour of the United States forces him into alarmed dislike. Agatha's problems, which represent James's, are central and every aspect is honestly faced of the novelist's feelings towards the English that have been revealed in his notebooks, essays and letters, even to her horror, like James's own, of the English slums and drunken poor, which Agatha alleges had no equivalent in the States. Yet even in this tale there is no recognition of the complexity of English life in the Victorian Age, and Sir Rufus Chasemore is shown (like all Englishmen in James who are not creative artists) to be simple-minded and rather stupid. We remember that Henry James told his sister that 'The English are the only people who can do great things without being clever' – a grudging admission that shows a basic inability to recognize intelligence unless it is shown by the continental signs of cleverness such as articulateness and philosophizing. One can't help recalling a momentary flash of honesty and insight in Alice James's diary, kept in England, when she remarks on the un-American quality of *civility* in all classes in Victorian England, even the poor, and how visiting Americans 'actually don't perceive the difference' coming fresh from the 'hard, gritty, rugged interchange which passes for manners at home' concluding 'when suddenly brought face to face with all this complexity, what can they do but seek refuge in blindness?' Henry James as a novelist overcame the temptation to take refuge in blindness, or in cowardly denigration as patriotism, or in colonial obsequiousness. He tried and often succeeded in doing his duty as a novelist.

Jackson Lemon was misguided in believing that American brains and wealth crossed with aristocratic English stock would produce a superior strain for America to breed from: all it produces is a general disaster, and frustration for the American partner, just as Mrs Headway's success in grafting herself on to English rank and breeding is going to end the Demesne line. Trollope had taken the view in several books that American girls could be successfully integrated into English High Society if they were prepared to sacrifice their American connections and anglicize themselves. This James seems to have felt obliged to reject, as we have seen. He even, in the tale *Lord Beaupré*, has a reverse case – the English heroine turned down the young peer to live in New York as the wife of an American stockbroker (it is true he is made out to be a very unusual stockbroker, fond of old books and a good amateur water-colour artist), and we aren't shown the outcome. James's insight in registering such pessimism was surely just – in actuality, the Anglo-American marriages in High Life of the late Victorian and Edwardian eras did nearly always break down, with the American leaving her noble husband and divorcing or being divorced. Edith Wharton chose to treat this classic situation in her last, but unfortunately unfinished, novel which critics have thought one of her best. James moved over to another but less direct anti-English attack in tales and the late novel *The Tragic Muse*; in these the indictment of English society is made not through Americans but artists – James uses sculptor, painter, novelist, illustrator (the painter being generally portrait-painter who, like the illustrator, is a convenient representative for novelist). James's anti-English resentments and compulsive drives to

embody these in fictions using symbolic figures get satisfaction
from showing the artist as victim of English Puritanism and
Philistinism, of a national lack of respect for artists and their
work, and of the absence in England of intellectual life in the
world of the country-house and London Society. That there
were other societies in England beside 'the Prince of Wales set'
and the studio James seems to have been unaware; and seeing
that he was so widely received in country-houses and in London
drawing-rooms and dining-rooms this was also ungrateful,
though perhaps, judging by such tales as *The Figure in the Carpet*,
The Middle Years and *The Death of the Lion*, he felt he had not
in those quarters got the recognition he deserved. But
prejudiced and partial as it was, it was a picture or myth
evidently dear to him and fruitful for composition. The most
extended is the brilliant novel *The Tragic Muse*, whose theme
is the contrast between the rewarding life and valuable roles
of painter and actress compared with the waste lands of English
career diplomacy and the Houses of Parliament. But the young
M.P. who gives up his seat to become a portrait-painter is sent
to Coventry by his kin and cut out of the will of his father's
old friend who is prepared to finance Nick's political career but
says (improbably) 'The pencil, the brush, they are not the
weapons of a gentleman.' In *The Death of the Lion* a great
novelist is virtually killed in a country-house called Prestidge
by the claims of the guests and hostess on the sick man, and
the unique manuscript of his last and greatest novel is lost by
them, while they fête and promote vulgar popular novelists.

The most deadly of all this group concerning the artist as
American, so to speak, in its anti-English hostility, takes place
entirely in the studio, that is, the international real world of
the creative talent, as opposed to the English social world which
Major and Mrs Monarch bring with them as they seek
employment as models for an artist who lives by doing illustrations for novels. The couple are described by him as people
formed by country-house life, and through them that culture
takes a symbolic beating. To start with, having lost their money
they have also lost their place in society. And even trying to
use them as models has almost ruined the narrator and done
his talent probably irreparable harm, we learn. He finally
breaks with them in some painful scenes by first rejecting them
in favour of two working-class models for his society characters,

and then obliging them to accept the role of servants to these models; and thus, having humiliated them as much as possible, he turns them out to starve, with evident satisfaction. Just as there was nothing to be said in favour of Nancy Headway or Daisy Miller except that they were American, so there is almost nothing to be said against Major or Mrs Monarch as against Lady Demesne and Sir Arthur, except that they are upper-class English, but this is enough to irritate and even anger the narrator. They do not arouse any sympathy in him though they have adjusted to destitution without self-pity or complaint, they behave with dignity in humiliating circumstances engineered by the narrator, and voluntarily do menial services; Mrs Monarch even shows touching magnanimity to the Cockney female model, as the artist himself recognizes. Yet he feels justified in treating them brutally and the last sentence of the tale records that he enjoys the memory of having humiliated and rejected them. No doubt James saw a satisfying symbolism in the story, whose germ was in real life an anecdote of his friend's, the half-French artist George du Maurier, and the name 'Monarch' is of course suggestive. They were punished, one must conclude, for being representatives of, as the artist says, 'the social life of their country' (not 'my country' or 'our country', as one would expect, thus making my point that James thought of his representatives of the arts as non-English). Yet it is this social life which James had elected to share, evidently not without psychological strain, as a work that approaching never to perfection, yet does not strike cold. Was his anger with the English due to disappointment? He told an American friend that for an American 'A position in (English) society is a legitimate object of ambition' and objected to being not considered to be middle-class by English middle-class people, but in his works, though the only American artist is the first one, Roderick Hudson, the English ones are always at odds with a hostile attitude to English Society so that they are equivalent to the American visitors who embody all the James family's reactions to England. Unlike Major and Mrs Monarch, the Cockney woman and the Italian barrow-boy who become ideal models *are* found sympathetic by the artist, but they of course live in a world outside his socially, though they somehow serve him for inspiration in interpreting drawing-room life. He sees them either as embodiments of dramatic ideas or, when not posing, as diverting him – he *uses* them but of course they never represent a challenge, they have no bearing on his personal life.

I would suggest that it is James's sense of not being on sure ground and his lack of any deeper knowledge of and response to the whole English subject than aesthetic or prejudiced that makes him so prone to make use of other novelists, truly English novelists, to provide a scaffolding from which to work or a framework within which to construct with a difference. Dr Leavis in *The Great Tradition* shows another kind of relation of James's to an earlier novelist, the use of *Daniel Deronda* (and it should be said of *Middlemarch*, also and not less) in creating *The Portrait of a Lady*: suppose George Eliot's Dorothea, with her Puritan Evangelical conditions and her ignorant demands on life, had been instead of a young English lady a New England young lady, also the product of a Puritan culture (though a different one) and with ambitions not to be satisfied by a conventional happy marriage? James cannot translate that theme into American life without bringing his heroine into contact with England and Europe (in fact George Eliot had taken Dorothea to Rome on her honeymoon for the same purpose, as a challenge to the Puritan disability, and James reveals his indebtedness wholesale by parasitic passages and derived images). Yet while the American characters are full of life and spirit and variety, the English ones – Lord Warburton, his sisters and his brother the Vicar, the man about town Mr Bantling – are all thin and conventional, and their conversation dull. Put Lord Warburton beside Sir James Chettam and you have shadow beside substance – George Eliot thoroughly understands Sir James, his strong points as well as his limitations, his full life as a landowner, magistrate, son, neighbour and husband and by the end of the book Dorothea, like the reader, has acquired an unexpected respect and esteem for him; but by the end of *The Portrait of a Lady* we know no more about Lord Warburton than at his first appearance, in fact less, because his sudden marriage at the end is unexplained and his impulse to marry Pansy a little before, in order to have access to his old flame, her step-mother, is so out of character as to be incredible.

It isn't that James isn't a real novelist with the power to create action, characters and dialogue, it is that where the English are concerned he doesn't have the same insight, intelligent understanding and confidence as he has with the Americans and the French, perhaps not even enough interest in them. This isn't innate disability, it is conditioning. We may recollect Conrad's remarkable and wide-ranging successes in rendering English life and character – successes ranging from the civil servant and his family in *Chance*, his numerous naval captains and officers and crews, to the Kentish country-folk in *Amy Foster*, Winnie and her mother and the other Londoners in *The Secret Agent*, for instance. These are all genuine and they 'speak the language'. But think of James's dreadful attempt at Cockneys like Millicent Hemming in *The Princess Casamassima* – a novel with evident roots in Dickens and unconscious transplantings from *Little Dorrit* – I mean Millicent is dreadful in her impossible speech. But there is something even more deplorable in that novel, the scene where the American-Italianate Princess, in her rented English country-house, has the whim to pass off Hyacinth Robinson, the little East End artisan, on her callers as one of their own class (a class which at that date – 1886 – was a caste). And this at a time in history when not only clothes and their cut but a man's hands, air, gait, expression – the whole physique – indelibly stamped him and when moreover an Englishman had only to open his mouth and utter to be classified socially beyond a doubt. Conrad would not have made such an error, he was a keen observer and not blinkered by any prejudices (here, in James's case, as usual, that the English were thoroughly stupid). It does suggest that James must have been still in such essential matters an alien in England, or else was so romantically carried away by his conception of Hyacinth as a *perfect gentleman* spiritually that it needed no more than his belief in the stupidity of the English to make such an absurd hypothesis seem plausible.

Thus James's assumptions of the dullness, simplicity and obtuseness of the English prevented him from observing the complex realities of the English scene. How *could* people so unforthcoming, he felt, so limp, living contentedly in such a stupid, pernicious social system, so offensively reserved in manner, etc. – as he constantly notes in his letters and personal writings – and as his sister kept before him – how could *they* have the right to own this covetable country with its beauties natural and man-made, its historic past and its literature? (One sees this resentment even more strikingly in Hawthorne's *Our Old Home*, etc.) James saw only the national uniform

Englishmen and women; he was far from being able, like
Dickens and George Eliot and Trollope and even Conrad to see
the wide differences within the English whole, differences
which were felt by the English themselves as tremendous local
differences, regional ones, differences of class and within each
class (as Trollope noted in *The Darlings* between clergymen),
a gulf even between the Oxford and the Cambridge educated
– so that Miss Emily Davies, who founded Girton, wrote to a
friend that she was well acquainted with the difference between
the cool Cambridge manner and the kind, gushing Oxford one
– such differences which made the English mutually objec-
tionable and only united against foreigners and Americans,
differences that were the breath of life to all our Victorian
novelists. Moreover, James seems to me to recognize only two
classes – the gentry in general and London slum-dwellers
and registers a horror at the aspect of the latter that
compensates for his admission that the English were a
handsome race, unlike an equivalent American crowd which is
stamped by 'the business face', as he wrote. Thus he fell back
on reflecting types that had been created for him by English
novelists.

Therefore James was largely dependent on English literature
for his usable knowledge of the English people. He was also
dependent on English novels for a painful sort of knowledge
of how the Victorians thought of Americans. This, though I
have never seen it noted, is mainly a debt to his predecessor
Anthony Trollope who decided the nature of James's treatment
of the America–England subject. In his interesting obituary
essay on Trollope (1883), James admits that Trollope was
unusually qualified to write about America (which he had
visited five times) and that he did it excellently; he also admits
to a knowledge of and interest in a number of Trollope's novels
(some of which he had reviewed), and of all those which contain
American characters. James there recognizes that the American
girl entered English fiction with Trollope (who twice married
her to English noblemen) and that not only was the theme of
the Anglo-American marriage one of Trollope's subjects but
the whole Anglo-American conflict. We may even say with
some confidence, I think, that it provided the inspiration
for transporting another Europeanized brother and sister, in
The Europeans, into a New England society, where another

hypothetically married titled siren is seen at work, also with a scandalous artist brother, and are likewise rebuffed and return to Europe. Trollope, though not much of an artist as a novelist, as James complained, was a shrewd and thoroughly initiated sociological observer of the English scene – which James also noticed with respect. What he did find useful was Trollope's dealings with what is now assumed to be James's theme, the intercourse between the English and visiting Americans. James's pleasant remark that 'No less than twice, and possibly even oftener, has Trollope rewarded the merit of a scion of the British aristocracy with the hand of an American girl' is perhaps a little joke, or else implies irony, for in Trollope's novels the American girls, it is very clear, feel that the reward is all theirs, and are troubled only by a sense of unfitness for their elevation. This must have been hard for a James family member to bear, and no wonder Henry James liked to show in his earlier tales and novels that Boston nymphs found English noblemen not good enough to accept (though James's romanticism found its outlet, in gifting American girls from first to last – as in the early *Last of the Valerii* and the late *Golden Bowl* and others in between – with noble or princely Italian husbands; after all, James's American girls are princesses by right anyway).

But Trollope's shrewdness hit too many marks, in a quite unmalicious way, to be ignored. And Trollope couldn't be written off as ignorant of America and Americans, and James admitted that as regards 'transatlantic knowledge' Trollope 'has all the air of being excellent' and that in this respect 'on the whole, Trollope does very well'. But from the point of view of the son and brother of James, Trollope had done very ill. Provocation is constant; in 1864, Trollope wrote *Can You Forgive Her?* (a novel which James shows close knowledge of) where the nephew of the Duke of Omnium, who was characterized by a pleasant line of ironic conversation, Jeffrey Palliser, entertains the heroine at dinner by saying 'I do hate the Americans. It's the only strong political feeling I have. I went there once, and found I couldn't live with them on any terms... Oh; it's jealousy, of course. I know that. I didn't come across a cab-driver who wasn't a much better educated man than I am. And as for their women, they know everything.' And Trollope elsewhere in the same novel pokes fun at

Hawthorne's complaints in *Our Old Home* of the offensive buxomness of English matrons, because it is so unlike the leanness of New England women. He is quite equal to seizing on the characteristic patriotic American note, which is seen in Hawthorne's intensely serious sketch for his last novel: 'It must be shown, I think, throughout that there is an essential difference between English and American character, and the former must assimilate itself to the latter, if there is to be any union' – the note of a characteristic aggressive complacency that amused and disgusted Victorian writers like Dickens and Trollope as much as what was felt to be the English effortless superiority maddened Americans like William James and Henry Adams. Trollope's double-barrelled weapon in such a dialogue as this in *The American Senator* (1877), two years before James finally settled in England, hit both the American assurance of being an improvement on the English with the American conviction of being entitled to claim the privilege of English status. Trollope's real service was to make James reconsider what would otherwise undoubtedly have been more complacent and unthinking acceptances of traditional American attitudes, traits and declamations, such as were exemplified by the James family. Trollope, while amusing himself and his readers by registering such attitudes and rhetoric in at least four of his novels, had made it impossible for an intelligent man like James to endorse them directly. James's feelings had necessarily to be subtle, and James, taking precautions, had to decide how much he must concede. This is a very valuable service for one novelist to have rendered another, though naturally James doesn't acknowledge it. James had to define his position about the points raised by Trollope regarding American crudities and ideological follies, which, in his general optimistic intention I have quoted (to stand above the mêlée) he would not otherwise have done.

To sum up: several of James's major sources of fiction were the result of the difficulties and disabilities that he had to struggle with as an American of his time. In treating them he drew on the deepest of his feelings and thus the resulting works have a vitality and interest that are absent from his purely aesthetic and intellectual tales and novels, or parts of novels, which tend to be either bloodless intellectual exercises or aesthetic word-spinning, lacking the personal engagement of the other category which have much more convincing detail and forcefulness of expression. These deeper preoccupations were either directly or indirectly the source of the greatest part of his best work (though no one would know it from Edel's biography). Henry James as a novelist overcame the temptation to take refuge in blindness, or in cowardly denigration as patriotism, or in colonial obsequiousness. He tried and often succeeded in doing his duty as a novelist. And insomuch as his inspiration and the feelings he expresses in this main line of his fictions are indeed American he was a truly American novelist if not what Melville would have desiderated or even recognized as such.

A note on literary indebtedness: Dickens, George Eliot, Henry James

Though the more one thinks about it the more inevitable it seems that the Romantic period must have discovered the sentimental uses of ancient Rome, with its melancholy and morally suggestive débris, discovered it, I mean, as a sympathetic literary background for the lovelorn or heart-broken, I have not found any instances of such a literary formula till the next age. Though indeed Childe Harold took his bleeding heart to Rome (remarking 'the orphans of the heart must turn to thee') and there appears to have adumbrated the general idea without precisely getting down to it. Whenever it was hit upon and by whom, however, to the Victorian novelists it seems to have become well known, as witness these three different but successive treatments of the theme:

(1) Little Dorrit would often ride out in a hired carriage that was left them, and alight alone and wander among the ruins of old Rome. The ruins of the vast old Amphitheatre, of the old Temples, of the old commemorative Arches, of the old trodden highways, of the old tombs, besides being what they were, to her, were ruins of the old Marshalsea – ruins of her own old life – ruins of the faces and forms that of old peopled it – ruins of its loves, hopes, cares, and joys. Two ruined spheres of action and suffering were before the solitary girl often sitting on some broken fragment; and in the lonely places, under the blue sky, she saw them both together. *Little Dorrit* (1857)
(2) She had been led through the best galleries, had been taken to the chief points of view, had been shown the grandest ruins and the most glorious churches, and she had ended by oftenest choosing to drive out to the Campagna where she could feel alone with the earth

151

and sky, away from the oppressive masquerade of ages, in which her own life too seemed to become a masque with enigmatical costumes.

To those who have looked at Rome with the quickening power of a knowledge which breathes a growing soul into all historic shapes, and traces out the suppressed transitions which unite all contrasts, Rome may still be the spiritual centre and interpreter of the world. But let them conceive one more historical contrast: the gigantic broken revelations of that Imperial and Papal city thrust abruptly on the notions of a girl . . . whose ardent nature turned all her small allowance of knowledge into principles, fusing her actions into their mould, and whose quick emotions gave the most abstract things the quality of a pleasure or a pain; a girl who had lately become a wife, and from the enthusiastic acceptance of untried duty found herself plunged in tumultuous preoccupation with her personal lot. The weight of unintelligible Rome might lie easily on bright nymphs to whom it formed a background for the brilliant picnic of Anglo-foreign society; but Dorothea had no such defence against deep impressions. Ruins and basilicas, palaces and colossi, set in the midst of a sordid present, where all that was living and warm-blooded seemed sunk in the deep degeneracy of a superstition divorced from reverence; the dimmer but yet eager Titanic life gazing and struggling on walls and ceilings; the long vistas of white forms whose marble eyes seemed to hold the monotonous light of an alien world: all this vast wreck of ambitious ideals, sensuous and spiritual, mixed confusedly with the signs of breathing forgetfulness and degradation, at first jarred her as with an electric shock, and then urged themselves on her with that ache belonging to a glut of confused ideas which check the flow of emotion. Forms both pale and glowing took possession of her young sense, and fixed themselves in her memory even when she was not thinking of them, preparing strange associations which remained through her after-years. Our moods are apt to bring with them images which succeed each other like the magic-lantern pictures of a doze; and in certain stages of dull forlornness Dorothea all her life continued to see the vastness of St Peter's, the huge bronze canopy, the excited intention in the attitudes and garments of the prophets and evangelists in the mosaics above, and the red drapery which was being hung for Christmas spreading itself everywhere like a disease of the retina.   *Middlemarch* (1872)

(3) Isabel took a drive alone that afternoon; she wished to be far away, under the sky, where she could descend from her carriage and tread upon the daisies. She had long before this taken old Rome into her confidence, for in a world of ruins the ruin of her happiness seemed a less unnatural catastrophe. She rested her weariness upon things that had crumbled for centuries and yet still were upright; she dropped her secret sadness into the silence of lonely places, where its very modern quality detached itself and grew objective, so that as she sat in a

sun-warmed angle on a winter's day, or stood in a mouldy church to which no one came, she could almost smile at it and think of its smallness. Small it was, in the large Roman record, and her haunting sense of the continuity of the human lot easily carried her from the less to the greater. She had become deeply, tenderly acquainted with Rome; it interfused and moderated her passion. But she had grown to think of it chiefly as the place where people had suffered. This was what came to her in the starved churches, where the marble columns, transferred from pagan ruins, seemed to offer her a companionship in endurance and the musty incense to be a compound of long-unanswered prayers. There was no gentler nor less consistent heretic than Isabel; the firmest of worshippers, gazing at dark altar-pictures or clustered candles, could not have felt more intimately the suggestiveness of these objects nor have been more liable at such moments to a spiritual visitation... Even when Pansy and the Countess were with her she felt the touch of a vanished world. The carriage, leaving the walls of Rome behind, rolled through narrow lanes where the wild honeysuckle had begun to tangle itself in the hedges, or waited for her in quiet places where the fields lay near, while she strolled further and further over the flower-freckled turf, or sat on a stone that had once had a use and gazed through the veil of her personal sadness as the splendid sadness of the scene – at the dense, warm light, the far gradations and soft confusions of colour, the motionless shepherds in lonely attitudes, the hills where the cloud-shadows had the lightness of a blush.   *The Portrait of a Lady* (1881)

Little Dorrit is, as Mr Trilling has shown us, one of Dickens's finest novels, and we can see at once that the first extract has the virtues of Dickens without his frequent weaknesses. A simple idea is forcefully but not crudely expressed and *not sentimentalized*; though 'old' is decidedly overworked, still, the simplicity of technique is felt to guarantee the genuineness of the passage, and in fact we see on second reading that 'old' is used in different senses and has the effect of adding, as by a play upon words, some subtlety, like the pun in the title of *Hard Times*. In the last sentence the rhetoric, which in the previous sentence has been collapsing into verse, pulls itself together again and rounds off with a neat word-picture in poetic prose with a dying fall, where the images and idea they impart are economically brought into play together. The ruins of old Rome are the objective equivalent of Little Dorrit's former prison-life, moreover the operative words 'ruined', 'broken fragments' and 'lonely' in this last sentence are symbolic as well as literal sense, the discontinuity that Little Dorrit suffers from in her life, since it became prosperous, being reflected in her apprehension of the discontinuity of the concrete city's existence that surrounds her and brings home to her her plight. The idea, in short, has been used persuasively and with some delicacy, though it remains mainly a good idea with the rhetoric between us and the girl whom we are being told about and who remains the occasion for the rhetoric rather than, as it should be, acting it for us.

George Eliot, we know on much internal evidence, had read and used – that is, was unconsciously influenced by – Dickens. In reading *Little Dorrit* it is pretty clear that this striking passage impressed her by its vivid and condensed symbolism and gave her the idea of using the ruins of Rome as not merely the background, nor merely the symbolism, but the precipitating emotional experience for her heroine. Like Little Dorrit a young girl whose life has lost continuity, Dorothea realizes on her honeymoon in Rome as she enters into the full consciousness of her surroundings that marriage with Mr Casaubon has wrecked her own 'historical' life – brought disorder into the ideas of life that had guided her hitherto, shattered her hopes and made chaos of her emotional make-up. As 'Rome' is brought to her consciousness as a thing of many different and incompatible cultures, all at odds spiritually with each other and all alien, unacceptable and frightening to herself with her narrow Swiss-Protestant education and her provincial young-ladyhood, so she senses without clearly formulating for herself the fact that life now she is Mrs Casaubon is something which she cannot assimilate or understand or bring into any relation with her ideals. This is not at all simple like Little Dorrit's situation and bears about the same relation to the Dickens original as higher mathematics does to simple arithmetic. The most obvious difference is that this is not rhetoric, the author is not pointing to a girl and telling about her, we are sharing Dorothea's experience of disorder in the depths of her being. Impossible to paraphrase the passage without changing and diminishing its meanings, for it is a complex kind of poetry, working on several different planes at once. Here is *the* example I should choose to illustrate what we mean by declaring that in the nineteenth century the novel took over the function of poetic drama. It is impossible to do the passage justice out of its context, for much of the earlier part of the novel has been preparing us for it and its roots are in Dorothea's past. We are to recollect, for instance, the earlier chapter where Dorothea is introduced to her future home and 'found the house and grounds all that she could wish', the dismal and old-fashioned manor house (symbolic of its master, Mr Casaubon) 'had no oppression for her, and seemed more cheerful than the casts and pictures at the Grange, which her uncle had long ago brought home from his travels... To poor Dorothea these severe classical nudities and smirking Renaissance-Correggiosities were painfully inexplicable, staring into the midst of her Puritanic conceptions: she had never been taught how she could bring them into any sort of relevance with her life.'

The general gist of this highly complex passage seems then to be a sounding of Dorothea's disturbed condition which was both precipitated by and dramatically enacted by the concept 'Rome'. The 'sordid present' of the Papacy with its Catholic culture had profoundly shocked her Puritanic character; while the conflicting pasts – classical, represented by the statues whose 'marble eyes seemed to hold the monotonous light of an alien world', typifying Mr Casaubon, and the Renaissance, in 'the eager Titanic life gazing and struggling on walls and ceilings', standing for her own struggles for a fuller life – seem to embody the painful state of the 'girl who had lately become a wife' and who has to combine preconcieved ideas of submissive 'duty' with unimagined reactions to her situation ('tumultuous pre-occupation with her personal lot'). Clearly it is to this that the 'Forms both pale and glowing' refer, which 'took possession of her young sense, and fixed themselves in her memory even when she was not thinking of them, preparing strange associations which remained through after-years', as also the 'vast wreck of ambitious ideals, sensuous and spiritual, mixed confusedly with the signs of breathing forgetfulness and degradation'.

If the passage is found to be obscure and incoherent, that is because those are qualities of Dorothea's feverish condition which is being recreated for us by the methods of poetry; actually the passage yields its meaning unambiguously to the reader who is prepared to take the trouble and does not demand the logical sequence of descriptive prose, such as we get in the Dickens passage. What we get here is the simultaneous presence of all the different layers of perception and emotion

that make up Dorothea's unresolved crisis. The fact that she
has no control of her experience but is at its mercy is given
in the psychologically apt description 'images which succeed
each other like the magic-lantern pictures of a doze', and
thereafter the sentence moves frankly into the recreation in
poetry of the fantastic fever of her state, 'a sordid present'
where all the sense-images and their emotional correlations are
fused, with the final triumphant 'red drapery' of St Peter's
'spreading itself everywhere like a disease of the retina'.

If (2) is an example of how a great writer constructively uses,
by extending and deepening, an invention of a less profound
artist (1), then (3) is, in its relation to both the others, an
example, however engaging and accomplished, of the parasitic.
It would never have been composed, that is clear, if the Dickens
and the George Eliot passages had not been there to provide
the inspiration and the execution; we could see that even if we
did not know in other ways that Henry James had read, been
impressed and obviously influenced by, both these novelists.
(3) does not, like (2) in relation to (1), carry the stamp of the
integrity of the truly creative; it is the use of a great piece of
literary creation by a writer who has read it with admiration
and envy and consciously or unconsciously made it his own by
imitation. This is the commonest of events in the production of
poetry, novels, literary criticism and music. The signs are always
dilution, sentimentalization or vulgarization of the original,
lack of unity and drive so that the force of the original is wasted
and dispersed, and – because the unique original occasion for
the creation of the admired piece of work is absent – an obvious
lack of rooting. (3) has become picturesque instead of poetic.
The integration of Dorothea's experience of Rome's complex
culture with her experience of being a bride and a disillusioned
wife – the one shock reinforcing because recreating unmistakably
the other – is replaced in Henry James's version by an external
picture full of sentimental touches and 'charm' – e.g. 'taken old
Rome into her confidence' – and where the general replaces the
particular, the abstract the concrete – e.g. 'a spiritual visitation',
'the suggestiveness of such objects', 'she felt the touch of a
vanished world'. Instead of clinching like Dickens and George
Eliot he ends by wandering off altogether from his theme into
an Impressionist painting, any effect he has achieved (vague,
general and inchoate as it was) being thus completely dispersed.

In fact his eye and attention are directed throughout to making an appealing picture in which Isabel really counts for nothing. There is, significantly, a Paterian quality, in his use of cadence and phrase and the merely aesthetic intention, about the final sentence. Isabel's disenchanted situation after marriage, imitated from Dorothea's, is merely staged against a sympathetic backdrop of Roman ruins and Romantic Catholicism; the passage as a whole is insignificant and disappointing, betraying its derivativeness everywhere but showing no justification for imitating one of George Eliot's most striking creative achievements, which is in her a key-passage and a crisis in a profound work of art. Nor has it even the virtues of the admirable Dickens passage, which James also had clearly possessed himself of and unconsciously drawn upon in (3). So unrealized is Isabel's postulated suffering state that no suffering, no feeling at all, is conveyed to us, we are only presented with a composition of vaguely melancholy charm, lacking the firm handling of an original conception shown by both (1) and (2) and which stamp them as first-hand. Having started with this passage from *The Portrait of a Lady* I went on without any effort to make a list, covering several sheets, of passages and effects in it directly parasitic upon passages in *Middlemarch* and Daniel Deronda.

The whole question of indebtedness in literature (as distinct from 'influence') is not only interesting but important and seems to have received little attention. As my analysis of these three passages has shown, I hope, there are two distinct kinds of indebtedness, that exhibited by George Eliot and that betrayed by Henry James. I might make the point briefly by putting it like this: as (2) is to (1) so is *Wuthering Heights* to *Lear* and *Macbeth*, or *Pierre* to *Hamlet*, or *Washington Square* to *Eugénie Grandet*, or *Pride and Prejudice* to *Cecilia*, or *Belchamber* to *Vanity Fair*; while as (3) is to (2) so is *Quality Street* to *Cranford*, or *The Cenci* to Shakespeare, or *Childe Harold's Pilgrimage* to various poems of Wordsworth's, or Mr E. M. Forster's story *Other Kingdom* to Meredith's *The Egoist*.

The fox is the novelist's idea: Henry James and the house beautiful

'The production of a novel finds perhaps its nearest analogy in the ride across country; the competent novelist presses his subject, in spite of hedges and ditches. The fox is the novelist's idea.' So Henry James wrote in those early sketches, *English Hours*, perhaps to our surprise if we have ever taken seriously Mr Eliot's dictum that 'James had a mind so fine that no idea could violate it.' Though not an idea-hunter like Aldous Huxley or Meredith, for instance (novelists whom we associate with the abuse of 'ideas'), yet James throughout his *Notebooks* is always to be found stressing 'the idea' as the essence of the story, for him, and until we have grasped that idea we cannot understand the intention of the story. But he had also some overall ideas which his works as a whole embody (though no one would think so to read Leon Edel's biography), and some of his ideas in this sense have never received the attention they deserve and indeed require. As he wrote in his *Notebooks* in 1885: 'One does nothing of value in art or literature unless one has some general ideas, constituting a motive and a support.' The idea I should like to discuss I will call for convenience by his own term, The House Beautiful, which was the original title of his short novel *The Spoils of Poynton*; it is an Idea which he started early and chased throughout his literary life; it provides an opportunity to examine his treatment of a key theme which reveals and perhaps explains his development or changes of attitude up to the end almost of his career. The International Theme was an important one to him and has had as much critical attention as it needs, but The House Beautiful is at least equally interesting and quite as central to James's deepest concerns. To trace its development and implications

is to understand what an idea can mean to a major novelist
and how it can inspire some of his most profound and vital
work. It also helps us, I think, to decide what some of his more
ambiguous later works, such as *The Golden Bowl* and *The Spoils
of Poynton*, are really concerned with.

I'll start at the beginning of his life as novelist. *Roderick Hudson*
takes as subject the development of an American artist in the
mid-nineteenth century, and the relevant problems of artistic
creation. The young American sculptor is taken by his patron
to Rome, where the action mainly takes place, because a
sculptor could not come to maturity in New England. Why in
Rome? Because 'only there [Roderick] really found what he
had been looking for from the first', the sufficient negation of
his native scene for Rome is 'the natural home of those spirits
with a deep relish for the element of accumulation and the
infinite superpositions of history'. And in relation to Rome we
have some analysis of the practice of art – there is not only the
case of Roderick but also that of other Americans – the
industrious water-colourist who succeeds in cultivating his
genuine little talent; the New England amateur, Roderick's
abomination, the young lady who paints flowers moralistically;
and the Franco-American sculptor Gloriani who 'represented
art with a mixed motive, the mere base maximum of cleverness'.
But it soon struck James that it was England and not Rome
which was that 'natural home' for his purposes. His *Notebooks*
record in 1881 how when he had made a tour in Somerset:

It was the old houses that fetched me...These delicious old houses
on the soil over which so much has passed and out of which so much
has come, rose before me like a series of visions. I thought of a
thousand things; what becomes of the things one thinks of at these
times? They are not lost, we must hope; they drop back into the
mind again, and they enrich and embellish it. I thought of stories, of
dramas, of all the life of the past – of things one can hardly speak of;
speak of, I mean, at the time. It is art that speaks of those things; and
the idea makes me adore her more and more. Such a house as
Montacute, so perfect, with its grey personality, its old-world gardens,
its accumulations of expression, of tone – such a house is really, *au fond*,
an ineffaceable image; it can be trusted to rise before the eyes in the
future.

Only two years later, in *The Siege of London*, we find the
International Theme treated in connection with the ineffaceable

image, which is now a symbol of what the English governing-
class has to offer in exchange for the good looks, smart clothes
and liveliness of the American woman. James has already noted
here what was to be for him an essential fact, the disparity
between the House and its present owners. The Demesne estate
as well as the mansion with its library of precious books that
no one opens is presented only as symbolic of its owners and
their class. This illustrates the spirit of *The Portrait of a Lady*
two years earlier, which, like the early story *An International
Episode*, writes down the value of an English peer with a park
nine miles round and a moated castle. The peer is unworthy
of this inheritance, that is the point in all these fictions. In *The
Portrait of a Lady* the future of the House is seen to have passed
into the possession of worthier, American, owners – Gardencourt, the symbolic early Tudor house, is described as having 'a
name and a history', the history then given being simply an epit-
ome of English history, concluding 'how, finally, after having
been remodelled and disfigured in the eighteenth century, it
had passed into the careful keeping of a shrewd American
banker, who had bought it originally because it was offered at a
great bargain: bought it with much grumbling at its ugliness,
its antiquity, its incommodity, and who now, at the end of
twenty years, had become conscious of a real aesthetic passion
for it'. So early had James cherished the obsession of the
American acquiring the English heritage without forfeiting his
Americanness (later the dream was to include buying up
Europe too to enrich America – Verver's 'American City').

The country-house as history-and culture-emblem in *The
Portrait of a Lady* is supplemented there by the false House
Beautiful assembled (again the centre of action is Rome) by
the bad American type Osmond, the 'sterile dilettante'.
Osmond is the 'irritable man of taste' (he owes something to
Gowan who blights his wife's life and has the same poisoned
tongue and to Gardencourt also). He, like the companion
figure of the ineffective young Rosier, represents the mere
collector who later on in James's scheme is more explicitly
defined as the opposite of the *artist*. The earliest example of
the collector is Robert Acton in *The Europeans*; his New
England mansion is filled with Chinese works of art collected
during his business life in the East, which indicate the extent
of the alleged cosmopolitanism of their owner who in fact

remains the tame Bostonian he always was, just as in *The Tragic Muse* collecting beautiful pieces as his life's work left the inferior George Dallow quite unmodified. In contrast Rowland Mallett, in James's first novel, gives up collecting European works of art of the past in order to sponsor in the person of the young sculptor Roderick Hudson the living art of his own time and nation, finding himself involved thereby in the most agonizing personal problems and faced with fundamental moral questions. The functionless collector stands aside from life and like Osmond prides himself on his 'taste', but Rosier, who has become less effete since his desire to marry Osmond's daughter has brought him to the point of sacrificing his collection, has an instinct for authenticity, *but also* a sense of uncatalogued values, which his devotion to brittle wares had still not disqualified him to recognize and he is struck by the fact that while Osmond 'had a good deal of taste', some of it was very bad (as exemplified by his yellow Empire *salon*). The way in which 'taste' and 'values' are used here, ostensibly in a technical sense but with an overtone that sounds in another world, that of the spirit, indicates the kind of parable James is working towards and which achieves more interesting, pregnant and integrated forms in the period 1888–90 with the stories *A London Life* and *Mrs Temperley* and the novel *The Tragic Muse*, the period of some of his best and most profitable work.

In *A London Life* the House (Mellows) is not merely the House of History like Gardencourt, it is the English country-house that, while representing a dignified, rich cultural heritage from the past, is positively defiled by its present (it is now in the possession of the Edwardian 'Prince of Wales set'). The point lies again in the contrast between the house and the owner, ultimately between the English Past and the Social Present. In fact Laura, the serious American girl whose fast sister has married the owner of Mellows, makes precisely these reflections as the story opens: 'there were strange voices that frightened her – they threw out ugly intimations'. They made her look with critical eyes at the charming school-room in the noble old house, a house

which betrayed the full perception of a comfortable, liberal, deeply domestic effect, addressed to eternities of possession...she had noted the incongruity that appeared to-day between Lionel Berrington at thirty-five and the elements that had surrounded his younger years

...she marvelled at the waste involved in some human institutions (the English country gentry, for instance) when she perceived that it had taken so much to produce so little. The sweet old wainscoted parlour, the view of the garden that reminded her of scenes in Shakespeare's comedies, all that was exquisite in the home of his forefathers – what visible reference was there to these fine things in poor Lionel's stable-stamped composition? When she came in this evening and saw his small sons making competitive noises in their mugs...she asked herself what *they* would have to show twenty years later for the frame that made them just then a picture. Would they be wonderfully ripe and noble, the perfection of human culture? The contrast was before her again, the sense of the same curious duplicity (in the literal meaning of the word) that she had felt at Plash....She had often been struck with it before – with that perfection of machinery which can still at certain times make English life go on of itself with a stately rhythm long after there is corruption within it.

This basic disaster, the disparity between what the House implies and what the people in possession now are, provides James with one of his 'general ideas'. *A London Life* has its logical sequel in *The Spoils of Poynton*, where he investigates the owner and his situation in all its cultural implications, as I shall presently show.

Meanwhile, the year after *A London Life*, *Mrs Temperley* takes up another aspect, as regards America, of the theme of the false House Beautiful where it had been left in *The Portrait of a Lady* and is important both in reference to the first novel *Roderick Hudson* and the last one, *The Golden Bowl*. The story had been originally called *Cousin Maria* which conveys the same intimation to the reader as Hawthorne's title *My Kinsman Major Molineux*. Maria Temperley the Californian matriarch, representative of the American new rich, is the fore-runner of Adam Verver in buying up Europe – in buying up not only its artifacts but also princely foreigners to marry their daughters. Like Osmond she is, and in the same way, a sinister figure, refusing her daughter the husband of her choice, but she carries the idea of the mere *collector* a stage further: she is shown also as specifically the *anti-artist*. In his very first novel James had voiced unambiguously his concern, as one devoted to the career of artist, for the conditions that make art possible; Roderick Hudson the promising American sculptor is financed and in more important ways assisted to fulfil his promise by the rich American

Rowland Mallett. Mallett had started as a collector but is no longer satisfied merely to acquire paintings and statues, even with the object of presenting them to his nation. He has come to realize that Art must be kept alive as a going concern. Mrs Temperley is the opposite kind of art-patron: she settles in Paris in a splendid *salon* which she has filled with treasures, some of them even contemporary work for she employs the most eminent painters and sculptors to take the family likenesses. But her object is not to serve art, only that art should advance her ambitions by making the right social setting for the family's apotheosis. For this only the work of the recognized, successful artist will do. Her cousin is a struggling young American painter, loving and loved by her eldest daughter Dora, but it is a match she won't consider, he is not good enough socially, not likely to become a famous painter and even if he were would not suit her purpose. She won't even hear of his painting Dora; she has turned her back (we are to understand) on American Art and has no intention of fostering the unknown artist, that is, the possible art of the future. It is Dora – who is 'full of perception and taste in regard to the things *he* cared about. She knew nothing of conventional signs or estimates, but understood everything that might be said to her from an artistic point of view' – who keeps him, isolated in America, in touch by writing to him from Paris of the latest concerts, 'the new pictures and the manner of the different artists'. So that in blandly condemning Dora to old-maidhood Mrs Temperley is felt to be not merely cruel to her daughter like Osmond to his: she is dealing death to art – that is, American painting in particular, Art in general and Literature perhaps most of all, for the tale forces itself on one as a parable and James commonly employs the context of Art to convey his concern for the creative writer, to portray his own situation. And the young painter formulates very severe judgments on his Cousin Maria, who is repeatedly said to incarnate the then typical American woman's ambitions and outlook – she is in fact the trans-Atlantic equivalent of that other symbolic Edwardian figure Aunt Maud in *The Wings of the Dove*, that bland incarnation of 'Britannia of the Market-Place'. Cousin Maria represents a society where the wealthy set a value on those works of art whose possession confers status, while despising the contemporary practitioner, a fatal situation for the arts.

And a year later, in *The Tragic Muse*, in what is it seems to me the climax of James's work, we get the fullest, most unambiguous and most pregnant statement of his position. This is a novel written in the lucid, witty style of his earlier work and which conducts its argument, a highly complex and subtle one, without either the obscurity or the windiness of his last phase. Also, more than any other of his novels, it renders the contemporary situation, that essential structure of a wealthy and stable English society, nominally educated, but hopelessly deficient for the artist, leading James to define the conditions that make the practice of the arts possible and even to show why the arts are essential to the life of the nation if it is not to sicken and decay. Here again is the House Beautiful – Julia Dallow's Palladian mansion (significantly now named not Mellows or Gardencourt but *Harsh Place*), whose treasures were collected by her late husband – he had cared for nothing else and was a rather unpleasantly inferior person (the mere collector). Moreover, as all the art treasures of the Place are antiques of one period, apparently eighteenth-century French, the effect is oppressively artificial and museum-like – the present contributes nothing and they are not even English art, much less an inherited aggregation with family associations. And worse still Julia, the society beauty and political hostess, values them only as possessions – as she says, she 'hates art', she resented as degrading her husband's preoccupation with it even as a collector. Like Mrs Temperley she is the anti-artist. The artist is her cousin Nick Dormer in whom Julia recognizes a future statesman only and therefore a desirable husband for an ambitious rich woman to invest in. At the opening of the book we see Nick getting 'refreshment' from an exhibition of modern sculpture in Paris, frowned on by his mother, who is an aristocrat and the relict of a Liberal Cabinet minister, Nick's mother represents another aspect of contemporary English Philistinism, she deplores Modern Art in general on moral grounds, like the well-born wife of the Author of 'Beltraffio'. Nick's mother urges him to marry Julia and thus acquire with Harsh Place wealth, power and status, calling it 'the first house in England'. Tempted, Nick reflects: '"The first house in England", she had called it; but it might be the first house in Europe, the first house in the world, by the fine air and high humanities that should fill it. Everthing that was beautiful in the place where he stood took on a more delicate charm; the house rose over his head like a museum of exquisite rewards.' But Nick's difficulty is that he 'was conscious of a double nature; there were in him, quite separate' two men. If one of them is a rising young politician desired therefore as a husband by his ambitious cousin and susceptible to the material charms of her splendid Place, the other is the incipient artist whose conception of truly serving the State is to use his talent to paint portraits in the modern style – that is, to restore the art of portrait-painting from the Academy art level to which it had sunk and to maintain a great humane tradition. This other Nick knows where his deepest satisfaction lies: 'This was, after all, in his bare studio, the most collective dim presence, the one that was most sociable to him as he sat there and that made it the right place however wrong it was – the sense that it was to the thing itself he was attached.' So when his mother, pressing him to propose, looks round Julia's drawing-room and says: 'If you're so fond of art, what art is equal to all this? The joy of living in the midst of it – of seeing the finest works every day? You'll have everything the world can give.' What he means is revealed when Julia, on accepting his proposal, endows him with 'poor George's treasures', and he says at once, expressing *his* valuation of them: '"Give them to the nation"' (to her chagrin), and irritates her by commenting on her idea that the possession of George's treasure will help him to paint (as an amateur): '"But how little you know about it – about the honourable practice of any art."' His world is solidly against him except for his Oxford friend Gabriel Nash who adds *the aesthete* to the combination that figures round the House Beautiful. Gabriel at first provides Nick with the moral support to make his decision to renounce politics for portrait-painting but not, it turns out, from a genuine concern for painting: the aesthete is never seriously devoted to art, he is serious only about living effectively or rather showily, a passion for 'Art' is merely one of his attitudes. Charles Dickens's Hugh Skimpole plus Oscar Wilde is probably James's source for Gabriel Nash. We see as the novel develops that the aesthete is as distinct from the artist as is the collector. Gabriel Nash eggs Nick on from a cheap desire for the scandal of an M.P. resigning his seat in order to paint; thereafter (except for a Mephisto-like effort to involve Nick in an affair with the actress) he loses interest and appropriately fades out of the book as Nick's devotion to his *métier* hardens. Long before the conclusion of *The Tragic Muse* the Aesthete has been finally placed (we remember Henry James's reaction to Wilde whom Nash resembles): 'A fatuous cad'. And let me here reject forever Mr Quentin Anderson's identification of Nash with Henry James Senior. For though Nash is, to begin with, used, in wonderfully comic scenes, to expose the Philistinism of the English governing class there is never any doubt of the shallowness of what he represents and he is soon placed in situations where he is felt to be obtuse, slightly vulgar and an embarrassment to Nick and his cause.

Nick's comments on the museum collected by George Dallow reveal the contrast between a mere collection of dead, alien objects, however beautiful in themselves and however intelligently selected and arranged, and something coherent and *belonging* that is the equivalent of a Literature, such as is represented by the English portraits in the National Gallery to which Nick goes for support and refreshment – we are told that in his isolation and despair 'he plucked right and left perfect nosegays of reassurance' there. This is the kind of Art he believes in; and 'bent as he was in working in the modern, which spoke to him with a thousand voices' means that he wishes to extend and maintain the tradition by keeping it alive in practice. There is a parallel activity in this novel to portrait-painting; it is the Theatre, in discussing which James is able to go more thoroughly into the question of what constitutes a Tradition. A tradition in an art, James argues, can exist only in the memory and devotion of its practitioners who represent the continuity necessary (he actually uses the phrase 'a continuity of tradition' to describe the Theatre); he specifies the *Comédie Française* and, for lack of such a tradition in England, what is represented by the fitting performance of Shakespeare (an ideal rather than an actuality, James suggests, deploring what the English stage did with its talented performers). And Miriam Rooth, the spirited intelligent creature who schools herself to become a great actress, contrasts with her rival Julia Dallow, who runs a political *salon* because without having the least understanding of politics she sees in the political field the road to social dominance (she is determined to have a Prime Minister for her second husband) – Julia 'loathes Art', as she says, because she lives in a society which has no use or respect for the arts: '...the arts. Did you never hear of them?' Nick is driven to say to her early on in the book.

Julia's brother Peter is the diplomat who completes a quartet with Nick the artist, Miriam the actress and Julia the Society hostess. The diplomat thinks himself devoted to the Theatre in the same sense that Nick is to painting, a devotion symbolized in fact by his passion for Miriam which after all turns out to be not much of a passion since he cannot bring himself to make any sacrifice for it. The diplomatic mind – the governing-class mentality and culture, that is – can do no more than patronize art as an aesthetic entertainment. Peter will give money but not himself, and like the *poseur* and aesthete Gabriel Nash he is eventually revealed to be a hollow man. 'The diplomatic mind' is finally placed by Nick thus: 'Dry, narrow, barren, poor, he pronounced it in familiar conversation with the clever secretary; wanting in imagination, in generosity, in the finest perceptions and the highest courage.' And the political world represented by the careerist Mr Macgeorge, by the disinterested mummy Mr Carteret, by Julia's *salon*, is painfully sterile. The period temple-ruin with its elegant eighteenth-century interior, seems to me an infinitely more satisfactory image than the alleged triumphs of his later phase – the Ivory Tower, or the pagoda that opens the second volume of *The Golden Bowl* or the Palladian church that is supposed to represent Prince Amerigo. Unlike these it is not dragged in but seems a necessary adjunct of the mansion and it does not need elucidation. In this Waste Land of Society, politics and diplomacy, which is the English governing-class world as James saw it, the Studio stands out as the place where creative work is done, where the real drama of life is enacted and where Art and Life are fed. It is in Nick's studio that Julia, who in one of James's most memorable and most painful scenes, encounters Miriam who, by refusing to defer to her, drives her out with the realization that Nick is an artist after all, not of her world or kind, and that she must break with him. In this society the stage and painting are shown as the only sources of creative life and freedom as Nick and Miriam are the only effective figures in the book, and of these the one is a renegade from the governing-class and the other is a cosmopolitan Jewess. Thus *The Tragic Muse* is James's most revolutionary statement of his appraisal of England at the end of the nineteenth century and at the same time his most positive contribution to the problem of regenerating such a civilization. And he shows here, too, a far subtler understanding of the nature of art (all arts being one and, as Nick says, 'any ground that's gained by an individual is of use and suggestion to all the others') – he states the problems of a creative artist in a Philistine society. The problems of the arts that relate to the artist, actor and dramatist and their relations with the public, the status and function of the arts in a Philistine governing-class ('"the pencil – the brush? They're not the weapons of a gentleman", said Mr Carteret') are threshed out in both conversation and symbolic action as nowhere else in literature, offering us the highest level of serious discussion of these subjects. Nick's 'double nature' of politician and painter is symbolic of the external conflict, for the politician is shown to be the antithesis of the creative artist and Nick has to fight an internal battle (he is not the Artist as Roderick Hudson was but rather Everyman). This essential opposition is finely brought out in the early dialogue between Nick and Nash in Paris, when Nick still trying to enter Parliament (while Nash is arguing against the Parliamentary sphere of action) remarks that the sight of *Notre Dame* makes him 'want to build a cathedral' to which Nash pointedly retorts: 'You can't build them out of words.'

'What is it the great poets do?' asked Nick. '*Their* words are ideas – their words are images, enchanting collocations and unforgettable signs. But the verbiage of parliamentary speeches!'

In Nick's ashamed confessions of what his political speeches are and how they work on his audiences James is enforcing the point made here, that the use of language by the politician and the journalist is radically different from the creative artist's – the discussion of language – poetry versus journalism – the scope of the argument about Art... (Du Maurier). Soon after *The Tragic Muse* and closely related to it we have in the short story *The Real Thing* (1892), the most unambiguous precipitation of James's feelings about the artist and the country-house world. The story is related by the artist, and the world of good society is seen only from the position of those who minister to the arts, Nick's true world is the centre and there is the real life. Merely by fulfilling their function the artists and their models 'place' the civilization of the English governing-class as it had been more circumspectly judged in the previous novel.

The tale clinches the moral of *The Tragic Muse*, setting the artist firmly in his studio and in a life-and-death struggle with the Edwardian upper-class world, presenting the people of that world as mere imitations of life, like wax-works but unlike them endowed with a blighting power – what James's friend Edith Wharton meant when she ascribed to 'the quality of making other standards non-existent by ignoring them'. We see in *The Real Thing* that it is only the morale and the criticism provided by fellow-artists and critics that makes the artist's work possible. To this development of the theme belong the stories about the novelist's life – *The Death of the Lion* where the upper-class world at the country-house called *Prestidge* kills the writer and makes away with his great unpublished novel; stories like *The Next Time* and *The Middle Years* showing the hopelessness of the writer without an understanding public; and many others. The problem, how to keep the arts alive, how to maintain an intelligent public, was bound to be a vital concern to James as a novelist and we can see from his letters as well as his books how much thought he gave to it and how bitterly he felt his own plight.

We must bear this in mind, what has been the subject and intention of the main body of his work, when we consider the rather puzzling and obscure work he began in 1893 with an entry in his *Notebook* giving the 'germ' as he liked to call it of the real-life story on which *The Spoils of Poynton* is based. When he began work on the book he called it *The House Beautiful*, a useful indication of his theme, and when he ran the story as a serial in *The Atlantic Magazine* in 1895-6 he gave it the title 'The Old Things', another useful clue and which, like Dickens's title *Hard Times*, has a double meaning. It is a pity that he should have finally substituted the misleading and affected title *The Spoils of Poynton*. As the original title shows, no less than *Cousin Maria* it is offered as a moral fable. Poynton is more than Harsh Place or Gardencourt inasmuch as it contains incomparable treasures for which all Europe has been ransacked, with which Mrs Gereth, like George Dallow, has made exquisite interiors; 'in selection and comparison', we are told, 'refined to that point, there was an element of creation'. She is not the mere collector, but embodies a more interesting situation: she not only loves her treasures but has devoted her life to acquiring and maintaining them. She has also sacrificed Life to them, for she is contemptuous of people who do not 'know the marks', and indifferent to their feelings; worse she has failed with her son the lawful owner of the treasures. Poynton is in danger, for young Gereth, in the manner of his class and time, is a Philistine devoted only to sport and has accordingly chosen a bride out of Waterbath, the home of Brigstocks 'from whose composition the principle of taste had been extravagantly omitted'. 'Taste' as we have seen is a key-word that in James's language has the widest possible extension: he was certainly not a subscriber to the 'the wall-paper will save us' school of thought. The Brigstocks' absence of taste in interior decoration has its more serious implications, it is linked with ugly manners, stupidity and spiritual obtuseness, just as the house of Mr Carteret in *The Tragic Muse*, an earlier Waterbath, with its grained woodwork, oilcloth and Landseers was an 'interior that expressed a whole view of life' and serves to convey the deadening futility of his political activities. The brilliantly witty writing that conveys all this so magnificently reminds us that real wit depends on the possession in the writer of serious standards deeply felt. The aesthetic horrors of Waterbath denote the collapse of that phase of English cultural history: the Waterbath Brigstocks are incapable even of the art of self-expression ('Mona belonged to the type in which speech is an unaided emission of sound') and are instinctively hostile to anyone different from themselves, to anything they cannot comprehend. They feel it a threat to themselves.

The fable is clear enough: Poynton [= Point on] Park is the European heritage, containing the highest achievements of the past in creating beauty, which can be acquired and transmitted only by those who are prepared to make sacrifices for the ideal; but it has now fallen into the hands of the modern Englishman who in late Victorian times James saw as an uncultivated, inarticulate type, 'one who had never taken the least pride or pleasure in his home' and whose room 'was the one monstrosity of Poynton', furnished with 'eighteen rifles and forty whips', and whose bride will ruin Poynton with vulgar additions in the spirit of the age. Mrs Gereth rightly appeals to Fleda, who has studied painting in the Paris studios and who also 'knows the marks', to 'save' her son and Poynton, but Fleda is routed by 'the awful Mona who is *all* will, without the smallest leak of force into taste or tenderness or vision'. From then Poynton is doomed and the fire that guts it is inevitable – even the precious crucifix cannot be salvaged from the disaster, and the burning of the house of treasures with which the tale ends is made to seem as horrible as an auto-da-fé. The House Beautiful has been destroyed in the negligence of its owners – the moral of the fable is plain enough.

There are two interesting elements that the tale adds to James's previous dealings with the Idea. One is that Fleda, who represents, very feebly, the potential modern practitioner of the arts, notes of Poynton, as Nick Dormer had done of Harsh Place, that it is 'an impossible place for *producing*; no art more active than a Buddhistic contemplation could lift its head there' – at Poynton 'neither ink nor water-colour' could be profitably employed. She comes to realize that Ricks, the meagre home made by the poor maiden aunt in the dower-house out of her inherited plenishing, was also an achievement and a truer one than Poynton – that the best kind of taste is to make a success of life by living and not by devoting oneself to beautiful Old Things. This is the weakest part of the book for though we are *told* so we are not shown it and must take the spiritual beauty of the dead spinster and her little house on trust. In contrast how thoroughly the *limitations* of the collector's achievement are conveyed in a phrase: when Fleda in her anguish seeks refuge in the perfect period bedroom Mrs Gerard had arranged for her, we are told that 'the age of Louis Seize suddenly struck her as wanting in taste and point'. The other new element is unsatisfactory for another reason. Fleda has a sister Maggie married to a provincial curate and thus fated to live in 'the mean little house in the stupid little town'; the nature of their home is symbolized by the 'old but rather poor' stopped Dutch clock which she believes was poor Maggie's chief wedding present and 'at the evening meal Fleda's brother-in-law invited her attention to a diagram, drawn with a fork on too soiled a tablecloth, of the scandalous drains of the Convalescent Home'. I suppose this is how the social-reforming aspect of Victorian England impressed Henry James, just as the Established Church of the time suggested to him an inferior antique clock that won't go and that together Owen, Mona, Fleda and the curate represented for him the possibilities of the younger generation of the educated middle class. But he doesn't see that the curate's indignation, his passion for ameliorating, a passion that can ignore so flagrantly the demands of Gracious Living, is the one bright spot in this depressing history, that *he* alone points to a possible live future as neither Mrs Gereth the collector nor the Philistine Owen nor the ineffectual Fleda, standing on a point of punctilio, nor the ghost of the maiden aunt, ever could. And if we compare *The Spoils* with *A London Life* from which it is a development we can see that there has been a recent impoverishment in James's art in every way, typical of what happened to it in his late phase. Compared with the highly individual Laura Wing, Fleda is only a misty spot in the middle of a diagram; compared with Lionel Berrington, Owen Gereth lacks character and outline, while Mrs Gereth in comparison with old Lady Davenant is, one can see, only an idea suitably clothed. It is the Regency relic Lady Davenant who gives the earlier story its moral poise, incarnating both the wisdom of age and the outlook of a once intelligent aristocratic society (the 'sort of indifference that is philosophical and noble', Laura feels) – but then James had observed Lady Davenant in his early days in England, felt the impact and drawn the inferences. Except for Watersouth (based on a visit to Fox Warren whose horrors he had recently experienced) there is nothing like the concrete detail of the earlier fiction about Poynton, nothing like the temple on the lake and the studio in *The Tragic Muse*, a novel which is both better art and better argument than *The Spoils*.

To Mrs Gereth and her husband the question, hitherto paramount for James, of keeping the arts honoured and alive in the present, in the person of the artist, did not occur. Nor does it to the Ververs in *The Golden Bowl*. Mr Verver's object in life, his plan for American City, is a gigantic preposterous version of George Dallow's and Mrs Gereth's enterprises – it is simply to buy up *all* the works of art of the old world and develop them in a museum in his native place, thus apparently doing a supreme service. In the light of what James had been saying all his life about the museum and the collector we surely cannot take this account of Mr Verver's ambition as anything but ironic: 'It hadn't merely, his plan, all the sanctions of civilization; it was positively civilization, condensed, concrete, consummate, set down by his hands as a house on a rock...this

museum of museums, a palace of art.' There has never been
any ambiguity hitherto about what James thought of the
Palace of Art – and Henry James must have known Tennyson's
poem on the subject. Mr Verver's project has been condemned
in advance by all James's work. Verver is at the furthest point
from the original enactment of the problem in Rowland Mallett
– that scrupulous New Englander who abandons a less
ambitious version of Mr Verver's scheme in order to keep the
arts going by assisting the young sculptor, assisting him by
everything he has to give, by much more than money, by
sacrificing even his hopes of personal happiness. The Ververs
cart about with them, in their globe-trotting acquisitive minds,
the kind of 'pieces' George Dallow collected for his Museum
at Harsh Place. And the word 'museum' to characterize the
Verver plan is the placing one. It is a dreadful museum of which
poor Charlotte is shown as guide at the end of the novel,
showing, you remember, ugly (albeit unique) vases to bored
visitors while reeling off her dreary patter – and she is
condemned to accompany it to American City as punishment
for her sin, while Maggie and her purchased husband, the
poor Prince with *his* functionless life – a round of clubs and
country-house parties enlivened by adultery – are left behind
in *their* London museum, whose priceless pieces were inspected
and approved by Mr Verver the last thing before he sailed.
To me the effect is of two separate hells, a *Huis Clos* on each
side of the Atlantic, and it seems to me that the intention and
moral of *The Golden Bowl* is unambiguous, whatever James may
have thought he was doing. Is it likely that James, who had
consistently treated this theme in all its aspects all his life, should
suddenly cease to 'press his subject' and abandon his fox-hunt
for a Grail Quest? Is it likely that the author of *The Tragic
Muse* and *Poynton* meant to convey, as has been alleged so often,
that there is a spiritual value in Adam Verver's activities; and
that 'museum' and 'palace of Art' should suddenly become
innocuous terms from James's pen, from him who was, as we
know, so intelligently interested in contemporary French
painting? The Ververs are made to seem like patrons of
Duveen, infinitely less progressive even than Mrs Temperley.
They never commission or entertain live artists, as Cousin
Maria did on principle, although her principles were wrong
ones.

There is in fact no reason to suppose that James's outlook had

changed in his last phase. Later than either *The Tragic Muse*
or *The Spoils of Poynton*, only six years before *The Golden Bowl*
itself, we have one of his last novels *The Awkward Age* where
part of the theme of *Poynton*, though marginally only, is taken
up still more convincingly. That is, what is the condition of
that culture that shall be the House Beautiful, that culture that
lives and grows with the life of the time and is the opposite
of the Academy and the artificial museum? In *The Awkward Age*
Mitchy, an English Adam Verver as regards great wealth,
simple goodness, and lack of ancestors, is staying in the
inherited Suffolk home of the unpretentious old friend Mr
Longdon. A country-house of great charm but which has
merely grown an accretion of family possessions, in the hands
of honourable gentlemen who cultivated their neighbours and
lived finely but usefully, it is presented as the true House
Beautiful, something that Mitchy recognizes he can never, with
all his wealth and 'taste', acquire. In the drawing-room:

He was at first too pleased even to sit down; he measured the great
space from end to end, admiring again everything he had admired
before and protesting afresh that no modern ingenuity – not even his
own, to which he did justice – could create effects of such purity.
The final touch in all the picture before them was just the painter's
ignorance. Mr Longdon had not made his house, he had simply lived
it, and the 'taste' of the place – Mitchy in certain connections
abominated the word – was nothing more than the beauty of his life.
Everything, on every side, had dropped straight from heaven, with
nowhere a bargaining thumb-mark, a single sign of the shop...
'Therefore', Mitchy went on, pausing once more, as he walked,
before a picture, 'I won't pull the whole thing down by the vulgarity
of wishing that I too had a first-rate Cotman.'

The enviable Cotman had obviously not come out of 'the
shop'; Mr Longdon's Suffolk forbears would have patronized
their East Anglian artist as a matter of course in his life-time,
before his pictures became museum-pieces acquired with the
sale-room – at least I take this to be James's point, though of
course we know that Cotman actually died in poverty for lack
of patrons. There is then, I'd say, in spite of the sophistical
interpretations that have been put upon *The Golden Bowl*, an
absolutely unbroken consistency of treatment of James's Idea.
His analysis of the problem of producing and maintaining a
Literature (which he often found it convenient to discuss as

the generalised form 'Art') in the modern, Anglo-American society, was consistently serious, profound, acute and impassioned. His first novel, *Roderick Hudson*, concentrated, we saw, on the problem of *becoming* an artist, in particular of becoming one if the artist had been born into a nation without a tradition of art. It was James's own youthful problem, of course, and it ceased to be of interest to him once he had solved it for himself, as he so soon did. But the problem which centres round Rowland Mallett and all that it implies, *that* is what he then saw to be the real issue and which was to preoccupy him all his life. The theatre interested him, for a time to the exclusion of every other form of literature, because he saw in it the one place where the creative writer and the general public could still meet – his tales about men of letters show he recognized the hopelessness of a similar condition ever occurring in literature, in his time, even for the short-story writer if he were serious – and not a journalist – his own novels when serialized had been found disastrous by several magazines and his files were not readily marketable. He saw like Gissing, that the time had come when the uncompromising, original writer or artist could hardly any longer even earn a living – he understood the psychology of the bestseller-writer to which he devoted several short stories, and he recognized the strategy of the fashionable artist, as in the case of the clever sculptor in *Roderick Hudson* who is materially successful because he has made his art into something comparable to the *haute couture*; he forecast the incidental results of writing for success in the case of the Master in *The Lesson* who, putting social prestige and financial success foremost to support his lady wife and a family, has sapped his creative power. In *The Tragic Muse*, and elsewhere, James said that to bring about a change in social assumptions and values was the only hope for the survival of the creative practitioner of the arts, and that the survival of the artist was essential if a nation is to have a society in which life shall be at once fine, profound, sensitive and spiritually healthy. As both an American and an Englishman he felt, and shows in his *oeuvre*, a great writer's sense of responsibility for the future of both societies knowing that *his* art, because it works through words, the language of social intercourse, is the one that affects our lives the most. This is the spirit in which he confided to his *Notebooks* in 1889 rather bitterly, his 'desire that the literary heritage, such as it is, poor thing, that I may leave, shall consist of a large number of perfect things illustrative of ever so many things in life – in the life I see and know and feel – and of all the deep and the delicate – and of London, and of art, and of everything; and that they shall be fine, rare, strong, wise – eventually perhaps even recognized'. When we examine his discussion of these problems, his understanding of their complexity and importance and his attitude to them, I think we cannot help feeling how immeasurably more intelligent, responsible and imaginative he was in this respect than any other literary artist of his time, English *or* French. He shows the value for a novelist of having 'some general ideas, constituting a motive and a support', and 'the success with which he can press his subject'. In his *Notebooks* he exhorted himself: 'Be an artist, be distinguished, to the last.' And I must say, I think it evident that he was.

Henry James: the stories

Henry James's short stories and *nouvelles* are out of print, so any publisher willing to devote some of his meagre allotment of paper to giving us any of that unique body of literary treasures deserves our gratitude at once. But whether Mr David Garnett, who selects the volume just published, is equally praiseworthy, is another matter. We all have our personal favourites among the stories and no anthologist could satisfy everyone, of course, but it seems to me that the questions to raise in respecting such a selection are – Will it help the reader new to this author to enjoy him and so want to explore the *oeuvre* for himself? or the uninitiated who is at sea among the novels – will it help him to find his bearings and get some insight into the nature and aims of this difficult art? I am afraid Mr Garnett's choice, backed by Mr Garnett's Introduction, will be more likely to put the novice off and certainly won't offer any critical hints to those who feel lost in a fog. In fact, you can see this is so from the press it has had, the lip-service paid to the genius of Henry James rarely being backed by first-hand judgment and genuine appreciation, even among our higher reviewers.

Mr Garnett has based his anthology on the appeal of quantity instead of quality, restricting himself to the shortest stories in order to get so many in. This seems to me a mistake: instead of fourteen stories, half of which are not worth owning (some worth reading once, some not) surely eight or nine first-class specimens of greater length would have been preferable. It seems hard on an author to have some of his worst pieces thrust in the public eye simply because they are short. For Henry James undeniably wrote some poor, some silly and some downright bad stories, and Mr Garnett has dug them up (though there are some very good short ones, such as *Greville Fane*, which he has apparently overlooked). Thus of those he reprints, *Paste* is an adaptation of one of Maupassant's slickest stories, and is hardly less shallow than its model; *Sir Edmund Orme* is a feeble, uncharacteristic effort – written for The Yellow Book and not even up to inclusion there; *The Private Life* is an earlier exercise, I should say, for *The Sacred Fount* and is silly in the same way; *The Tree of Knowledge* is a bore; *Maud-Evelyn* seems to me unprofitably unpleasant in the same way as *The Altar of the Dead* and some of the other stories written at that period – morbid is the nearest word to describe them; *The Diary of a Man of Fifty* and *The Marriages* are fair specimens of a class in which his work offers many more interesting examples; *Owen Wingrave* is a respectable piece that fails to rise to its possibilities. *Brooksmith* is a whimsical expression of James's social ideal, and nothing more. *The Pupil* was worth reprinting if only to show that James can offer as lively and amusing a surface as any writer in the language: it is the only specimen in the anthology that introduces the author of *The Portrait of a Lady* and *The Bostonians*, the brilliantly witty novelist whose range and scope is so much wider than the conventional account of him, with its emphasis on *The Sacred Fount, The Ambassadors* and so on, admits. Only *The Real Thing, The Abasement of the Northmores* and *The Jolly Corner* are selections from the best level of his work, and that reach down to its core. And dispersed as they are, what effect can they have on the reader who does not already know how to relate them to the body of James's significant writings?

In the Introduction we can put our finger on the mistaken assumptions that have directed Mr Garnett's choice. What are we to make of this final exhortation to the reader?:

Henry James had no unusual understanding of psychology, no abnormal faculty of analysing the human soul. His characters are just as much alive as the people we meet in hotels or at the houses of our friends, but no more. They are not heroic or larger than life; characters whom to meet once is to know intimately for ever like... James's characters are ordinary people seen as indistinctly as we see people in real life; but the attitudes in which we meet them are revealed in all their complexities, with all the possible implications, so that we can grasp the situation as we seldom can in life.

Is this an attempt to make James acceptable to the great Boots public by assuring them that he 'creates' 'people in real life' just like Trollope and Priestley? Surely Mr Garnett must know it his duty to warn the innocent reader off any attempt to take James as a naturalistic novelist. The briefest account of him should include mention of his descent from Hawthorne, that he is a novelist in the same tradition as Melville; should allude to his deliberate stylization of life; notice the techniques he devised for conveying his special interests, his recurrent symbols, his preoccupation with the ideal of social life and the function of the artist in it. How anyone professing to write about James could pen the first sentence of the paragraph I have quoted is beyond belief. The son and brother of psychologist-philosophers, James was of a highly introspective habit himself – nothing is plainer – and he had the intuitive understanding of psychology that we find in all great literary artists. Such painful triumphs in morbid psychology as the short story *Europe*, the well-known *Turn of the Screw*, and the study of the relation of the heroines of *The Bostonians*, leap to the mind, but the real refutation of Mr Garnett's unpardonable obtuseness is in the very texture of Henry James's best work. And what are the 'ghost' stories but expressions of his psychological bent? the 'ghost' being a convenient symbol for the oppressive atmosphere of moral pressure, such as the family ghost that kills the hero of *Owen Wingrave*, or for the guilty conscience, as in *Sir Eustace Orme* (both reprinted here) or for some morbid state. In Mr Garnett's last choice, *The Jolly Corner*, the 'ghost' symbol is explicitly used to embody 'the other self' of the hero, and so might have served to introduce the reader to one of this novelist's principal artistic devices.

The value of *The Jolly Corner* would have been multiplied if beside it an anthologist had placed, say, *The Lesson of the Master* (a mere twenty-five thousand words for which we would gladly have forgone *Paste* and suchlike). These stories are both attempts by James to justify to himself the line he took. The horror the expatriate sees in his New York mansion is the self that James felt he would have become if, instead of settling to live the life of a writer in Europe, he had taken his place as an American in the contemporary world of business and politics. James had no doubt that *that* would have been disastrous; but there was another alternative. The Master, Henry St George, so like the actual Henry James in name, talents and appearance ('beautifully correct in his tall black hat and his superior frock coat') is unlike him in two ways

– he has made a financial success of novel-writing by deliberately writing below his own best level, and he has lived the normal life. 'I've had everything. In other words, I've missed everything', says the Master to his disciple, who replies:

'You've had the full rich masculine human general life, with all the responsibilities and duties and burdens and sorrows and joys – all the domestic and social initiations and complications. They must be immensely suggestive, immensely amusing', Paul anxiously submitted.
'Amusing?'
'For a strong man – yes.'
'They've given me subjects without number, if that's what you mean; but they've taken away at the same time the power to use them. I've touched a thousand things but which one of them have I turned into gold? The artist has to do only with that – he knows nothing of any baser metal. I've led the life of the world, with my wife and my progeny; the clumsy conventional expensive materialized vulgarized brutalized life of London. We've got everything handsome, even a carriage – we're perfect Philistines and prosperous hospitable eminent people. But, my dear fellow, don't try to stultify yourself and pretend you don't know what we *haven't* got. It's bigger than all the rest. Between artists – come!' the Master wound up. 'You know as well as you sit there that you'd put a pistol-ball into your brain if you had written my books!'

This is the more interesting possibility than that treated in *The Jolly Corner*, and it produced a much finer and more complex story. The counterpoise to the mature and successful Henry St George is the young novelist Paul Overt (the author of *Roderick Hudson*, as it were); at the Master's urging he makes the sacrifice of the human goods. Both the Master and Overt are Henry James potentials, played off against each other. This story is not like *The Jolly Corner*, a simple statement whose artistic effect depends entirely on playing on the reader's nerves; this is a drama, the tension arising from the uncertainty the reader is kept in and finally left in. The series of surprises in the structure are not the surprise of the trick plot of the well-made story of the Maupassant–Kipling–W. W. Jacobs type. The ambivalence, which is personal and inside James himself, conditions the structure: the uncertainty Henry James felt remains to the end and is expressed in the final ambiguity – what indeed was the lesson of the Master? It is one of the most remarkable works of art.

Moreover, it exhibits one of James's favourite techniques, the structure built on alternative selves. It is a device for conducting psychological exploration in dramatic form. Even *The Diary of a Man of Fifty*, Mr Garnett's first choice, which he says has a charming flavour of Turgenev, is stamped as unmistakably James's, slight as it is, in the mathematical elegance with which its case is presented. The elderly soldier who is the diarist and had blighted his life by leaving the Italian Countess, sees acted out by their younger selves, presented in the same relation – in the forms of the dead woman's daughter and a young Englishman – the opposite solution to the diarist's. I dwell on this technical device because it is a key one – it is a different thing from his use of the portrait as the idealized or dead or false self, which occurs in a great many novels and stories, starting with the very early *nouvelle Watch and Ward*. It is not merely a device or literary formula, or, like the portrait, the symbol of an intellectual idea, but a method of artistic procedure. It enables an exploration of certain possibilities of life to be presented dramatically, with the tensions, the contrasts and the psychological surprises that make a work of art instead of a narrative. It is obvious that such a method implies a very considerable degree of stylization of the raw material of life, a very special approach to characterization. Henry James takes the trouble to make this clear in many different ways, most of all in his use of symbolic names (as Overt above; and *The Death of the Lion* takes place in the country-house named Prestidge) – the only one most readers seem to notice is that of the Princess Casamassima – and symbolic figures, such as the Figure in the Carpet, the Beast in the Jungle, the Golden Bowl. How unkind, then, of Mr Garnett to go out of his way to inform his readers that Henry James is not a different kind of novelist from the circulating-library average. Can he have inspired the blurb which describes this selection as 'the best introduction to the work of "the old magician" for those who have not yet fallen victims to the enchantment'? Enchantment is the character of the appeal made by, say, Mr De La Mare's writings, but it seems to me a great injustice to Henry James to suggest that that is the nature of the interest his work has for us. His stature is that of Tolstoy, Conrad, the great international masters of the novel, and it is misleading to imply that he offers us, even in his short stories, anything less serious than a profound apprehension of life.

Of course if you take random dips into the shortest stories, as in this volume, you risk overlooking everything vital. Mr Garnett has put none of the keys into his reader's hands. Who would suppose from *The Abasement of the Northmores* that Henry James had written a whole body of stories about the life of the writer and the novelist – the artist, as he more generally considers him – and that these contain some of his liveliest, wittiest and most deeply felt writing, besides embodying some of his fundamental ideas? *The Author of 'Beltraffio'*, *The Figure in the Carpet*, *The Lesson of the Master*, even *The Coxon Fund*, *John Delavoy*, *The Middle Years*, *The Next Time*, *The Death of the Master*, are all more central than the one of the series reprinted; an introducer should at least have referred his readers to them. *The Real Thing* is fortunately here: it was an anecdote of Du Maurier's that provided James with a congenial theme – he made it a fable expressing his contempt as an artist for the English country-house culture and its social values. Characteristically, it is much deeper than it looks and will bear endless pondering. It links up with the novel *The Tragic Muse*, where he develops his theory of the function of artist and actress and their pre-eminence in a world of politics and society.

The account Mr Garnett gives of James's development is also misleading. 'He began as a painstaking writer for American magazines and most of his early stories are singularly feeble. He did not, at first, know how to write and he contrived stories with little imagination or knowledge of human beings. He developed slowly. He was thirty six-years old before he published the first story included here...' The author of *No Love* and *The Sailor's Return* has, naturally, a high standard. Still, I feel that the greenhorn should be told that before the date of the first story Mr Garnett thinks printable, James had published *Roderick Hudson* (1874), an accomplished and adult novel on a theme full of interest; *The American* (1875), also a novel showing considerable powers; and had got on well with *The Portrait of a Lady*, one of the finest novels in the language; that he had written many short stories of permanent literary value, of the highest interest in themselves and also of great importance to the understanding of his work – such as *Madame de Mauves*, *Daisy Miller*, *An International Episode*; and that, above all, he had written the remarkable *nouvelle The Europeans*, whose perfection, seriousness and originality as a work of art is surpassed by nothing he composed later. Continuing with a sneer at James's debt to Hawthorne Mr Garnett ends 'It was just that sort of nonsense that he escaped the following year when he came to live in Europe. A year in Paris, meeting Flaubert, Turgenev, Maupassant and Zola altered him.' Yet his correspondence shows that he was disappointed with these men of letters and disgusted with their *milieu*, that he thought their novels inferior to George Eliot's and soon decided to abandon France in favour of a permanent home in England. What he learnt from the French seems to have been mostly what to avoid, and what more valuable it was that George Eliot, for instance, could do. He was more in Dickens's debt than Turgenev's or Zola's, still more than anything else he was rooted in his native tradition (his volume on Hawthorne in the English Men of Letters Series shows how seriously he took his forerunner), a tradition which included Bunyan.

No, I can't agree with Mr Garnett that his volume is 'the best introduction to reading James at all'. There was a more modest and much better one, published by Nelson in the fabulous days of the sixpennies and sevenpennies and which, in its indestructible blue binding and excellent print, could until recently still be found on second-hand stalls. It contained *Daisy Miller, An International Episode* and *Four Meetings*, stories stimulating, amusing and exquisite in themselves, which would make sense together, and illustrate in the most apprehensible way James's principal subject, the International Theme. No one who picked up that volume could suppose James a discouraging author or form any false views about the nature of his art. And that reader would be launched painlessly on the right path – qualified to appreciate *The Portrait of a Lady* and to graduate to *The Golden Bowl*, to recognise the interest of such relevant works as *Pandora, Lady Barbarina* and *The Reverberator*. I remember Nelson's cheap reprint with gratitude, for it lay around the house when I was a child and was my own introduction to Henry James.

Finally, I should like to register a protest against a gratuitous and worse than unjustifiable display of animus. Out of a four-page introduction Mr Garnett devotes two paragraphs to insulting American critics of Henry James in general. He says: 'If American critics admire James they do so with a bad grace; they admire in spite of the fact that he learned to write in Europe, that he preferred to live in England, that he was "snobbish" and wrote, sometimes, about our upper classes, that he did not seize every opportunity to criticize the world... The theme of every American critic (even Mr Van Wyck Brooks) is that Henry James abandoned his birthright and never became at home in England' etc. I suppose I have read as much writing on Henry James in books and periodicals as Mr Garnett, since it is a subject I take particular interest in, and I can find no justice in his attack. Surely it was *only* Mr Van Wyck Brooks, among critics of any standing at all, who ever abused James as an expatriate, and the essentially international character of James's genius has long been a commonplace of American literary criticism. As for the other charges, I don't recollect any but extreme Left-wing writers taking that line, and if it comes to that we have equally to blush for Communist 'literary' criticism of the same stamp. No country is responsible for ideologically prompted critics. *Pace* Mr Garnett I should venture that except what has appeared in the pages of *Scrutiny* *all* the intelligent criticism of Henry James and all the hard work on him has been done in the land of his origin. Yvor Winters (in *Maule's Curse*), Edmund Wilson, Quentin Anderson, F. O. Matthiessen, among many others, have left us in no doubt of the high and able evaluation of James's art current in the United States. When *The Hound and Horn*, the former highbrow review of Harvard, produced a number in honour of James, though it is true some of it was not very inspired criticism, yet I distinctly remember that the only really offensive contribution was by our Mr Stephen Spender. And Mr Garnett does not exactly deserve a bouquet from James's admirers for his present effort.

The institution of Henry James

This is a very welcome edition of an American book that appeared a year or two ago, an anthology of critical articles on Henry James collected from periodicals and of chapters culled from books. Perhaps it is not so well done as it might have been – its interest is less intrinsic than historical. We are given as a start an essay of 1879 ('Henry James, Jr.'), a fine specimen of complacent provincialism, and can see the various phases of James's reputation to date and the evolution of a serious critical approach to his art. In 1898, we are told, he was virtually unknown in America. In 1918 Mr Eliot began his memorial notice '...James will probably continue to be regarded as the extraordinarily clever but negligible curiosity'. Whereas in 1943 Mr William Troy ends his essay '...no great wonder that more and more people are turning to Henry James'. Between the nadir of '98 and the zenith of the last decade journalistic criticism exposes itself more shamefully than over any other great writer. In 1912 intellectual brilliance was represented by Sir Max Beerbohm's 'parody',[1] reprinted from *A Christmas Garland* – this is the period when the idiosyncrasies of James's late style stuck in the public throat and any journalist could get a laugh by making gestures of crude intention behind James's back. The viciousness of such a 'parody' lies in its endorsing the vulgar account of James as unreadable, unprofitable and preposterous. Mr Dupee regrets that Wells's attack (in *Boon*, 1915) could not be reprinted too; contemporary with Beerbohm's piece, this illustrates the malice that the successful writers of the Wells–Bennett–Maugham era felt for the novelist who had devoted his life to his art, exercising incredible industry with no material reward (unless we reckon the O.M. bestowed on his deathbed). On top of this he had to face vulgar unprovoked attacks in his old age by journalists like Wells. He minded deeply. No one can read unmoved his letters to Wells about *Boon* [Mr Percy Lubbock comments with desolating fatuity, in his notes to *The Letters of Henry James*, 'H.J. was always inclined to be impatient of the art of parody'.] The letters to Howells in 1888 and '95, to Howard Sturgis in '99, and to Gosse just before his death about the failure of the collected edition of his works, show the impressive courage and dignity that James had developed to sustain him against the kind of treatment noted above.[2]

We see here how very different is the tone of pieces of the same period by Eliot and Conrad (and Pound, whose notices of 1918 were reprinted with later criticism in *Make It New*, and might very profitably have been drawn upon by Mr Dupee). It is encouraging to see that those creative writers who were also literary critics, as distinct from journalists and academics and social men of letters, were all along able to respond to James at his own level of seriousness. Conrad, for instance, in 1905, is here seen to have jumped the whole historical process with his note on James as 'The Historian of Fine Consciences'. Similarly, Pound in *The Little Review*, 1918, could see that 'there was titanic volume, weight, in the masses he set in opposition within his work... His art was great art as opposed to over-elaborate or over-refined art by virtue of the major conflicts which he portrays.' At the same date Mr Eliot was writing 'The real hero, in any of James's stories, is a social entity of which men and women are constituents... He is the most intelligent man of his generation.'

Conversely, the journalists are still where they were – all the phases of criticism of James that you find in this anthology are now simultaneously present in layers. The 1904 essay, 'In Darkest James', is just the kind of bright journalism that you might find in the literary weeklies today; or Mr Van Wyck Brooks, who is shown in 1925 damning James because his characters are not true to (the man-in-the-street's impression of) life and because Brooks cannot comprehend their motives – how often we still meet that. In 1927 Mr Pelham Edgar, in what is unfortunately a standard work but really a monument of misunderstanding, shows that he has missed the whole point of James's studies of the International situation (p.141f.). We can feel that criticism has at any rate progressed if we compare the chapter from *The Method of Henry James* (1918) by Joseph

Warren Beach, the pioneer critic of James's 'art', with the best
work in the same field in recent years. Beach makes painstakingly
one point after another about 'method', without ever seeming
to get anywhere or to make the only kind of criticism that
matters, that which adds to our ability to read the work: he does
not understand the author's intention, he is not an interpreter.
Nowadays, at the top level, critics of James, as Mr Dupee says
in his Introduction, 'discourage any reading that takes a part
of his effect for the whole'.

Everyone will be glad to have Mr Eliot's hitherto inaccessible
pieces on James. Popularly, Mr Eliot's contribution to James
criticism has been limited to the famous sentence, now thirty
years old, 'He had a mind so fine that no idea could violate
it', which has been a battle-ground ever since. Some said it
means nothing, others that it supported their representation of
James as an aesthete, and others that it is demonstrably untrue,
since James's mind was in fact the prey of his father's eccentric
system of ideas, to illustrate which the son composed his novels.
Now we can read the sentence in its context, where it seems
to have been thrown out as an exasperated attempt to
distinguish James from the Merediths and Chestertons who
cluttered the foreground of literature at the time. The essay
dates, and contains many odd judgments e.g., 'Henry was not
a literary critic' – who that has read even James's essay on
Baudelaire in *French Poets and Novelists* would not demur?). It
nevertheless puts its stresses in the right places; one I have
already quoted, the other is contained in his title, 'The
Hawthorne Aspect'.

The essay of 1917 on 'The Aesthetic Idealism of Henry
James' introduces a familiar note: James's art is identified with
Pater's. And wherever aestheticism is still prevalent, poor James
is thus misconceived. The hangover from the nineties represented
by Mr Cyril Connolly is still at the stage of seeing in James's
prose no more than a Paterian surface:

the dialect of Pater, Proust and Henry James, the style that is common
to mandarin academic circles given over to clique life and introspection.
The dead literary English, with its long sentences, elaborate similes
and clever epithets. (Introduction to *The Rock Pool*)

James's late style (for he developed several styles in the course
of his very long career though the journalists seem not to have

observed this elementary fact), ridiculous to a 'Max' and elegantly decadent to a Connolly, is now felt by serious readers to be, like his other idiosyncrasies, a language we have learnt to take for granted – once we are at home in it it presents no difficulty but is felt to be as effective an instrument, and one as informed with life, as the language of Hopkins or Shakespeare. The serious, the vicious aspect of this assimilation of James to Proust and Pater is that James is assumed to have, like them, replaced moral values by aesthetic ones, to be, as one critic in this book accuses him of being, 'ugly with the absence of moral energy and action'. That it refutes this falsification of James's work is the value of the criticism that puts James back into his place in the New England tradition. While there is a good deal collected by Mr Dupee of purely American interest – contributed by those for whom the Question of Henry James was whether his art is American and therefore sound, or un-American and therefore decadent – even that has its point for the rest of us because it shows in sum, very convincingly, that, as the editor says, 'James turns out to be a continuator of the severe ethics of New England.' Unfortunately there is no extract from Mr Yvor Winters' book on the influence of the New England ethos on American literature, *Maule's Curse* (1938), where the chapter devoted to James, called 'The Relation of Morals to Manners', still seems to me the best treatment of the subject. Another way of showing James's American roots is the essay here by Constance Rourke on 'The American', taken from her pioneer work *American Humour* (1931), where she made a study of the American folk-lore that fertilised American literature.

After aestheticism, the hard-boiled twenties, cock-sure and shallow, are seen 'placing' James. Then was produced the formula that explained away his art as a purely mental production of the jig-saw order of achievement. The distinction of *locus classicus* is perhaps to be claimed for Richards's *Principles of Literary Criticism* (1925) – the passage is not reprinted here but echoed in more than one place:

Certainly it is a serious charge against much of Henry James, for example, that when the reader has once successfully read it there is nothing further which he can do. He can only repeat his reading. There is often a point at which the parts of the experience click together, the required attitude is achieved, and no further development is possible.

This was evidently a bright idea being handed round by frequenters of the smart literary circles. Gide must have picked it up there:

nothing really alive nourishes him, and James extracts only from his brain what he knows to be there, and what his intelligence alone has put there... The skillfully made network spun out by his intelligence captivates only the intelligence... James, in himself, is not interesting; he is only intelligent... all his characters are like the figures of a clock, and the story is finished when they have struck the curfew. ('From an unsent letter to Charles Du Bos', American publication, 1930)

There is no sign in his 'letter', reprinted here, that Gide has read anything of James whatever (Connolly has the grace to admit in *The Condemned Playground* that he could never manage to get through James's books). Evidently this kind of judgment was a formula for dismissing a novelist for whom such people could have no use, whom they could not make the effort to comprehend, and to whom they felt impelled to display superiority. Mr Matthiessen's mind seems also to have been informed in the Richardian twenties: 'James's novels', he tells us here, in the essay on *The Ambassadors* from his recent book (reviewed in *Scrutiny*, Spring, 1947), 'are strictly novels of intelligence rather than full consciousness'. But even an academic nowadays breathes a livelier critical air than of old, and another way of proving that criticism achieves something is to compare the results of Matthiessen's industry with those of the Lubbocks and Pelham Edgars of the past.

This brings us to the day before yesterday. Yesterday saw the reversal of Mr Matthiessen's dictum that in James's novels 'there is none of the welling up of the darkly subconscious life that has characterized the novel since Freud'. Mr Edmund Wilson and Mr Stephen Spender find James's works a Freudian field-day. Of course every great writer is reinterpreted in the light of contemporary interests (and fashions), but how sound the more recent presentations of James will look tomorrow is still to be decided. Thus when Mr Spender finds that 'the monologues [of *The Golden Bowl*] dip into an abyss where they become part of the unconscious mind of Europe', and that 'His technical mastery has the perfection of frightful balance and frightful tension: beneath the stretched-out compositions there are abysses of despair and disbelief: *Ulysses*

and *The Waste Land*' (1936) – one may well raise an eyebrow.
Mr Wilson, writing at the same date but keeping closer to the
texts, has a surer poise. One may not agree with his
interpretations, and in point of fact his account of *The Turn of
the Screw* (as an hallucination of the neurotic governess who is
narrator) has, I seem to remember, been shown not to hold
water by several critics. But when he proceeds to build up a
theory of an ambiguity in presentation by James very
generally, he is certainly drawing attention to a feature of
James's work that most people, preferring to simplify, find it
convenient to overlook, and which culminates in his valuable
point that 'the element of irony in Henry James is often
under-estimated by his readers'. Mr Wilson's criticism is tough
as opposed to the 'aesthetic' apprehensions of Mr Matthiessen,
but, being alive and disinterested, he succeeds in infusing a new
sense of reality into James's works whereas the other's kind of
attention seems to empty James's art of significance. Mr Wilson
puts substance behind his final claim that James 'is in no
respect second-rate, and he can be judged only in the company
of the greatest'.

As for the criticism of today, represented here by Mr William
Troy's 'The Altar of Henry James' (1943), it seems to have
been fertilised by the new school of Shakespearian criticism
that followed on *The Wheel of Fire*. To see in a great part of
James's novels and stories a body of work of the same nature
as Shakespeare's is at least less misleading than to judge them
as Victorian prose fictions which aim at imitating a social
surface. While the novels of the eighteenth and nineteenth
centuries, with a few exceptions, were descended from Addison
and Defoe, with some admixture of a debased stage comedy,
there is quite another kind of novel, created by Emily Brontë,
Melville, Conrad and Henry James, among others, which
makes use of the technique of the dramatic poem. If Mr Troy
seems to be laying too much stress on James's symbols, he has
to correct a long tradition of crass insensitiveness to the whole
intention of James's art. 'It is clear enough', he writes, 'that to
the present generation James means something more than
to the generation of Van Wyck Brooks and Lewis Mumford or to
the addled and intolerant generation of the thirties. Also clear
is that what he means is something different'. 'As in any
authentic artist', he continues, 'the "meaning" in James is

contained in the total arrangement and order of his symbols, and in the novel everything – people, events, and settings – is capable of being invested with symbolic value'. Excellent as is his theory, he does not seem to me to carry it out in the right way; he makes no such convincing and illuminating analyses as Mr Quentin Anderson in the essay on Henry James that appeared in *The Kenyon Review* for Autumn, 1946. The weakness of the study of symbols is that the text tends to get less attention, instead of a fresh concentration of attention. Nevertheless, elementary and uncertain as is Mr Troy's handling of James's 'symbols', one can see how fruitful the approach might be. To recognize in James's novels and *nouvelles* art of the same nature as *Measure for Measure*, to see that they are in a tradition of medieval and Elizabethan drama transmitted through Shakespeare, Ben Jonson and Bunyan (and so Hawthorne), is to make their meaning accessible, as it never can be if they are approached on the assumption that they are the same kind of thing as the writings of Trollope and Thackeray. This is to put James's work on a plane where the highest claims can be convincingly made for it.

The editor prints also Mr Auden's poem *At the Grave of Henry James*, presumably as an illustration of the Snob cult of James. Mr Zabel's contribution, 'The Poetics of Henry James' (1935), subscribes, in so far as it says anything, to the general conspiracy to find James's Prefaces profoundly illuminating, but fails to produce any paraphrasable explanation of why they should be held to be so. Mr Jacques Barzun's essay, 'Henry James, Melodramatist' (1943), an attempt to show that romantic and violent drama is a basic element in James's writings, has some point inasmuch as it takes the wind out of the sails of those who would dismiss James as 'the last refinement of the genteel tradition' (as in an essay reprinted by Mr Dupee on 'Henry James and the Nostalgia of Culture', 1930). But the superficiality of his thesis is apparent once he applies it to a specific work – *Washington Square*, which he interprets as crudely melodramatic:

And its force is derived from the essentially melodramatic situation of a motherless daughter victimized by a subservient aunt and a selfish father – a being for whom the melodramatic epithet of "fiend in human form" is no longer sayable but still just.

This is to misrepresent James entirely and to do blatant injustice to the American *Eugénie Grandet*. James's triumph lies in doing without Balzac's sentimentality about the *jeune fille* and in creating an infinitely subtler situation than Mr Barzun credits him with presenting. The father is not a villain – James takes pains to secure sympathy and respect for him, it is significant that he is linked with the 'Republican simplicity' of the ethos of old New York, and he is introduced to us as 'a thoroughly honest man'. The suffering is shown to be on both sides, a tragedy of the relations between an exceptionally brilliant father and a commonplace but worthy daughter. The two are bound by natural affection, but the clever father, his history being what it is, can only take an ironic tone with his dull and inarticulate child. In the one crisis of her life this acts as an insuperable barrier between them. There is complete mutual misunderstanding, symbolised by the icy waste among the mountains, with night descending on them, where they find themselves at odds so painfully, in a memorable scene. He alienates her confidence while doing his best for her welfare, and though the fortune-hunting lover 'had trifled with her affections', it was her father who 'had broken its spring'. It is the father's tragedy too, for he has destroyed his only natural link with life. To ignore the complexity of a distinguished work of art like *Washington Square* and to assert instead that it is something crude and commonplace is to impoverish James's creation. That is the result of concocting a theory about a writer's work and then making a text square with it.

It is the distinction of the essay of Mr R.P. Blackmur's here, 'In the Country of the Blue' (1943), that it starts with the texts – James's tales about artists – and extracts a theory from them. Noting James's fondness for the theme of 'the artist in conflict with society' and making the point that 'the artist is only a special case of the man', Blackmur concludes: 'James made the theme of the artist a focus for the ultimate theme of human integrity'. It was James's own experience as an artist – the letters I quoted above are evidence – that qualified him to feel this struggle from the inside. Typically he dramatizes it in the choice between being a Henry St George, the Master who has succumbed to the temptations of a Philistine society and ruined himself as a novelist, and being a Paul Overt – or a Nick Dormer (in *The Tragic Muse*) or a Ray Limbert (in *The Next*

Time) or a Neil Paraday (in *The Death of a Lion*) – a kind of ascetic, saint and martyr. But why, while admitting Conrad's accomplishment as novelist, did James complain to Ford Madox Ford that Conrad's works left a very disagreeable impression on him? Was it that Conrad rubs in so intolerably the inescapable isolation of every man?

Henry James's heiress: The importance of Edith Wharton

The unfinished posthumous novel of Edith Wharton – *The Buccaneers* – should at least serve to bring up this author's name for evaluation. It is incidentally quite worth reading if you are an amateur of the period now in fashion again (the seventies). It would have been far more worth publishing if Mrs Wharton's literary executor had supplemented his appendix by a memoir and critical essay designed to introduce the present generation to her best work, scarcely ever read in England – for to the educated English public Mrs Wharton's novels are those of her last ten years and known vaguely as the kind of fiction which was published serially in *Good Housekeeping*. But her characteristic work was all done long before, early enough for one of her good novels to have been published in World's Classics in 1936, more than thirty years after it was first printed. It was as the historian of New York society of the nineties that she first achieved character and eminence as a novelist, on the dual grounds, as she said, that it was 'a field as yet unexploited by any novelist who had grown up in that little hot-house of traditions and conventions' and had been 'tacitly regarded as unassailable'. In her rapid growth as combined social critic and historian she continued to strike roots outwards and downwards until she had included in her reach the lowest levels of rustic, urban and manufacturing life. And her work was no mere historical fictionizing, she was a serious novelist. She was also an extraordinarily acute and far-sighted social critic; in this she was original and appears still more so when we think with what an effort this detachment must have been achieved by the child brought up to believe it her ambition to become, like her mother, the best-dressed woman in New York, and who was married young to an anti-intellectual society man.

By a combination of circumstances she was peculiarly qualified to undertake such work. Her interesting auto-biography[1] documents her cultural origins for us. There we are told that the best people in New York, among whom she was born, had the traditions of a mercantile middle class whose 'value lay in upholding two standards of importance in any community, that of education and good manners, and of scrupulous probity in business affairs'. This society was leisured, and satisfied with a moderate wealth – she never in her young days encountered the gold-fever in any form. It con-centrated on the arts of living that radiate from home-making. It was resolutely English in culture (speaking 'pure English', importing tutors and governesses, reading the English classics and deploring contemporary American men of letters) and habitually travelled abroad (unlike Boston) though keeping aloof from the English Court and society. She grew up to see this society disintegrate from within, its values succumbing to spiritual anaemia – 'the blind dread of innovation and the instinctive shrinking from responsibility' that she noted as its chief weaknesses and which left politics to be the prey of Business – even before its standards were overthrown by the invasion from without of the predatory new rich. Her quick intelligence made her aware of the import of changes that even an insider at the time could only have sensed, her literary ambition encouraged her to try to fix them in the novel, and her early environment and family traditions gave her a position from which to survey changes in the social scene, a code by which to judge the accompanying shift in *mœurs*, and values by which to estimate profit and loss. Her admiration for Henry James's work, later her great intimacy with him, provided her with a spring-board from which to take off as an artist.

For her literary career began, as she said 'in the days when Thomas Hardy, in order to bring out *Jude the Obscure* in a leading New York periodical, was compelled to turn the children of Jude and Sue into adopted orphans; when the most popular magazine in America excluded all stories containing any reference to "religion, love, politics, alcohol or fairies" (this is textual); the days when a well-known New York editor, offering me a large sum for the serial rights of a projected novel, stipulated only that no reference to "an unlawful attachment" should figure in it...and when the translator of Dante,

Professor Eliot Norton, hearing (after the appearance of *The House of Mirth*) that I was preparing another "society" novel, wrote in alarm imploring me to remember that '"no great work of the imagination has ever been based on illicit passion"!' It was equivalent to the literary England of Trollope's beginnings, yet Edith Wharton without any bravado assumed that because she did not depend on literature for her income she should ignore its 'incurable moral timidity' and the displeasure of her social group. 'The novelist's best safeguard is to write only for that dispassionate and ironic critic who dwells within the breast', she wrote. The likeness to Jane Austen is revealed in that, and borne out by her decision, after writing several dull psychological novels, to make a novel out of what she knew best, the fashionable New York of her married life 'in all its flatness and futility'. In doing so she was taking up Henry James's work where he left it off with *The Bostonians* and *The Portrait of a Lady*. And in this novel she turned, as she noted, from an amateur into a professional novelist. The American novel grew up with Henry James and achieved a tradition with Mrs Wharton. He, she points out in a passage of great interest,[2] was never at home in twentieth-century America – 'he belonged irrevocably to the old America out of which I also came' and whose last traces, as she said, remained in Europe whither he fortunately went to seek them. 'Henry James was essentially a novelist of manners, and the manners he was qualified by nature and situation to observe were those of the little vanishing group of people among whom he had grown up, or their more picturesque prototypes in older societies – he often bewailed to me his total inability to use the "material", financial and industrial, of modern American life'. And she instances James's failure to make plausible Mr Verver in *The Golden Bowl* or 'to relate either him or his native "American City" to any sort of reality'. She might have instanced her own Mr Spragg and his Apex City in contrast, those fully realized symbols which make the later creations Babbitt and Main Street seem unnecessary as well as crude work. Unlike James, she rightly felt herself qualified to deal with the society that succeeded 'the old America' and she stayed to write its natural history, to write it in a form as shapely and with a surface as finished

as if she had had a number of predecessors in her chosen task.
These works had the advantage of being 'readable' as Jane
Austen's and even George Eliot's were and as *The Ambassadors*
was not. It is profitable to observe how, in *The Custom of the
Country*, she makes use of James's technique and yet reaches
a public unwilling or unable to wrestle with his formidable
novels.

She was early convinced that the virtue had gone out of 'the
old America' of her ancestors – 'When I was young it used
to seem to me that the group in which I grew up was like an
empty vessel into which no new wine would ever again be
poured'. So when she decided to make a novel out of the circle
in which she lived she chose to depict it in terms of 'the slow
disintegration' of Lily Bart, one of the 'wasted human
possibilities' who form, she declared, 'the underpinning [on
which] such social groups (the shallow and the idle) always
rest'. No doubt it was her own experience that enabled her
to isolate the destructive element in such societies – 'the quality
of making other standards non-existent by ignoring them...
Lily's set had a force of negation which eliminated everything
beyond their own range of perception'. These explanations are
from the subsequent introduction. In the novel (*The House of
Mirth*, 1905) this analysis is present in solution – in terms of
dialogue, dramatic situation and the process by which the
exquisite Lily Bart slips down into annihilation. For in these
novels Mrs Wharton never ceases to be first of all a novelist.
Her social criticism is effected in the terms that produced
Middlemarch society and the Dodsons in *The Mill on the Floss*,
and often challenges comparison with analogous effects in Jane
Austen:

Mrs Gryce had a kind of impersonal benevolence: cases of individual
need she regarded with suspicion, but she subscribed to Institutions
when their annual reports showed an impressive surplus.

In her youth, girls had not been supposed to require close supervision.
They were generally assumed to be taken up with the legitimate
business of courtship and marriage, and interference in such affairs
on the part of their natural guardians was considered as unwarrantable
as a spectator's suddenly joining in a game. There had of course been
'fast' girls even in Mrs Peniston's early experience ; but their fastness,
at worst, was understood to be a mere excess of animal spirits, against

which there could be no graver charge than that of being 'unladylike'. The modern fastness appeared synonymous with immorality, and the mere idea of immorality was as offensive to Mrs Peniston as a smell of cooking in the drawing-room: it was one of the conceptions her mind refused to admit.

[Of the much-divorced but 'ineradicably innocent' beauty from the West] The lady's offences were always against taste rather than conduct ; her divorce record seemed due to geographical rather than ethical conditions ; and her worst laxities were likely to proceed from ⌐ wandering and extravagant good nature.

The feature of most permanent interest in the book is the systematic portrayal of the various groups in New York society. These are created with zest and an abundant life, surprisingly lacking animus: even distaste is lost in ironic apprehension. And no group or character is wantonly dragged in, each has an indispensable function in advancing the plot. They range from the timid millionaire of the old school, Percy Bryce:

After attaining his majority, and confirming into the fortune which the late Mr Gryce had made out of a patent device for excluding fresh air from hotels, the young man continued to live with his mother in Albany ; but on Jefferson Gryce's death, when another large property passed into her son's hands, Mrs Gryce thought that what she called his 'interests' demanded his presence in New York. She accordingly installed herself in the Madison Avenue house, and Percy, whose sense of duty was not inferior to his mother's, spent all his week-days in the handsome Broad Street office, where a batch of pale men on small salaries had grown grey in the management of the Gryce estate, and where he was initiated with becoming reverence into every detail of the art of accumulation.

through the established 'good' society – smart Trenors, dowdy Van Osburghs, and their parasites like the divorcée Mrs Fisher – to the various social aspirants, such as the new-rich Gormans:

Mrs Fisher's unconventionality was, after all, a merely superficial divergence from an inherited social creed, while the manners of the Gorman circle represented their first attempt to formulate such a creed for themselves,

the comic Wellington Brys and the financier Rosedale (not stock size) down to the outermost darkness of Mrs Norman Hatch from the West, 'rich, helpless, unplaced', living in the Emporium Hotel whence she endeavours to launch herself into the bosom

of society. [There is an invaluable pre-Sinclair Lewis account
of fashionable hotel life of the time.]

The environment in which Lily found herself was as strange to her as
its inhabitants. She was unacquainted with the world of the
fashionable New York hotel – a world over-heated, over-upholstered,
and over-fitted with mechanical appliances for the gratification of
fantastic requirements, while the comforts of a civilized life were as
unattainable as in a desert. Through this atmosphere of torrid
splendour moved wan beings as richly upholstered as the furniture,
beings without definite pursuits or permanent relations... Somewhere
behind them, in the background of their lives, there was doubtless
a real past, peopled by real human activities: they themselves were
probably the product of strong ambitions, persistent energies,
diversified contacts with the wholesome roughness of life ; yet they
had no more real existence than the poet's shades in limbo.

Lily had not been long in this pallid world without discovering that
Mrs Hatch was its most substantial figure. That lady, though still
floating in the void, showed faint symptoms of developing an
outline... It was, in short, as the regulator of a germinating social
life that Miss Bart's guidance was required; her ostensible duties as
secretary being restricted by the fact that Mrs Hatch, as yet, knew
hardly any one to write to... Compared with the vast gilded void
of Mrs Hatch's existence, the life of Lily's former friends seemed
packed with ordered activities. Even the most irresponsible pretty
woman of her acquaintance had her inherited obligations, her
conventional benevolences, her share in the working of the great civic
machine; and all hung together in the solidarity of these traditional
functions...

Mrs Hatch swam in a haze of indeterminate enthusiasms, aspirations
culled from the stage, the newspapers, the fashion-journals, and a
gaudy world of sport still more completely beyond her companion's
ken... The difficulty was to find any point of contact between her
ideals and Lily's.

Such a combination of sustained anthropological interest
with literary ability was hitherto unknown to fiction except
in *The Bostonians*. Mrs Wharton had all the qualifications that
Galsworthy so disastrously lacked; to place *The Forsyte Saga*
beside one of her characteristic novels is to expose it.

The Custom of the Country (1913) is undoubtably her masterpiece.
[It should have been obtainable in a cheap edition or
'Everyman' long ago.] Here the theme is explicitly 'social
disintegration'. But now the 'good' New York society has
shrunk to a sideshow, the centre is consciously occupied by the

moneyed barbarians; they lack both a moral and a social code but are fast acquiring the latter by imitation. Whereas old New York (like Henry James's Boston) by keeping itself to itself had evolved an independent culture, new New York is shown trying to construct an imitation of European culture by copying its social surface, by acquiring it by marriage, by buying up its antiques and by reproducing its architectural masterpieces at home:

Bowen, from his corner, surveyed a seemingly endless perspective of plumed and jewelled heads, of shoulders bare or black-coated, encircling the close-packed tables...During some forty years' perpetual exercise of his perceptions he had never come across anything that gave them the special titillation produced by the sight of the dinner-hour at the Nouveau Luxe: the same sense of putting his hand on human nature's passion for the factitious, its incorrigible habit of imitating the imitation. As he sat watching the familiar faces swept toward him on the rising tide of arrival – for it was one of the joys of the scene that the type was always the same even when the individual was not – he hailed with renewed appreciation this costly expression of a social ideal. The dining-room at the Nouveau Luxe represented, on such a spring evening, what unbounded material power had devised for the delusion of its leisure: a phantom 'society' with all the rules, smirks, gestures of its model, but evoked out of promiscuity and incoherence while the other had been the product of continuity and choice. And the instinct which had driven a new class of world-compellers to bind themselves to slavish imitation of the superseded, and their prompt and reverent faith in the reality of the sham they had created, seemed to Bowen the most satisfying proof of human permanence...

Small, cautious, middle-class, had been the ideals of aboriginal New York; but...they were singularly coherent and respectable as contrasted with the chaos of indiscriminate appetites which made up its modern tendencies... What Popple called society was really just like the houses it lived in: a muddle of misapplied ornament over a thin steel shell of utility. The steel shell was built up in Wall Street, the social trimmings were hastily added in Fifth Avenue; and the union between them was as monstrous and factitious, as unlike the gradual homogeneous growth which flowers into what other countries know as society, as that between the Blois gargoyles on Peter Van Degen's roof and the skeleton walls supporting them.

The writing is unbrokenly taut and incisive, with sustained local vitality. The hero reflects on his 'aboriginal family' – 'Harriet

Ray, sealed up tight in the vacuum of inherited opinion, where not a breath of fresh sensation could get at her', 'hardly anything that mattered to him existed for them, and their prejudices reminded him of sign-posts warning off trespassers who have long since ceased to intrude'. Instead of the downward drift characteristic of *The House of Mirth* we are initiated into the triumphant social and material progress of Undine Spragg, type of the new as Lily Bart was of the superseded. Thanks to an inborn lack of either moral sense or introspective qualms Undine hauls herself to the top of the ladder, trampling husbands, family decencies and social codes underfoot, perpetually violating in all unconsciousness even her own moral professions. Yet Undine is not a monster. She is felt to be less of one than Rosamund Vincy, George Eliot's masterpiece on the same pattern, and there is a stimulus to be derived from the display of her tactics. The pattern of this novel lends itself to a kind of irony congenial to Mrs Wharton – the latent irony that is to be discovered in certain kinds of situation: the clash between civilized and primitive *mœurs*, between pretence and actuality, intention and achievement. Her novels are rich in social comedy, displayed with something like Jane Austen's enjoyment, though the victory does not, as in the latter's works, go to the finer spirits.

The next novel in this line is *Twilight Sleep* (1927), which displays the chaos that followed on the establishment of a society based on money without any kind of traditions. It is inferior to the earlier work in its tendency to come down on the side of the farcical in the study of Pauline Manford, whose optimistic progress through life is symbolized in the title. '"Of course there ought to be no Pain...nothing but Beauty... It ought to be one of the loveliest, most poetic things in the world to have a baby", Mrs Manford declared, in that bright efficient voice which made loveliness and poetry sound like the attributes of an advanced industrialism, and babies something to be turned out in series like Fords.' Nevertheless it compares favourably with Huxley's and other novels treating of the same kind of life. Pauline, whose millions were made in the Middle West from the manufacture of motors, appears intended to embody the crude virtues of the invaders of pioneer stock, for with all her innocence of culture and her belief in activity for its own sake and her muddled passion for universal spiritual progress – in spite of this she seems to have a respectable aspect too. For opposed to her is the next generation, represented by her daughter-in-law and her social group, whose insolent irresponsibility and empty vice set off whatever it was worth admiring – some moral positive or intuitive decency? that at least kept the family from going to pieces – that Edith Wharton felt even a Pauline Manford retained but was then (in the twenties) melting away under her eyes: the last stage of the social disintegration she had analysed and chronicled and turned into art. She had lived, she felt, to see disappear 'the formative value of nearly three hundred years of social observance: the concreted living up to long-established standards of honour and conduct, of education and manners'.

This sequence leads up to the fiction of Scott Fitzgerald, Faulkner and Kay Boyle, among others, and without it their writings cannot be understood by the English reader. This school depicts (Faulkner and Kay Boyle with approval) a kind of life, without roots or responsibilities, where value is attributed only to drunkenness and allied states of excess. This phase of American culture is conveniently illustrated by the career of the late Harry Crosby. Mrs Wharton's autobiography contains a first-hand account of the earlier half of this cultural disintegration. Read in sequence, after *The Education of Henry Adams* and Henry James's *A Small Boy and Others*, and before Malcolm Cowley's *Exile's Return*, it provides the English student with part of this indispensable background to American literature – the cultural history of literary America which, if Van Wyck Brooks's *The Flowering of New England* had been executed by an able critic, would now be complete to date in five volumes.

Later on she attempted to supplement her sequence by historical studies – *The Age of Innocence* (1920) and *Old New York* (1924) – of the static society of her grandparents' days. But the historical novel necessarily bears about the same relation to art as the waxwork, and in any case her talents found congenial only the contemporary and the changing. Here she has to reproduce 'the old New York way of taking life "without effusion of blood"'.

Nevertheless there are good things in both books. One remembers the analysis of

That terrifying product of the social system he belonged to and believed in, the young girl who knew nothing and expected everything.

His own exclamation: 'Women should be free – as free as we are,' struck to the root of a problem that it was agreed in his world to regard as non-existent. 'Nice' women, however wronged, would never claim the kind of freedom he meant, and generous-minded men like himself were therefore – in the heat of argument – the more chivalrously ready to concede it them. Such verbal generosities were in fact only a humbugging disguise of the inexorable convention that tied things together and bound people down to the old pattern. In reality they all lived in a kind of hieroglyphic world, where the real thing was never said or done or even thought, but only represented by a set of arbitrary signs, as when... The result, of course, was that the young girl who was the centre of this elaborate system of mystification remained the more inscrutable for her very frankness and assurance. She was frank, poor darling, because she had nothing to conceal, assured because she knew of nothing to be on her guard against... But when he had gone the brief round of her he returned discouraged by the thought that all this frankness and innocence were only an artificial product. Untrained human nature was not frank and innocent; it was full of the twists and deferences of an instinctive guile.

After this sequence she ceased to write novels worthy of herself. Partly she was growing old, partly, as she wrote in her memoirs, she should have ceased to write because 'the world she had grown up in and been formed by had been destroyed in 1914'.

But her work is by no means so limited as this may have suggested, even though suggestions have been made that she turned Henry James's early work from a sport to the beginning of a tradition, that she was the nearest thing to an American Jane Austen, and the archetype of a Galsworthy. As far back as 1907 she had shown, in *The Fruit of the Tree*, her recognition of the general social problem and her refusal to limit her subject-matter to the moneyed or educated strata of Americans. Heaven knows where she got her knowledge of mill-towns, but here, though the novel is uncertain in intention and now only readable in patches, she revealed the split between the capitalist ruling class and the oppressed mill-hands, the worthlessness of the lives of the one and the misery of the lives of the other. Nor do we know how she aquired the material for that moving study of the sufferings of the respectable poor, the short story *Bunner Sisters*. Mrs Wharton's presentation of the poor [of New York in the horse-car period in this story, of the hill-farm folk in

Ethan Frome (1911) and of the New England rustics in *Summer* (1917)] is like George Eliot's in its sympathy and its freedom from sentimental evasions, but without the latter's large nobility that throws a softening light on all wretchedness. She is prone to end on a note of suspension in fierce irony that was not included in George Eliot's make-up. Mrs Wharton, with her unmannered style and impersonal presentation, solved the problem of tone by ignoring the reader altogether. These three *nouvelles* might well be issued in England in one volume, everyone interested in literature ought to read them at least once – they are works of art, and historically they have some importance. She was the first to outrage the accepted pretence of seeing the New England countryside idyllically. Hers was informed realism. 'For years I had wanted to draw life as it really was in the derelict mountain villages of New England, a life even in my time, and a thousandfold more a generation earlier, utterly unlike that seen through the rose-coloured spectacles of my predecessors, Mary Wilkins and Sarah Orne Jewett. In those days the snow-bound villages of Western Massachusetts were still grim places, morally and physically: insanity, incest and slow mental and moral starvation were hidden away behind the paintless wooden house-fronts. *Ethan Frome* was written after I had spent ten years in the hill-region where the scene is laid, during which years I had come to know well the aspect, dialect and mental and moral attitude of the hill-people'. In consequence *Summer*, and the inferior but better known *Ethan Frome*, stand, along with the Scottish specimen, *The House with the Green Shutters*, in the *Wuthering Heights* category.

Mrs Wharton's interest in the contemporary social scene then was deep and wide as well as acute and witty. *Silas Marner* is rightly considered a classic of our language, but except for the accidental advantage of having a more attractive social picture to reproduce – a mellower setting, less ungracious *mœurs*, a more comely dialect – it seems to me inferior to *Summer*. The village of North Dormer, 'abandoned of men, left apart by all the forces that link life to life in modern communities', where only those remain who can't get away or who have drifted back wrecked, completes Mrs Wharton's social survey. Outside North Dormer is the Mountain, the home of a colony of squatters, bad characters and outlaws, who represent the limits of degradation to which society can sink – they have neither material civilization nor moral tradition. Mrs Wharton declared that they were drawn in every detail from life. She was bold enough to seize on the Mountain for an unforgettable symbol that few novelists would have cared or dared to touch (it was received, she recorded, 'with indignant denial by reviewers and readers'). And the understanding shown in these three stories of the workings of uneducated, rustic and similar inarticulate kinds of minds is more convincing than George Eliot's, even as hers is more plausible than Hardy's, both these last having a suspicious tendency to humorous effects and George Eliot besides being never quite free from a shade of superiority in her attitude to intellectual inferiors.

Edith Wharton's value seems to me therefore not merely, as Mr Edmund Wilson said in a recent article ('Justice to Edith Wharton', *The New Republic*, June 29 1938) that she wrote 'in a period (1905–1917) when there were few American writers worth reading'. I am convinced that anyone interested in the cultural basis of society, and anyone sensitive to quality in the novel, will find this selection of her writings I have made of permanent worth and unique in character. The final question then is, what order of novelist is she? – i.e., not how permanent but how good? She was, until her decay, a tough-minded, robust artist, not the shrinking minor writer or the ladylike talent. It is characteristic that she should refer to 'that dispassionate and ironic critic who dwells within the breast' of authors, and equally so that she should have considered the unencouraging atmosphere (indifference to her literary success and disapproval of her choosing to write) of her family and social circle, and the adverse reviews she received from outside, stimulating to talent, just as she accepted the severest professional criticism as valuable. This, she said, was better for fostering literary ability than 'premature flattery and local celebrity' and having one's path smoothed; one contrasts this with Mrs Woolf's claims for the creative temperament. She was a born artist; of the work of her prime she could justly say 'My last page is latent in my first'. Of how many novels in the English language before hers can that be said? She had the advantage of being a solidly-educated lady frequenting the most cultivated society of England and France. As an artist she had Henry James behind her work, whereas Sinclair Lewis, when he later attempted similarly to epitomize his environment in fiction, had only H. G. Wells behind his. She was remarkably intelligent: it is easy as well as more popular to be wise after the event (like Sinclair Lewis) but it takes a kind of genius to see your culture from the outside, to diagnose what is happening and plot its curves contemporaneously as she did. Jane Austen never got outside (of course she could never have imagined doing so): her social criticism is all from the inside and remains indoors without so much as a glance out of the window. It is not only that in Jane Austen social forces never come up for comment or that she accepts the theory of the rich man in his castle and the poor man at his gate, but that she can mention the enclosure of the commons as the natural subject of conversation for the gentlemen at dinner – just that and no more. Yet there can be no question that Jane Austen was a great novelist while Edith Wharton's greatest admirer would not claim that title for her. What makes a great novelist? Apparently not intelligence or scope or a highly-developed technique, though, other things being equal, they often give an advantage. But what then are other things?

Again, compare Edith Wharton with George Eliot. George Eliot was a simple-minded woman except where great sensitiveness of feeling gave her a subtle insight – even her learning was deployed with solemn simplicity. Undeniably Mrs Wharton had a more flexible mind, she was both socially and morally more experienced than George Eliot and therefore better able to enter into uncongenial states of feeling and to depict as an artist instead of a preacher distasteful kinds of behaviour. Her Undine Spragg is better sustained and handled than the other's Rosamund Vincy. Undine's sphere of action is dazzling and she always has a fresh surprise for us up her sleeve in the way of moral obtuseness; it was cleverer to make Undine up at the top of the tree with her only disappointment that her last husband couldn't get made Ambassador (on account of having a divorced wife) than to involve herself in disasters like Rosamund: the manifold irony of worldly success is more profitable than any simple moral lesson and artistically how much richer! Mrs Wharton writes better than George Eliot, who besides lacking grace rarely achieves the economy of language that Mrs Wharton commands habitually. Her technique is absolutely right and from the works I have instanced it would be difficult to alter or omit without harm, for like Henry James she was the type of conscious artist writing to satisfy only her own inflexible literary conscience. Now George Eliot in general moves like a cart-horse and too often takes the longest way round. But again it is George Eliot who is the great novelist.

I think it eventually becomes a question of what the novelist has to offer us, either directly or by implication, in the way of positives. In *Bunner Sisters*, *Summer*, and some other places Mrs Wharton rests upon the simple goodness of the decent poor, as indeed George Eliot and Wordsworth both do in part, that is, the most widespread common factor of moral worth. But beyond that Mrs Wharton has only negatives, her values emerging I suppose as something other than what she exposes as worthless. This is not very nourishing, and it is on similar grounds that Flaubert, so long admired as the ideal artist of the novel, has begun to lose esteem. It seems to be the fault of the disintegrating and spiritually impoverished society she analyses. Her value is that she does analyse and is not content to reflect. We may contrast Jane Austen, who does not even analyse, but, having the good fortune to have been born into a flourishing culture, can take for granted its foundations and accept its standards, working within them on a basis of internal relations entirely. The common code of her society is a valuable one and she benefits from it as an artist. Mr Knightley's speech to Emma, reproving her for snubbing Miss Bates, is a useful instance: manners there are seen to be based on moral values. Mrs Wharton's worthy people are all primitives or archaic survivals. This inability to find any significance in the society that she spent her prime in, or to find 'significance only through what its frivolity destroys', explains the absence of poetry in her disposition and of many kinds of valuable experience in her books. She has none of that natural piety, that richness of feeling and sense of a moral order, of experience as a process of growth, in which George Eliot's local criticisms are embedded and which give the latter her large stature. Between her conviction that the new society she grew up into was vicious and insecurely based on an ill-used working class and her conviction that her inherited mode of living represented a dead-end, she could find no foundation to build on. We may see where her real strength lay in the critical phrases she uses – 'Her moral muscles had become atrophied' ['by buying off suffering with money, or denying its existence with words'] ; 'the superficial contradictions and accommodations of a conscience grown elastic from too much use' – and in the short story 'Autres Temps...' a study of the change in moral codes she had witnessed since her youth. Here the divorced mother, who had for many years hidden her disgrace in Florence, returns to America to succour, as she thinks, her divorced and newly remarried daughter. At first, finding the absence of any prejudice against divorce in the new America, she is exalted, then she feels in her bewilderment ' " I didn't take up too much room before, but now where is there a corner for me?" Where indeed in this crowded, topsy-turvey world, with its headlong changes and helter-skelter readjustments, its new tolerances and indifferences and accommodations, was there room for a character fashioned by slower sterner processes and a life broken under their inexorable pressure?' And finally, depressed by what she feels to be the lack of any kind of moral taste, she loses her illusions about the real benefits of such a change, she finds it to be merely a change in social fashions and not a revolution bringing genuine enlightenment based on good feeling. She explains to an old friend: 'Traditions that have lost their meaning are the hardest of all to destroy... We're shut up in a little tight round of habit and association, just as we're shut up in this room... We're all imprisoned, of course – all of us middling people, – who don't carry freedom in our brains. But we've accommodated ourselves into different cells, and if we're moved suddenly into new ones we're likely to find a stone wall where we thought there was air, and to knock ourselves senseless against it.' She chooses to return to Florence, 'moving again among the grim edges of reality'.

Mrs Wharton, if unfortunate in her environment, had a strength of character that made her superior to it. She was a remarkable novelist if not a large-sized one, and while there are few great novelists there are not even so many remarkable ones that we can afford to let her be overlooked.

Edith Wharton: *The House of Mirth*

The real strength of *The House of Mirth* goes into the analysis of what was wrong with the protagonist Lily Bart and why. Lawrence Selden's awareness of Lily Bart is critical though appreciative. He reflects:

everything about her was at once vigorous and exquisite, at once strong and fine. He had a confused sense that she must have cost a great deal to make, that a great many dull and ugly people must, in some mysterious way, have been sacrificed to produce her. He was aware that the qualities distinguishing her from the herd of her sex were chiefly external: as though a fine glaze of beauty and fastidiousness had been applied to vulgar clay. Yet the analogy left him unsatisfied, for a coarse texture will not take a high finish; and was it not possible that the material was fine, but that circumstance had fashioned it into a futile shape?

This is too near the author's own attitude to Lily Bart to be any help in looking critically at the problem of values involved, for the novelist never arrives at a judgment and never examines impartially the confused and conflicting ideas that pass through Selden's mind here. She also is strongly drawn to justification through aesthetic satisfaction in a character, and in fact except in a physical sense Lily is not 'strong', she is fatally weak in character so that her undoing is really that she can't resist extravagance or bear deprivation of luxury that the novelist as much as Lily and Selden seems to feel is the birthright of the physically exquisite. But Lily is also one of 'the shallow and the idle', quite as idle as the rest of her class who, unlike her, have the money to be able to be so without getting into debt, and only relatively less shallow. What right has Lily to fastidiousness, we are impelled to ask with some impatience? Married to the man whose fastidious tastes meet her own but who is too poor to support her in the style she cannot do without – Lawrence Selden, who shrinking from marrying her therefore 'fails her' – she would have made both of them miserable and the marriage financially disastrous; her fastidiousness is just sufficient to make her draw back each time a sufficiently wealthy but dull or vulgar suitor is available. And the novelist shows that no better choice is likely to occur in such a society. Only the best would do for her, the novelist feels, like Lily herself; but the reader may well ask (and can't help asking, one would have thought) whether mere beauty and charm and good-nature, without ability, talent for anything but high fashion in living, or enough character to save herself from the fatal drift downward as she grows older and socially less desirable, should be allowed such high claims. The exquisiteness inevitably goes with weakness – always implicit in aestheticism – which can't always grasp the nettle or embrace and defeat hardships.

The representation of Gerty Farish, Lily's opposite, as necessarily dull, bornée and sentimental, reveals a bias in the opposite direction that confirms one's suspicions of Edith Wharton's own weakness revealed in such partiality (uncritical partisanship on the one side and a revelatory if unconscious hostility on the other). Lily is made interesting by being allowed to talk wittily, but though she is 'not nasty' she is not really intelligent either and her talk is merely 'social', her knowledge of everything but social arts merely superficial, a means to a social end. She has already been 'out' for eleven years when the novel opens so that to make a 'good' marriage to rescue herself from debt and bondage to her aunt has become urgent even to her dilatory dislike of facing facts. Gerty Farish, her relative, who *has* faced the fact of being poor and refused to be useless or dependent, is not 'exquisite' and therefore hasn't any sympathy from the author for her tenderness for her cousin Lawrence Selden; she is condemned also to life in a flat that is 'hideous': the novelist (who we know was an authority on period interiors and what was in that age known as 'the House Beautiful') seems, like Lily, to know no alternative to 'luxury' but 'squalor' and 'dinginess'. This is a real limitation of the aesthetic sensibility and the most obvious point in which it differs from the sensibility and taste – which is essentially imaginative and independent of money-values – of the true artist. It is true the novelist provides some excuse for Lily in the conditioning she has received from her mother to believe it inevitable to marry a man of fashion whose essential function is to pay the bills.

It is hard to have any sympathy for a woman (far from being a young girl now) who has no desire for any better life than the smart set's and whose hardship is in not being able to pay her gambling debts and dressmakers' bills and to satisfy her ambition to have smarter gowns and 'far more jewels than her hostesses'. Lily's weakness is principally that of always taking the colour of her surroundings, her virtue is in being unable to go through with the campaign of exploitation she has embarked on, so that each time she is robbed of the fruits of victory and is self-defeated until at the last repetition of this pattern she can only escape from her difficulties by an overdose of her sleeping-drugs, having lost everything. The only time the novelist cheats is when she tries to show Lily deeply moved by the working-girl's baby which arouses in her a quite incredible maternal impulse – she has always hitherto reflected her unloving, unnatural mother – we remember that earlier the spectacle of Rosedale's 'homely goodness in his advances to the child' (his hostess's little girl) which made him 'seem a simple and kindly being' had only given Lily's 'repugnance a more concrete and intimate form'. Her kind of social graces are essentially unmaternal and she cannot think of a husband as the father of her children or of herself as fulfilling herself as a mother, only as a triumphant beauty and an outstanding hostess. Like Cleopatra's, a similar but different case, it cannot be tragic because it arouses too many cynical considerations. The description of Lily at the end cherishing the dresses she had worn in her best days and the description of her ('She was like some rare flower grown for exhibition') is, one feels, exactly right, but the final pathos that follows, of her sinking into her last sleep feeling that Nettie Struther's child, which she had briefly seen once, 'was lying on her arm...but she felt no great surprise at the fact, only a gentle penetrating thrill of warmth and pleasure' rings utterly false and improbable.

Selden isn't the right man for Lily since he oscillates between idealizing her and so expecting of her what she is incapable of sustaining,[1] and a rejection of her whenever the actuality of her weaknesses and failings becomes inescapable to his trained lawyer's eye and cold nature. But Rosedale instinctively understands her because her ambitions and ideas about her rightful claims of life and a worthy function for herself are his own ambitions for his wife, and he justly sees that she could fulfil them for him and be satisfied and gratified herself. At the very end she realizes this and would have married him if she could, 'because, little by little, circumstances were breaking down her dislike for Rosedale'. Why she disliked him was because his materialism, expressed in forthright terms, made her see her own, which she expressed to herself in an evasive form, in a repugnant light.[2] 'I want my wife to make all the other women feel small...I should want my wife to be able to take the earth for granted if she wanted to. I know there's one thing vulgar about money, and that's the thinking about it; and my wife would never have to demean herself in that way.' 'Lily raised her head, brightening a little under the challenge. Even through the dark tumult of her thoughts, the clink of Mr Rosedale's millions had a faintly seductive note. But the man behind them grew increasingly repugnant in the light of Selden's expected coming.' Selden never comes to propose to her as she is expecting, and when she next meets Rosedale it is too late, her reputation is tarnished and he can't afford to indulge himself by marrying her or he would lose the social position he has laboriously acquired. It is his loss too, for he sacrifices to his social yearnings his aesthetic sense of Lily's uniqueness not only in beauty but in a fastidiousness otherwise unknown to him as a self-made financier:

It was as though the sense in her of unexplained scruples and resistances had the same attraction as the delicacy of feature, the fastidiousness of manner, which gave her an external rarity, an air of being impossible to match. As he advanced in social experience this uniqueness had acquired a greater value for him, as though he were a collector who had learned to distinguish minor differences of design and quality in some long-coveted object.

One would know this as from an Edwardian novelist's work anywhere (it is 1905). In fact, Edith Wharton is the English – or rather the American – Proust, and independent, if not earlier.[3] She inherited from Henry James of course. Compare and yet contrast *The Spoils of Poynton* (1896) where Henry James has raised the whole question of the collector and the connoisseur in a critical dramatic examination of values, as in *The Golden*

Bowl (1905) he shows a divided mind about it – the Ververs are chained to their possessions which they drag about Europe with them and the second Mrs Verver is finally shown to be their victim and they her punishment (the Museum). Maggie has had her princely husband bought for her by her father and he is part of the beautiful interior of the home in which *he* is imprisoned and which is our last glimpse of the – we are given to understand – now happy couple, the Prince having perforce no occupation but that of stallion and decoration in his wife's London mansion, having been pried out of his real life in Italy with the duties and occupations of his position there and, therefore, we feel convinced (against the novelist's opinion, but of course it is only through his account that we come to our conclusion), committed to further adventures in infidelity from boredom. When a novel fails to convince the reader of the inevitability of the conclusions the author has laid out for us, then it must be due to a discrepancy in the values that have been the basis for the fiction; or to the reader's inability to accept the author's value-judgments.

The Edwardian novelist's impulse to fix every character by its aesthetic milieu is a different thing from the Victorian novelist's habit of describing a character in his or her whole context (Dickens, Trollope, or George Eliot for example) and we see that this is because of the dissolution of class that the Edwardian novelist saw around him. In a society with strong and generally accepted and understood values, as in Jane Austen's, no such description of either kind is necessary. Edith Wharton notes that Jane Austen does not give background of costume, etc. In fact what Jane Austen gives, when at all, is what is necessary to make a critical judgment. Bennett and Wells are both true Edwardian novelists in this feeling that people can only be rendered by their possessions and their taste in material objects and the Edwardian novelist needs space and many words for this. Edith Wharton, on the other hand, renders the idea thus:

The glow of the stones warmed Lily's veins like wine. More completely than any expression of wealth they symbolised the life she longed to lead, the life of fastidious aloofness and refinement in which every detail should have the finish of a jewel, and the whole form a harmonious setting to her own jewel-like rareness.

This is not the usual gross passion for jewels but a comparatively respectable explanation of their fascination for a refined sensibility. But Lily can't separate her aesthetic pleasure in jewels from the acquisitive instinct, though not gross in her case but put in the refined light of her ideal claims on wealth. The underpinning of a society where such ideals are held at the top is shown in the working-girl's life at the club, and in the millinery establishment where Lily is reduced at last to learning the trade. The brief glimpse of the married working-class life, the woman satisfied with the minimum of a kind husband, a baby, a salvaged reputation and a flat 'extraordinarily small and almost miraculously clean' is not convincing, nor is the maternity rendered in these terms: 'Having passionately celebrated her reunion with her offspring, and excused herself in cryptic language for the lateness of her return, Nettie restored the baby to her crib', a young baby whom (one feels characteristically) Mrs Wharton shows as a matter of course to be bottle-fed. The final summing-up is perceptive but the positive, represented, we are assured, for Lily by her little visit to Nettie Struther's flat, is pitifully inadequate and unconvincing:

And as she looked back she saw that there had never been a time when she had had any real relation to life. Her parents too had been rootless, blown hither and thither on every wind of fashion, without any personal existence to shelter them from its shifting gusts. She herself had grown up without any one spot on earth dearer to her than another: there was no centre of early pieties, of grave endearing traditions, to which her heart could revert and from which it could draw strength for itself and tenderness for others. In whatever form a slowly-accumulated past lives in the blood – whether in the concrete image of the old house stored with visual memories, or in the conception of the house not built with hands, but made up of inherited passions and loyalties – it has the same power of broadening and deepening the individual existence, of attaching it by mysterious links of kinship to all the mighty sum of human striving.

Such a vision of the solidarity of life had never before come to Lily… All the men and women she knew were like atoms whirling away from each other in some wild centrifugal dance: her first glimpse of the continuity of life had come to her that evening in Nettie Struther's kitchen.

No: Lily shrank from a little poverty and deprivation to the point of more or less consciously taking an overdose of chloral;

the narrow life even of marriage with Selden on his lawyer's meagre salary would have been impossible for her.

The question the novelist doesn't tackle is how detrimental to Lily her innocence was – girls were bred to innocence in a Victorian society and were protected by conventions of behaviour towards them which preserved this till marriage and even afterwards in essence. In an Edwardian society this had become difficult to maintain as the conventions broke down with the rise of an ungentlemanly class and the claims of girls to 'amusement' before marriage of a more exciting kind than girls had previously been allowed, as well as their forming friendships with married women who 'initiated' them, as James notes of Nanda's friendship for the undesirable Tishy Grendon. Dickens had noted that the scheming woman in shady circles on the edge of Society, like Mrs Lammle, is similarly undesirable as a friend for the innocent Georgiana Podsnap, but in her society protection was inevitable and her parents are duly informed of her peril, in addition Mr Boffin has an eye on her at a critical moment. Nanda's mamma is deplorable not only for her own sinister designs on gentlemen of her circle, both financial and amatory, but in not saving her daughter from such threats to her innocence, and this exposure, though she is technically and morally innocent, is shown as spoiling her for the existing marriage market, when the man she loves, though morally reprehensible himself sexually, can't be bribed to marry her because she has lost her bloom for him, while the excellent and intelligent man who would willingly marry her, she can't bring herself to accept in spite of her affection for him and knowledge of his worthiness *because* he is willing to accept her deprived of her 'innocence'. Lily is innocent only in the sense of being ignorant of what her behaviour implies and will bring down on her. She more or less consciously uses her privilege as an innocent girl to protect herself from the consequences of her self-indulgences and a strategy for manipulating men, a recurrent situation in novels of Edwardian societies.

❦ The French novel

I am not going to give a historical survey of the French novel, nor to analyse all or even many of its best novels, which would be impossible in the short time I have. What I am doing in each of these lectures is to try to isolate a sequence of novels characteristic of the nation and so representative of its tradition thus established and to raise as required some of the social, political, economic, intellectual, historical and other changes which may be considered to have determined the nature and quality of the constituents of that tradition. The fact that the work of the novelist more than that of any other kind of artist, is partly determined by the age he lives in and his relation to it as well as by his personal experiences as a feeling, thinking individual – this fact should be a commonplace in studying a novel. I take the French novel tradition to be, like the English, normative, though a norm of the European whereas the English is essentially an insular, independent product, tied in each case to a unique social and political history, which evolved a tradition naturally by accretion and generally unconsciously in response to national development.

As I have previously argued, the English novel was originated by and developed for a middle-class urban public and a cultivated aristocracy in the eighteenth century, and it was a very fluid society where the middle class, unlike Germany and other European countries, constantly married into or otherwise rose into the aristocracy and where the younger brothers of aristocratic families were traditionally, ever since the Middle Ages, able to enter all professions and become merchants, without incurring social disability, and where the landowners traditionally lived on their estates for most of the year and in contact with their tenants of all grades, making local communities centring on the great house and parsonage complex, ideal for

216

a novelist needing a microcosm of society for his purposes. But this was the English system. The French system of the seventeenth and eighteenth centuries meant a court culture, creative artists dependent on aristocratic patronage, an aristocracy who were mainly absentee landlords, and a privileged society cut off from the values and disciplines of work. Thus the novelists had necessarily a predisposition to concentrate on an analysis of aristocratic conduct and manners and the artifices and refinements of feeling associated with courtly love, and tended to be of this class themselves. Hence a novel like *La Princesse de Clèves*, quite a native product and inconceivable in English at that or any other date, but a tradition persisting to the end of that courtly life, as seen for example in Laclos's *Les Liaisons dangereuses* and even long after the Revolution had swept the world of both away, was still a preoccupation of Stendhal's, and an important constituent of his novels. Such novels were characteristically written in letter form, the development of the letter being an aristocratic literary pastime, as the classical collections of letters by famous French writers of both sexes prove. Rousseau, though an original thinker, and a revolutionary one, wrote his novel, *La Nouvelle Héloïse*, like Laclos's novel, in letters, as a variation on the theme of investigating love as an absolute and the morality of love. *Les Liaisons dangereuses* had already specialized in a wholly French line, which we might call the morbidity or philosophy of love or the pursuit of sex and lust as an end in life, something that was outside the English novelist's interest and pursuit until this generation. The other strain in the classical French novel was contributed by the unpleasant realities of court life and its psychological pressures, which we see in the realism of Saint-Simon's *Mémoires* and the cynical *Maximes* of La Rochefoucauld which formed the social realities of so many eighteenth-century novels even in England. This fed into the French novel that wittily expressed fascination with the meanness and hypocrisies of man as a social entity which powers so many important French novels – Stendhal's, Balzac's, Maupassant's and Flaubert's for instance and even those of a Catholic novelist like Mauriac and is the preoccupation of Proust so much later – an absolute disillusionment with human nature that cannot be paralleled in eighteenth- and nineteenth-century English fiction. In Stendhal it takes the form of combining a sceptical realism as regards human nature with the other French strain, that of the analysis of aristocratic love (that is love in persons of refined mind and polite manners) – which implies a suspension of disbelief in idealism, a very French illogicality. Stendhal's other inconsistency is his admiration for Napoleon, seeing him (as we find with surprise at the opening of *La Chartreuse de Parme*) as a great liberator of Europe – not at all 'the Corsican tyrant' of English history. This boyish enthusiasm for *la gloire* where we would expect a realist's cold eye cast on mass murder to achieve the conquest of Europe, is also a French theme, even with novelists who, unlike Stendhal, had not been in the field with Napoleon (or anyone else), – a point of view instinctive, one supposes, in a country of successive revolutions and changes of government. England had had sufficient experience of revolution and civil war far back in its seventeenth century and since the restoration of Charles II the remembrance of that previous catastrophe has caused a tradition to this day of our revolution, whether political or social, being bloodless and generally gradual and shared by consensus. Thus the English novelists have been much less engaged politically than French novelists and no major English novelist has cared to associate himself with iconoclastic social theories, even of those who supported radical party politics.

To distinguish French from English even at the point where they are nearest: nothing could be further from the tone and spirit of Voltaire's neo-classic novel *Candide* than its exact contemporary, Dr Johnson's *Rasselas*. Similarly the Regency period in England was much closer to France in some ways than England was at any later time in the nineteenth century, and parts of most of Disraeli's novels, and his novel *Coningsby* as a whole, are remarkably like Stendhal (though I don't think it has ever been remarked) in centring on aristocratic society and seeing the whole social scene from an aristocratic point of view, and also in analysing its conduct and other character-istics with caustic wit (a French wit and not English humour, running in the French way to epigrams, sexual license and intellectual high spirits). But though Disraeli may have just had time to read Stendhal's novels before writing *Coningsby* and *Sybil* (there is no objective evidence that he did, unfortunately) – even if he *had* read Stendhal's novels, and even though he had the same enthusiasm for youth (noble youth that is) and respect for romantic love and its idealism, combined with this

psychological scepticism, all as in Stendhal, Disraeli is in the
end very different from Stendhal. To Stendhal the lower orders
exist only as devoted servants or as workmen for the aristocracy,
or are mere brutish peasants, and the bourgeoisie he felt to be
morally and spiritually worse than distasteful. No doubt such
was the nature of the reactionary Bourbon restoration after
Napoleon's downfall; and Stendhal was not a snob, but he saw
the aristocracy as the only remaining repository of a life-style
at once happy, refined and consciously individual. Disraeli was
living in a rapidly expanding as well as changing England and
no less than the other Victorian novelists I've mentioned did
he and his novels take a responsible attitude to the problems
of raising the condition of the workers and striving to achieve
social justice. And his – the English – attitude to the rising
middle class (ever since Defoe had proudly enunciated it at
the opening of *Robinson Crusoe*) was that they were the backbone
of the country's commercial prosperity and responsible for its
inventions in industry and that inter-marriage with the landed
gentry and nobility was beneficial to both sides. The compassion
for the underdogs so unfailing in Fielding's novels, as later in
Dickens's and George Eliot's, was also a characteristic of the
English novel and a development of the social conscience
promoted by Protestantism. The Catholic tradition of France
can almost be said to have had no effect on the novel and even
tributes to the Jansenist type of moral character are marginal
as in Stendhal's *Le Rouge et le Noir*. For one thing, the French
novel was necessarily written in the language of the court and
its subsequent classical stylistic development. If this meant a
gain in clarity, wit and elegance, it may be argued that it
meant also a limitation. My husband used to say that something seemed to him to have gone wrong with the development
of the French language between Rabelais and Racine, what
that was being in short the idea of the Académie Française.
One sees in Rabelais not only an uninhibited vocabulary and
freedom with language but also a rejoicing in its creative
potentialities, whereas Racine's genius is fatally restricted (to
Shakespeare's countrymen) by the narrow range of vocabulary
Racine permits himself or felt able to use, and one is only less
aware of this in French novelists because they rarely attempted
in fiction to enter the territory of tragedy, a territory open to
the English, Irish and Russian novel traditions, with their

highly developed, rich languages that were always in touch with the language of the people.

When the French novel ceased, in the nature of things, to be aristocratic in its preoccupations and style, it was taken over by the intellectuals who played an important part in French revolutions, and French intellectuals have always been a formidable race, setting up their scholars and drawing up principles and theories antecedent to practice, the opposite to the pragmatic English attitude to novel-writing. But whether because of a misguided theory, or because of the nature of French schooling with its insistence on some philosophic training and analysis of a literary work which extracts the apparent philosophic content for discussion and throws away the rest of the work of art, or because French intellectuals collected together in nineteenth- and twentieth-century Paris and lived in isolation from the real life of their country, whereas English eighteenth- and nineteenth-century novelists identified with the nation and lived it first-hand, the products of the French realists and still more of the naturalists strike an English reader as theoretic and lacking in something essential – humanity, perhaps. The naturalists were obliged by their theory to take an attitude to their subject matter that is inhuman – so that even Balzac and still less Zola in spite of their ambitions, couldn't do for their nation what Scott did for Scotland and Dickens for England or Tolstoy for Russia. *Madame Bovary* though a remarkable piece of writing and construction is spiritually desiccating and Flaubert's other novels even more so. Balzac is happiest, we can't help seeing, in pinning down the self-destructive and anarchic tendencies of human beings, their cruelty and even unmotivated animus to neighbours and close relatives; it is significant that while he is horrifyingly successful with depraved and evil characters he is unable to make his virtuous characters interesting or even plausible if they are not merely pathetic like Eugénie Grandet – suffering at the hands of others, not actively taking a stand to support the values they profess. The theme of *Le Lys dans la Vallée* is a very odd offer to a good woman. This is a defect he is unaware of but it is a considerable drawback to a novelist with such pretensions as the author of *La Comédie humaine*. We see why Victorian novelists like Charlotte Brontë, Dickens and

George Eliot all disliked the novels of Balzac and had no use
for him.

Another distinctive characteristic of the French novel is that
in spite of the French Revolutions and the declaration of the
Rights of Man etc., the re-establishment of the peasants on
the land and relevant changes in administration and laws, the
revolution turned out to be middle-class as regards literature
and residually aristocratic in social ideals and urban in
sympathies. The post-revolution novelists seem to have made
no equivalent to the realization of peasant life in other
European countries such as Turgenev's and Tolstoy's in Russia,
Verga's in Sicily, in England in the novels of George Eliot and
Emily Brontë and Hardy, and in Scotland in the novels of Scott
and Galt for example. Balzac admitted he in fact did not
understand the mind of the peasant, and Zola, even worse off,
was the child of an Italian family that settled in France – he
systematically assembled *data* for the purpose in notebooks.
George Sand's *romans rustiques* in the 1840s are pastoral idylls
with an artificial appearance of capturing the alleged patois
of her native countryside, and she volunteered that she too had
no idea of what peasants thought and felt, she worked by fancy
and it comes out as romance, though, like Hardy's Wessex
novels, she also notes for us rustic ceremonies and archaic
practices and beliefs of interest to antiquarians. Her remoteness
is the more surprising since she, the grandchild of the great
house, used, she says, as a child to play with the peasant
children and go into the fields with them with their flocks and
herds all day. Later training cut her off, it seems, and she
became a renowned figure in the revolutionary intellectual
world of French letters, in short, a member of the avant-garde,
a character we hardly know of in English letters until
Bloomsbury. George Eliot, whose life followed a similar pattern
to George Sand's, retained, like Hardy, and so many other
English novelists, those earlier associations and memories which
nourished an art not cut off from its roots. But a novel like
Fromentin's *Dominique*, a genuine if minor French nineteenth-
century classic (dedicated to George Sand), is centred on the
life of the aristocratic master of a country-house, but more than
half of it is devoted to his account of the abortive passionate
love of his early life and the rest to his resignation to the

second-best – subdued contentment in his domestic life and the round of duties in running his estate. The peasants and servants who surround him are shadowy figures, a background frieze playing no part in the theme though they are supposed to sustain him whereas, in an English or Scottish novel, they would be fully realized and take part in the action. One sees why England, where the squire played cricket on the village green with his tenants, the blacksmith and the villagers, was the envy and astonishment of Europe. This inter-penetration of classes in England was a great asset to the novelist, but traditionally from *Piers Plowman* the voice of the English peasant was heard in English literature, and England gave to the world the name as well as the concept of folk-lore. Yet without such a tradition Verga, unlike any major French novelists, when *his* family took him, a schoolboy, for two years to their country property in the interior of Sicily, recorded this experience as very important for him: 'I took part in the life of the peasants and had close companions of my own age whose background and characters impressed me deeply. I became very fond of those courageous people I used to see every day, and became involved in their dramas of passion and distress. Instinctively, I tried to understand them. Much later, those impressions of my youth returned with tremendous vividness, and I tried to hold them fast.' In fact, they were the origin of his best work – the novels of French type he tried first were inferior. It seems that such roots in the culture of the peasantry must be struck in one's formative period and depend, for their use to a writer, on sympathies which subsequently are not eradicated by an intellectual system. Pushkin, who was impressed not only by the Russian oral literature but the characteristics of the Russian peasants themselves and owed so much to his nurse in affection and inspiration, said he wanted his novel *Eugene Onegin* to be 'earthy' and 'folk-simple', importing into a novel of town and country-house life the values of the peasant culture as touchstones and wrote a novel which is not at all simple.

Thus *Middlemarch* is characteristically English in its conception of the personal history and development of the central character or cluster of characters who are shown to be an organic part of a total society – a society revealed from top to bottom and all characters shown as mutually dependent and as affected by the rest, and all equally seen with respect and compassion. This is true also of Dickens, of course. But Stendhal's great novel, *Le Rouge et le Noir*, is utterly unEnglish in its absence of respect for social order and in being without any idealistic weakness for human nature or natural ties. His hero, Julien Sorel, is a prosperous peasant's son but he is an *âme supérieure* and has acquired a hero-worship for Napoleon from an old soldier as well as Latin from the old priest, the only people he loves and respects. His family despises him as a weakling and ill-treats him, and we see nothing of any favourable side of the peasant *milieu*; the presumption is it had none. Julien escapes from it without regret by the whim of the local rich man, a snob, who sees in him a possible resident tutor for his little boys – a means of giving the family an aristocratic status. This kind of process is repeated, Julien climbing the social ladder by a series of ironic accidents from one world to another of French society which appears to have no overlap or reaction between the classes, strictly stratified as in Germany also. It is the very unattractive reactionary world of the Bourbon restoration after Napoleon's downfall and its odiousness, equal though different in each sphere, which is the justification for Julien's (to us) morally contemptible behaviour in each phase of his ascent. He remains loyal to his ardour for Napoleon and all he stood for, but the necessity to hide this in the new order of Church and Throne imposes on him a perpetual hypocrisy which he feels justified in maintaining by his increasing contempt for his contemporaries of all ranks as he gets to know them. He feels superior successively to the peasants, the bourgeoisie, the powers of the Church establishment and the young aristocrats, who have, unlike him, power deriving from property, money, birth and rank or office, basely acquired, and he therefore feels justified in deceiving *them* and profiting by his superior intelligence and tremendous napoleonic will-power. Thus he acquires perforce a philosophy of life and a strategy of action, which is to bring him to the top where he feels he rightly belongs, though in the process of doing so he deteriorates to the point where, with all the success he desired within his grasp, he finds that it is worthless to him and destroys himself through the eclipse of will. The knowledge that if he had been born earlier, under Napoleon, when all careers were open to talent and every soldier carried a field-marshal's baton in his knapsack, his path to success would have been guiltless and the success, *la gloire*, honourable, is an irony that has embittered him from the start. For after the Bourbon restoration there is seen to be no alternative to baseness and injustice except failure, or mediocrity which Julien refuses to accept as his lot, failure such as that of the disinterested Jansenist priest who is driven out of his place as head of the seminary by the enmity his virtues arouse. Between his spell in the rich bourgeoisie and that in the aristocracy, Julien samples the seminary as a means of self-promotion: he finds it to be only a microcosm of the France outside it, managed like that by hypocrisy and intrigue, arbitrary injustice, and hatred of anyone of superior ability or character. Of course this is Rochefoucauldian analysis, and the seminary becomes a model of the world. Julien, who appeals to women because of his apparent innocence and need for help, sees them only as a way of proving to himself his will is dominating, and he – never having known family love – cold-bloodedly embarks on love affairs with his first patron's innocent young wife, the mother of his pupils, and his later benefactor the Marquis's beautiful proud daughter whom he seduces though he dislikes her and thus forces the Marquis to agree to their marriage, with Julien's establishment in life as a nobleman. At the summit of his hopes Julien's downfall takes place – this, which would have been seen as a triumph of moral judgment in an English novel, a nemesis richly deserved and no tragedy – is presented by Stendhal as a last injustice to the napoleonic hero, though he has shot, with intention to kill, his first mistress for having, under orders from her confessor, written to the Marquis enlightening him as to this episode in his future son-in-law's earlier life, a letter which has precipitated the crash of Julien's ambitions. The underwriting of Julien as hero by the author is even heightened by Julien's subsequent attitude to prison, trial and impending execution: he despises the corrupt and stupid jury whom he sees as typical of society – the trial and court provide another model of French society – and will not assent to any steps by his friends and his mistress, though she is about to bear his child, any steps to secure his acquittal, because he is by now bored with the beautiful aristocratic Mathilde's adoration which he suspects to be self-deception and, resolute in superiority and detachment, he prefers death

to living in the France he has found it to be. The remarkable
psychological study, impressive in its consistency and insight, the
wit and the refusal to soften or excuse or overlook anything
whatever in anyone, is a triumph of the classical French novel.

Theology, we note, plays an important part in Stendhal's
novels as in those of our Victorians. The French Revolution,
preceded by the enlightenment of the encyclopaedists, brought
into being an environment of atheistic philosophy antagonistic
to religion which created tension between the Catholic Church
and progressive thinking in politics, philosophy and religion
which necessarily put the Church on the side of reaction, the
novelists ranging themselves on one side or the other. The
differences were more extreme than those in England between
High and Low Church or Protestant and Catholic, more
resembling those in our seventeenth century between Cavalier
and Roundhead where the difference consisted in invincible
religious, political and social positions. There was thus plenty
of tension in French life and thought to provide novelists with
subject-matter of the deepest concern to all, and in national
history the pride of a successful revolution of the people
followed by Napoleon's achievement of conquering Western
Europe.

A novel such as *Le Rouge et le Noir* shows how a major novel
of the nineteenth century with different material and traditions
nevertheless found a form comparable to that of the major
English nineteenth-century novels (such as *Middlemarch, Bleak
House, Little Dorrit*), though, *la logique* being a French characteristic, its method is to work through successive stages in
demonstrating the theme, rather than stating the theme
dramatically at the opening (as in the English) and developing
it simultaneously in different fields shown to be indivisible
socially.

This novel is not a sport; but one example of the tradition
so peculiar to France and bound up with its history, in this
case adapted to the special circumstances of France after
Napoleon's defeat. Its descendants can be seen to be on one
side in such a novel as Maupassant's *Bel Ami*, the history of
a cad who systematically exploits his amatory appeal to women
and moreover without any come-uppance. He is one of life's
successes, in fact. This is a diminished adaptation, not a
development, of Stendhal and the French tradition of

examining the psychology of sex. Another and more interesting descendant which is a real development of the Stendhal tradition is Camus's first novel *L'Étranger* (*The Outsider*), which starts its thinking where *Le Rouge et le Noir* left off, over a century later than Stendhal's; it is adapted also to the special circumstances of the author's native French North Africa, where the blinding sun and the French colonial mentality in a surrounding despised and feared Arab population are the determining factors. If Julien Sorel was justified in his belief that even a crime such as murder as well as moral sins, like his callous use of women who love him and rejection of family ties and loyalty, can be committed by a man who is nevertheless self-respecting, then what would happen if a man decided to live his whole life by this principle deliberately? For instance, Meursault has no feeling for his mother (thus violating a sacred French value), puts her into a home for the aged and does not visit her and when obliged to attend her funeral refuses to go through any of the motions expected on such an occasion as normal, since he feels nothing and believes hypocrisy is the real sin. He will not compromise with the human code in any respect. For instance he responds to his young mistress who wants to make the relation a real and permanent one through marriage by saying that marriage isn't serious, that is, he refuses to admit that love is more than sex or that religion and morality are real – or that life can't be lived by a man as a separate entity: Meursault's position is that of the uncompromising solipsist, who is nothing, we see, but a callous hedonist. His course is marked out in human terms by Camus with all the intelligence and systematic consistency of a French intellectual with a university degree in philosophy. Meursault's quarrel is really with the conditions for living as a human being anywhere and at any time and it leads him inevitably to prison and trial for wilful murder of an Arab. He can explain away all the events that were manifestations of his honesty, that are cited to look black against him in the trial and, convicted, *he* convicts society as unjust and hypocritical, refuses either to see priests or to answer his mistress's letters and feels quite happy awaiting execution in prison in the remembrance of his past happinesses which are recalled as entirely sensual. The solipsist is a man without a soul, we see. But Camus's introduction to the third edition of *L'Étranger* asserts that Meursault is not a monster but simply a man who won't play society's game by subscribing to its conventions – he simply, his author says, refuses to lie. Here we have a descendant of Molière's Alceste, a character Molière used to investigate the social nexus and its obligations – George Eliot described *Le Misanthrope* as 'the finest, most complete production *of its kind* in the world'; it must remain a subject of the greatest interest for any novelist, if by a novelist we understand the creative writer who is responsibly concerned for the social individual life of his age and the possibility of achieving happiness and fulfilment. Alceste, like Meursault, refused to accept the obligations of civility and practised uncompromising honesty, thus sacrificing his prospects of happiness and, quite logically, ultimately retiring in disgust to a hermit's life on his estate.

But Alceste was a high-minded man, while Meursault is a blindly selfish one, for he wants other people to exist but only for his own convenience or pleasure, without admitting obligation to them. Yet Camus endorses him to the extent of declaring that his Meursault is a modern Christ, the only one we deserve nowadays, because, he says, Meursault has a passion for the absolute and for truth. Camus was less than thirty when writing this in 1942 – a bad time in French history. If he had written no more novels, or no different ones, would we have considered him a novelist who mattered? *L'Étranger* is far inferior in humanity and art and wisdom to even a minor French classic like Constant's *Adolphe* which is one of its ancestors, I imagine – the analysis in depth of a young gentleman who, in the hope of finding happiness seduces a woman he doesn't love, ruining her life and loading himself with guilt and misery, but in that novel reasons are accounted for as due to his having a cold and ambitious father who is schooling him for a similar political career to his own.

But we know Camus was a true novelist because, as he evolved, he rethought his ideas and arrived at a more mature conception of the problem, giving us half-a-dozen years later an important novel in *La Peste*. Here it is demonstrated that man, though he lives individually, is inescapably a social being, and that he has impulses and needs that can only be called religious.

It is a very moving and complex book as well as one that asks the essential questions that face a writer who had lived through the Second World War. France, like Italy, was occupied by the enemy, and had to cope with many political factions and loss of morale, and its novelists and dramatists rose to the challenge. They asked the necessary questions, the fundamental ones, and allegorized them even before Paris was liberated.

The epigraph, from Defoe, states that it is quite reasonable to represent one kind of imprisonment by another. This alerts us to the symbolic nature of the setting – the beleaguered city, an ancient image (compare Bunyan's *The Holy War*) – historically, France occupied by Nazis (the plague equals the corruption of Nazism and the rats that carry it are the Nazi officials and the SS men), spiritually, the soul of man beseiged by the Devil, and philosophically, the challenge to any society of the recurrent threat of disintegrating forces – always present somewhere in the world (compare Conrad's *Nostromo*), illustrating the theory of historic cycles of growth and degeneration.

The chief opponent of the plague is the doctor but he needs assistance from all men of goodwill and especially those whose training fits them for it. First Rieux has to contend with officials who don't want the word 'plague' used, which will alarm the populace. He cannot get serum sent from Paris, the hospital arrangements are wholly inadequate. Rieux's allies are Grand who keeps the statistics and a friend, Tarrou (a writer), who collects documents and narratives to compile a history of the town during the plague, though he dies of it when it is nearly over. We learn at the end of the book that it is Rieux who has written this chronicle.

The town is declared in a state of plague and closed, families are separated, everyone, sick or well, is now imprisoned in Oran. The Church orders a week of prayer and puts up a distinguished scholar Jesuit to preach a long sermon explaining the plague is a judgment from God – the faithful need not worry. The Doctor and Tarrou agree in not being able to accept this. Tarrou asks him: 'Why do you show so much devotion to your work if you don't believe in God? Perhaps it will help me in my own case.' The doctor, in reply to Tarrou's questions, admits he doesn't believe in an all-powerful God, for obviously if he did he would leave the sick to Him to cure. As it is, his vocation is to protect people against disease and save them from death – because he can't get used to seeing people die – to save them if possible he puts himself at risk as a matter of course. This is his professional faith. The plague is a desperate defeat for him, but that is no reason for ceasing to fight. The doctor in return asks Tarrou, who insists on accompanying him on his visits to the sick, what makes him concern himself with those things – the writer replies that his 'morale' is the need to understand. The Jesuit joins the volunteer squad to help the doctor – 'I'm glad to know he is better than he believes.' 'Everyone is' says Tarrou. 'All that is necessary is to give them the opportunity.' The journalist Rambert says that though he fought in Spain against Franco, he realizes that it is nothing to have courage and risk one's life for an idea – heroism is easy. The real test is whether one can live and if necessary die for what one *loves* and now people are no longer capable of loving. The modern Christ is now not Meursault but shown in the role of the doctor, a man with a vocation, enduring selflessly in the plague-ridden city, devoted to safeguarding the community's philosophical content, and the characters, though representative – a Jesuit preacher, the doctor, an author, a journalist, a statistician and so on – are fully human and individualized. Many of the scenes are deeply moving and yet in spite of the dramatic and horrifying possibilities of the subject-setting, the telling is always controlled, nothing is exploited. This is achieved by having it written by Rieux, the doctor, with his professional discipline and impersonality. In *La Peste* the religious question is raised by Camus as inescapable, for Camus, like Conrad, is asking 'What do men live by?' – the basic question all serious users of the novel are obliged to consider if not directly then by implication. The author asks Rieux 'Why do you show so much devotion [to the sick] if you don't believe in God?' Rieux says, that to protect people against disease is his vocation because he can't bear to see them, particularly children, dying. If it is possible to save them he must put himself and his family at risk. Thus the creative mind is by its function also obliged to participate in salvation.

As the plague continues, popular morale declines, and arson, looting and immorality spread even to previously decent people. Despair and horror grip them, and religion is replaced by superstition. So Camus is in the best tradition of the French novel in showing no weakness for idealization of the common man – yet Rieux reflects that there is more to *admire* than despise in mankind. The conclusion spelt out for us is that we all carry the plague microbe within us and that health, integrity and goodness can only be achieved by unceasing exertion. What does the plague mean? It's life, that's all. But in spite of such a promising development in Camus, he did not go on like an English or a Russian novelist, to write a number of mature novels. *La Peste* is his last.

Camus's stress on Meursault's social crimes and state of mind in imprisonment is also an important part of the French novelist's contribution to the novel generally and the Russian novel in particular. *Le Rouge et le Noir* with its daring examination of the psychology of the social non-conformist and subsequent criminal, who is also offered as a moral superior to his accusers and who thus constitutes an investigation into the ethics of crime, could only have come at that date from a society that had been the result of a thorough-going revolution, declared the Rights of Man and given birth to the career of a Napoleon, thus questioning 'right' and 'wrong' and arguing the case for moral pragmatism. Hence followed such French novels as Hugo's *Les Misérables* and Dumas's *The Count of Monte Cristo* – exciting and vividly written novels which, immensely and widely read, aroused sympathy for the socially wretched and moral outcasts as victims of poverty and oppression and explore their psychological suffering. Hence Dostoevsky's novels, though of course founded in first-hand experience of the underworld of poverty, vice and crime, explore it on the theorizing systems so congenial to the trained French mind. *Crime and Punishment* starts with the university student with grievances against society committing a dis-interested murder of an old woman, a squalid money-lender and therefore, he feels, a louse living on the blood of the poor – to demonstrate that he rejects the moral judgments of an intolerably unjust social order and carries out justice indepen-dently of the state. But this act of uncompromising logic is shown in an unFrench development, to bring psychological punishment for thus flouting a basic human law. André Gide however developed the idea of the disinterested murder into the *acte gratuit*, as a game of ideas. Malraux, still in the French tradition, starts his novel on the abortive Shanghai revolution,

La Condition humaine, with the moral problem of the right to kill an innocent man in a just cause: the Chinese must nerve himself to murder a sleeping stranger in order to rob him of a document needed by the revolutionaries to secure a shipment of arms – Bakunin's law that in a good cause the end justifies the means.

La Condition humaine was a stirring success at the time it appeared (1933) because the Spanish civil war and Hitler's Germany and Stalin's Russia brought up, for the remaining civilized countries of the Western world, the subject of political violence and what that involved. Malraux who had inspected the Shanghai revolt on the spot and took part as a combatant in the war against Franco was able to serve up the subject of the moment in a new mixture – an exotic orient setting with scenes of bloodshed, torture, and sadistic sex, suspense and violence alternating with philosophic dialogue and ending by laying the blame on international finance, the popular villain of Left-wing thinkers. The novel was eventually made into a popular film, actually an improvement since in the novel the characters are shadow-puppets.

We see the degeneration of the modern French novel even more clearly in Sartre's case, a type of a more recent intellectual than those with a human face like Camus. Sartre declares: 'a technique of narration always involves a novelist's metaphysics. The critic's task is to elucidate the latter [the metaphysics] before appreciating the former.' This is of course doubly fallacious. The content cannot be separated from the form, and the novelist's philosophy can't be extracted from the novel and discussed by itself in isolation. Sartre believes it can because he is essentially uncreative, and what he writes are what I commonly call non-novels. He illustrates negatively my point that a novelist needs to have a well-nourished personal life as well as 'technique' and 'a metaphysic'. For instance, Sartre had no happiness in childhood and he says that the conflict of religions in his household made any religious belief impossible for him. Until the German occupation when he was to spend three months in an internment camp, he had never met any peasants or working men (in spite of his Marxist convictions) and seemed surprised that he found them human and conversable. His novels show a morbid dislike for women and impulses to degrade them. All these disabilities account satisfactorily for the fact that he and other French novelists like him wrote boring lengths of dreary fictions, but only some surprising degeneration of the French reading public made such novels sell so hugely that they made him a millionaire, it appears.

But isn't Sartre's complaint one that too has a French pedigree? One remembers the devotion to the art of the 'novel' by Flaubert and what disappointing results it had. Henry James, for all his admiration for *Madame Bovary* as a piece of art or criticism, felt obliged to stress what he saw to be Flaubert's limitations as a novelist. James concluded that Flaubert's attitude of eternal irony was a *refuge*, and that this ended in the failure of *Bouvard et Pécuchet*. Flaubert's other refuge, James thought, was to run away from the actual, human and new, so that 'he was absolutely and exclusively condemned to irony' – irony not being the appropriate response to man's struggle with fate and circumstance, I take it. James diagnosed Flaubert's situation as 'the comparatively meagre human consciousness struggling with the absolutely large *artistic*'.

It is the meagreness of the human in the contemporary French intellectual novels which, as in the case of Sartre and his kind, does not even have the artistic aim as in Flaubert's case, and is so disabling for the art of the novel, when the novel has been placed at the service of irresponsible political ideas. This abdication of the novelist's function was accompanied by 'turning to America', the United States of the twentieth century, for models instead of developing from the mature ones which were truly French, under the misguided belief that Americans represent the society of the future for Europe. Unfortunately the novels of the cruder American novelists were admired and imitated by up-to-date French and also Italian novelists. The tragedy is that these American models were totally inappropriate to Latin countries with their ancient cultures and totally different historical, social, religious and philosophic traditions. Their effect was to encourage the coarsening of feeling, crudity of thought and extreme cynicism that was the pursuit of the development of modern American society, a mongrel society classless by definition but whose members devoted themselves to the values of a vulgar ideal based on money and success without any of the restraints and doubts of our 'old' societies.

The French situation seems to show that a nation can not only produce a valuable and distinctive tradition of the novel, but also can lose it. This had happened to the dismal American novel tradition. The opposite is true in Russia where to date its great novel tradition has been revived by Pasternak and Solzhenitsyn in response to the creative writers such as Tolstoy and Dostoevsky. In the case of France the decline has been owing, I feel, to the limitations of the French tradition – first as being aristocratic in conception and later as the province of the intellectual theorist for whom philosophic ideas are the animating interest and not life itself experienced in its fullness and seen with humility.

The Russian novel

It's not difficult to establish that there existed a distinctive tradition of the Russian novel in its early classical days – though a late starter by the standards of the other traditions. This Russian tradition was so compelling and so satisfactorily national that it was able to survive the cataclysmic change from its origins in a society with an autocratic ruler and court, an old nobility of landowners supported by a peasantry of serfs, and a very small middle class, and all thoroughly imbued with the Orthodox Greek religion, to the modern communist state professing atheism, scientific materialism, classlessness and the rule of the proletariat: the major novels of post-Revolutionary Russia correspond remarkably with those of the old novelists. In *The First Circle* the conformist novelist of Stalin's Russia (Galakhov) who underwrites the regime volunteers – 'Is there any Russian writer who hasn't at some time secretly tried on Pushkin's frock-coat? or Tolstoy's Russian shirt?' More surprising still, we find that writers who are *not* Russian but are covering some of the ground already occupied by the Russians, have been drawn into the Russian orbit, deserting their own very different novel traditions for this foreign one. I'm thinking of novels like Conrad's *Under Western Eyes* (1911), Koestler's *Darkness at Noon* (1940), Malraux's *La Condition humaine* (1933) and Victor Serge's *The Case of Comrade Tulayev* (1948) – yet Conrad was an anglicized Pole, Koestler Hungarian, Serge a Belgian writing in French and Malraux, of course, French. Tolstoy, Dostoevsky and Turgenev served as models for the form and approach to the human problems these novels had to consider, and also their themes, and this though the Russian classical novelists were themselves originally indebted to French and English novels for their ideas of a novel. A recent biographer of Dostoevsky has declared: 'It is difficult to imagine the kind of writer Dostoevsky might have become had he not known the works of Dickens, Balzac and George Sand. He was more profoundly versed in European literature and more immediately an heir to it than any of his major Russian contemporaries.' Yet isn't it Dostoevsky we think of as the most characteristically Russian of them all? Tolstoy rightly insisted on the uniqueness of the Russian novel: he declared that Russian novels from Pushkin onwards deviate from the European form of the novel – 'the Russian artistic idea', he wrote, 'cannot be fitted into that frame and seeks for itself something new'. This is what the early Irish novelists said about the English novel, and Melville about his American generation.

So the question one asks is: What were the determining factors that decided the Russian novel's evolution? They were of course, speaking generally, the usual ones of political and social history, the nature and quality of its religious and social life, and its literary resources; but one feature we note as exceptional is the comparative lateness of the appearance of the Russian novel compared, that is, with England, France, America and Ireland. It was not that Russia suffered, as did Ireland and nineteenth-century America, from not having a sufficiently large reading-public to support a serious professional novelist: in early-nineteenth-century Russia there was such a demand for novels and even more formidable reading-matter that the gentry – who had had Swiss tutors and English governesses and therefore were able to speak French, German and English – greedily devoured the modern classics of each of these nations, and popular novels such as Dickens's were quickly translated for the Russian market, running as serials in Russian magazines even before being published in book form in Russian.

It was the attitude of inferiority to the progressive Western Europeans that made the Russians look there for culture, and a corresponding denigration of the Russian language as a medium for anything but conversations with servants and peasants, that held back the earlier development, as in other European countries, of a sophisticated native literature. But Russia had an ancient alternative literature in its oral literary tradition of exceptional richness of idiom and variety of kinds, kept alive as a tradition and language by its peasantry and communicated by serf nurses and professional tale-tellers to their landed employers: Count Tolstoy, the novelist's grandfather, bought a serf simply because he was famous for his knowledge of this oral literature and so that he could tell tales to the household – the whole household. The future novelist, we are told, thus fell asleep in childhood to the stories of folk-lore in prose and verse. It was the wave of nationalism that accompanied the European Romantic movement in literature and the discovery of folk-lore as literature by Scott, the brothers Grimm and others, and its cult in Europe, that made Pushkin turn to these native sources of inspiration when he and his circle decided Russia must have a national literature, which patriotic pride after the defeat of Napolean now demanded. But Pushkin, like Tolstoy and other Russian creative minds of the nineteenth century, looked to these sources not as antiquarian collectors as the folklorists did, but because they had in childhood received, like Scott, and the Irish novelists, but unlike the French, indelible impressions of the delight and imaginative stimulus in folk-literature, folk-music and folk-ways.

Russia was fortunate in having at this point in history a creative mind like Pushkin's – his was an exceptional intelligence in all matters bearing on literature, seeing, for instance, that literary and critical periodicals were necessary to educate a reading-public for supporting a literature. Thanks to the combination of an education in the literature of Western Europe *and* his emotional attachment to his nurse, a serf of course, who fed him with folk-lore all his life, and to the Russian countryside and all that this meant aesthetically, he was able to synthesize these opposing strains, and his novel *Eugene Onegin* (1830) dramatizes them. This was a theme so truly representative for Russians that it was adopted by all his immediate successors. It seems to me a great misfortune for Italy that it did not produce any literary figure as able and important as Pushkin or Goethe or the first generation English Romantics, Scott, Wordsworth and Coleridge – produced them, that is, at the right time to nourish and direct its modern literature. Dante of course came far too early for this. America at its outset, as an independent country severed from England, had a combination of high talent, and one determined to work out the form of a representatively national literature – American, not English – in Hawthorne, Fenimore Cooper and Melville, who also evolved a tradition of the novel adopted by their successors.

Pushkin did not understate the problems inherent in his undertaking, as we see from his novels and from his journals and letters. 'How fascinating these stories are', he wrote of the folk-tales. 'Each one is a poem. Nowhere has it been possible to endow our language with this Russian breadth as in a folk-tale.' But, he added, 'What must be done to learn to speak Russian *outside* the folk-tale?' This was the difficulty as the Irish novelists too found. The stylization of oral literary forms in all countries – the ballad, the historical epic, the Märchen, the legends, etc. – had conventionalized appropriate imagery and language, developed unity of narrative and sequences of motifs, and repetitive refrains, and they drew on extra-rational experiences excluded from neo-classical literature, such as dreams, visions and omens, but most of these forms and conventions are not easily adaptable for a sophisticated writer's purposes. Scott's 'Wandering Willie's Tale' in his novel *Redgauntlet* is a brilliant use of the techniques, style and language and the traditional content of the historical legend together with the supernatural elements of the Märchen, but it is a tale within the book, and not integrated into the novel, though the use of a *double entendre* makes it illustrative of Scottish life. Irish novelists have been more successful in working with folk-lore within the novel itself, but at the cost of using the Gothic novel and melodramatic action as the only appropriate container. A better solution was worked out by George Eliot and Emily Brontë who were countrywomen with both educated and folk idioms native to them, and who used these to convey cultural disparities in life-style, and as the cause of conflict. We see that something corresponding to this was adopted for *Eugene Onegin* and *Anna Karenina*. A biographer of Pushkin says this inspiration from the folklore 'was the balancing factor to the classical and French influences to which Pushkin was subject in his formal education, and it provided the impetus he needed to establish Russian as a literary language'. This situation is so important for literature, music and opera that we see Mussorgsky, for instance, who was born in 1839, declaring in his autobiography that it was through the influence of his nurse that he became familiar with the old Russian tales and that it was his familiarity with the very spirit of the life of the people that impelled him to extemporize music and made him aspire to write a music 'grown on our own country's soil and nurtured on Russian bread', thus escaping from what he described as the 'routine of international classical music'. In *Of Men and Music*, Mosco Corner the musicologist argues as to Dvořák's greatest work, his instrumental music, that Dvořák had two roots – the Viennese classical school, and the folk-music of *his* country and that of some other Slavonic nations; and that the classical influence was *intellectual*, but the other acted as a strong fertilizer on his melodic and rhythmic imagination. This suggests the radical contribution that can be made by the folk traditions to a sophisticated art, and indeed seems almost necessary to produce a great literature. We see the combination, in Shakespeare's plays as in those of other Elizabethans, of the classical and folk elements working together.

This applies still more to the language of the Russian novels. Pushkin discovered that, as he wrote, 'The daily speech of the common people is worthy of the deepest research', and he wished to bring into use for literature all the resources of the spoken Russian language. Earlier printed literature had used an artificial abstract style, Church Slavonic, produced for the purposes of theology and government. 'Our literature started suddenly in the eighteenth century', Pushkin wrote, but his mastery of spoken Russian established a new tradition. We can see it followed by Tolstoy in *War and Peace* where, Professor R. F. Christian tells us, the language of Tolstoy's soldiers and peasants is 'rich in colloquial words and idioms', while the language of country sports and country occupations is full of words not in the standard dictionaries at all. This constant renewal of the language of literature from the coinages and practice of those who have escaped the standardization of education is still occurring in Russian. 'To Solzhenitsyn, at a critical period of his development, the peasant woman's rearrangement of the commonplace building bricks of language into her own unselfconscious patterns exposed the very roots of the Russian language. The moment he heard her, he knew that he had arrived in the one place on earth where he would be able to graft his own literary language on to those deep roots. The freshness of Solzhenitsyn's prose derives from its unforced use of the hidden resources of the language.'

In 1965 Solzhenitsyn wrote an article by invitation on the development of the Russian language. Careful listening to peasant speech was only the first phase of his craft of writing. He wanted the vast potential of the Russian language for creative expressiveness developed, and urged the restoration of intrinsically Russian structures against the draining of its vigour by newspapers and bureaucrats' language. He specified as models 'the special liveliness which calls to us from Russian proverbs'. Andrei Sinyavsky, given a seven-year spell in imprisonment in 1965 for obstinate dissidence, published a remarkable work, *A Voice from the Chorus* (1976), drawn from the fortnightly letters he wrote to his wife from his labour-camp, recording his thoughts and feelings and his observation of the other prisoners. The voice is that of the poet and literary critic, but it is accompanied by snatches of anonymous prisoners' speech – in proverbs, comments on life, disputes, thieves' slang, the religious idiom of the old believers' popular and folk verses, bits of their conversation, newspaper jargon rehashed by the uneducated mind, and the inspired verbal orations of the tramps, common criminals, peasants and mechanics with whom he had to live, work and make friends. Sinyavsky found in their conversations poetry, tragedy, comedy and wisdom. His book is not a novel for it has no plot and no defined characters, but it is a potential novel – the raw material of a novel like Turgenev's *A Sportman's Sketches* – and it registers an element for lack of which literature dies, the voice of what Turgenev called 'Anonymous Russia', which has been brought into the Russian novel successfully. Margaret Mead, the American anthropologist, wrote some time ago with apprehension of the development of the language used by Americans, saying it had become no longer suitable to support a literature – it had become, she said, 'a one-dimensional public language, a language oriented in the description of external aspects of behaviour, weak in overtones'. And she complained also that modern American words 'lack the formal precision which comes from awareness of past and different usage'; that is, a language with no feeling for words and their historical associations. One sees this impoverishment in modern American fiction, among other places; it is a language invented for the purposes of journalists, politicians, trade-union officials, advertising and television, and we see how in England it has superseded the traditional spoken language and an American's ability to respond to English literature fully. Even more interesting is that Tolstoy remarked to Gorky: 'How will the peasants *compose* stories! Everything is simple, the words are few, and a great deal of feeling. Real wisdom uses few words.' He thus wrote his twenty-three tales on that model. We remember the help through such means given to Pierre Bezukhov by the peasant Karatayev in *War and Peace*, at a crisis of his life in the battle of Moscow. Solzhenitsyn recalls a similar truth in *The First Circle* when Nérzhin, a mathematician, hears the peasant Spiridon tell his life-story through the Revolution and Civil Wars and found there the basis for a radical rethinking of his views about life. Russian writers – and many of them, like Dostoevsky and Solzhenitsyn and Sinyavsky, have spent ten years in prison or exile from the centres of urban life – thus have become acquainted with a national reality of which the Russia of the drawing-room and study was only the superstructure, saving Russian literature from inanition. A drawback for the classical Russian novelists was that they had initially the disadvantage of an educated class that spoke French and thought in French. Dostoevsky, pillorying the man of letters whom he sees as abnegating his function, has him admit that 'we Russians don't know how to say anything in our own language' to explain why he quotes Pascal and other French writers instead of expressing his own ideas and in his own tongue. And though of course Stepan Trofimovich Verkhovensky is a figure of fun on the whole, he must have been plausible in the generation up to 1871, when *The Possessed* appeared.

Thus Pushkin was inspired to build his novel in verse, *Eugene Onegin* which took him eight years to write, on a basis of the contrasts, in character and setting, of the two Russias which we see perpetually recurring in Russian literature, the underlying tensions giving rise and force to a drama of action, and to a series of tragic situations due to the social conventions of the fashionable world. The tension is between the life of St Petersburg the court capital, fashionable and western-orientated, and the traditional life-style of the Russian countryside. From the capital comes the blasé Eugene Onegin to try his country estate as a relief from boredom and love-affairs, whereupon he makes friends with a younger neighbour Lensky, the typical Russian product of the period of the German university in the *Sturm und Drang* romantic phase. Lensky takes him to visit a country-house where live his fiancée Olga and her sister Tatyana with their widowed mother, and here Onegin encounters the peaceful round of neighbourliness and country pursuits relieved by books and music and love of nature. Tatyana inevitably falls in love with the aloof mysterious Onegin and being a Russian country girl of character – spontaneous, ardent and independent of convention – writes to tell him so. Onegin behaves well by his standards – he only consoles her by explaining he has no vocation for marriage and she would bore him. As a relief he flirts with her sister which results in a challenge from Lensky, furious at his friend's disloyalty. Onegin has no wish to fight Lensky, but the conventions oblige him to accept the pointless duel and Lensky falls dead in the snow, loading Onegin with guilt and remorse. He therefore goes abroad. Returning from his travels after a few years he is much struck at a ball in the capital by a great lady courted and deferred to by everyone and eventually recognizes in her Tatyana, now a beauty, a princess and a general's wife, the general being Onegin's cousin. The situation is now reversed, for Onegin falls in love with her – she, being now a married woman, is suitable for a conquest (we see the same situation in Vronsky's relation first with the young girl in Moscow, Kitty, and then with Anna, Karenin's wife at St Petersburg). But though Tatyana has only married to please her mother and still loves Onegin, she has not been corrupted by society life, nor is she romantic. Like Pushkin she has read Richardson and admires his Clarissa and like her tells her sister that though she still loves him she loves honesty more and will be a loyal wife – he has come too late; he is dismissed for ever and like Richardson's Lovelace he realizes that in his egotism and vanity he had thrown away his only chance of happiness. We are left to conclude that the true Russian qualities exist in the life of the countryside and not in the artificial world of St Petersburg, corrupted by cosmopolitan fashion. Pushkin registered for his posterity that 'living model' that Sinyavsky says is all important for the artist to discover – 'a life that corresponds to his thoughts. He looks at this country and he says "Mine!"' And Pushkin fixed some other notable characteristics of the Russian model – he both made his novel 'earthy' and 'folk-simple' in the language he used, but combined it with wit and intellectual originality, and high spirits playing over and around the tragedies. We see these qualities surviving into Solzhenitsyn's novels.

Pushkin's countryside versus capital, with their contrasting types of misguided, unhappy court-dandy and country-bred girls who became their victims, were taken over by Pushkin's admirer Lermontov in his remarkable novel *A Hero of Our Time* and passed on to Tolstoy (e.g. originally in his novella *Family Happiness* and in *Anna Karenina*), but Lermontov extended Pushkin's model by adding violent elements and actuating them in a suitable setting, the Caucasus with its mountain peaks, wild landscape and wilder native tribes. The hero of the ironic title is Pechorin, an army officer and a tougher type than Eugene, and explored as a case-history for his callousness and perverse cruelties.

In these novels – and in all the classical Russian novelists – we hardly meet any characters between gentry and servants or peasants except government officials. This illustrates other differences between the Russian novel and those of other countries in the nineteenth century – Madame de Staël recorded the absence in Russia of an educated middle class which, as she said, is the usual class from which artists sprang in other countries. It is also a class which novels in other countries were written for as well as about. Pushkin was noticing a related fact when he said that in Russia then literature was mainly the occupation of noblemen. The objection to this is that noblemen are essentially *amateurs* and don't practise literature as a profession. Pushkin himself was professional in spirit and intention but his domestic troubles and his compulsory court-duties distracted him and in fact brought about his early death, like Lensky's; and Lermontov's life was even shorter before the inevitable duel ended it. By the time Turgenev wrote *Fathers and Sons*, the next significant Russian novel, it was 1862, and the work of Tolstoy and Dostoevsky was still to come, whereas in France and England many major novelists had long been at work or finished it. Thus the Russian novel was comparatively late in arriving at fruition, but it had benefitted by using the results of the pioneer work already done by English and French novelists. But the Russians could use the novelists of Western Europe successfully because the Russians were truly creative minds and were not the second-rate novelists, described by Lawrence as 'old imitators', who write pastiches or who go on writing the same novel all their lives. Tolstoy said that but for Stendhal and Scott he could not have written his historical novel – but *War and Peace* is not a copy of either. A young man in *Cancer Ward* trying to find something to read in hospital writes 'In the last century there had been only ten Russian novelists, all of them great', but that in his Russia 'there were thousands, and when you did read one, it was as if you might just as well not have done. Nearly any book of any size got a prize the year after it appeared, then sank back for ever.' (Of course only novels passed by the state censorship get published unless smuggled abroad in manuscript.)

Pushkin and Lermontov, whose lives were cut short, wrote single novels, but the next generation (born in Pushkin's lifetime) wrote prose capable of many and large undertakings. In a country so obviously backward and badly managed, idealistic members of the younger generation were prompted by their university education and reading of progressive Western theorists to wish to import scientific, economic, political and social reforms, doomed to failure and tending from frustration to produce anarchic action versus authority. Turgenev, like Dostoevsky, saw the dangers and the potential tragedy. He selected for his finest novel this theme. *Fathers and Sons* opens with the return from the university to the country-house of the son of the house, Arkady, who is accompanied by his friend, a young doctor Bazarov whose lower-class manners deliberately challenge the code of his friend's aristocratic uncle, and is a trial to Arkady's admirable father. Bazarov intends to devote his life to promoting science and medicine and denies the existence of all values not utilitarian – he reduces love to sex, rejects natural piety, religion, poetry, tradition and all sentiment. But he is angry at finding himself human – unable to resist falling in love with a beautiful young widow because he finds he must 'recognize idealism in himself' and suffers because she has no use for him. He takes Arkady with him to pay a long-postponed visit to his old parents living in primitive Russian simplicity and who adore their only child but dare not show it as he is embarrassed by their affection and has nothing to say to them – a situation shown as painful in the extreme. Arkady, who is tolerant and inclined to be happy, marries a nice girl, the sister of Bazarov's love and is obviously going to be a more enlightened version of his father. Bazarov however dies of an infection in the course of his duties as a doctor leaving his parents heartbroken and knowing his life has been one of personal failure. Turgenev shows that the doctrine of scientific materialism in denying full humanity is a dangerous basis for a revolution or for any programme of social change, and we must appreciate the delicacy and economy with which he illustrates these truths and how evenly he holds the artistic balance between the generations and the classes, for Turgenev has much sympathy with Bazarov who is a kind of hero of his time without using Lermontov's phrase in the ironical sense. Bazarov has no personal ambitions but wishes to devote himself to improving the life and health of the peasants (who don't take to him) and furthering medical research for the sake of humanity – 'A good chemist is twenty times more useful than a poet', he says. Turgenev really admires his altruism while seeing the fallacies of the position he has taken up and its dangers since the Bazarovs were the new men, ripe to be recruited by anarchist societies and pointing forward to the Marxist–Leninist state that took over the 1917 Revolution. Turgenev's, Tolstoy's and Dostoevsky's greatness lay in the fact that they saw the novelist's function as a responsibility and an opportunity – like D. H. Lawrence they could say 'I write for the race' and like Solzhenitsyn they could be called 'the conscience of Russia'. Solzhenitsyn in this tradition wrote that a novelist has the ability to inform society 'of all that is unhealthy and cause for anxiety' and that 'this is his duty'. 'A writer who thinks differently from society represents an asset to that society.' And Russia has a splendid history of dissident novelists. 'For a country to have a great writer is like having another government', a character in *The First Circle* decides.

In *Anna Karenina* the tensions are incarnated in St Petersburg, the seat of the court and the centre of bureaucracy, looking westwards culturally, and Moscow, the heartland of Russia, where a society of old-fashioned Russian family life is maintained (Lermontov makes Princess Mary a Moscow girl while Pechorin belongs to the St Petersburg world). The two cities are connected by the railway, a no-man's land where the characters are at the mercy of their impulses, suffer from

nightmares or ominous dreams and where the disasters thus
foreseen eventually occur; the reader is haunted like the main
actors in the tragedy, by the peasant railway workman with
the sack on his back who appears finally in actuality at the scene
of Anna's suicide when she, inevitably, throws herself under the
train to punish Vronsky. St Petersburg is a world permeated
by falseness, adultery and intrigue, while Moscow-based life
is useful and spontaneous. These polarities link the dual
movements on which the novel is constructed – the tragic
downward spiral of Anna and Vronsky and the progress
upwards to serene fulfilment in family life and his relations with
his parents by Levin, with occasional cross-encounters between
a member of each side which mark their relative positions at
different points on these charts. In *War and Peace* the tensions
between families and individuals are contained in the larger
national movement of history – the resistance to the French
invasion, in which the lives of the characters are caught up.
This is the model of Pasternak's novel of the Revolution and
its aftermath, in the course of which Tsarist Russia is replaced
by general chaos in the Civil Wars, the fortunes of the
characters are similarly involved, and Zhivago as poet is
defeated by the collapse of social life, now reduced to a struggle
for survival, in which he tries to salvage the humane values on
which civilization depends. And in Solzhenitsyn's novels we see,
on truly Russian lines, an enquiry into what the values of
civilization are, and we are shown how they are clung to, even
in the most difficult conditions, as represented by those dying
of cancer or struggling in unjust imprisonment. In fact, in
The First Circle, Solzhenitsyn shows the thirst for and reaching
out towards these human aspirations even in the products of
a state that has been promoting scientific materialism and
atheism for a couple of generations at the expense of humane
values. But the classical Russian novelists did not produce any
rigid theory of the novel, like those of various successive French
novelists of the nineteenth century; such theories fatally constrict
their successors. The autonomy of the novelist and the uniqueness
of every novel was insisted on by Tolstoy, who declared that
War and Peace 'is that which the author wanted to and could
express in the form in which it has been expressed'.

It is the obvious misgovernment by a stupid administration,
the abnegation of duty by men of letters, a depraved

aristocracy and the young men looking for speedy solutions to the social injustice by political organisations formed for violent action, that is the basis of Dostoevsky's great novel *The Possessed* (*The Devils*). Here the countryside and its country town (the surprising Russian equivalent of the setting of *Middlemarch*!) are shown as a microcosm of Russia on the point of breakdown. Though peaceful on the surface at the opening, we are taken through a series of dramatic scenes increasingly tense and sinister till with mounting excitement the whole system explodes like a volcano under its internal pressures as morale disintegrates, the town is set on fire, the Governor breaks down and goes mad, and most of the leading characters are murdered or destroy themselves; some of these tragedies fill us with horror and others with unbearable pity. Most moving of all is the history of Shatov, desperately poor, whose emancipated wife Marie returns to him only to bear Stavrogin's child. The good Shatov accepts them both with joy, and this lull in the storm, with its implications of the Holy Family and the birth in the stable with its apparent promise of some happiness saved from the general wreck, makes the more intolerable the wanton murder of Shatov by the revolutionaries that follows next day and the death in consequence of his wife and her new-born baby as she runs distracted about the streets to find him with the baby in her arms. The final death, Stavrogin's suicide, without having solved for us the mystery of his unaccountable conduct throughout the novel, is disquieting as Dostoevsky so often is, leaving us with questions we cannot answer. At the centre of all the mischief is a figure animated by hatred and contempt, Peter Verkhovensky, a follower of Bakunin, who has returned from abroad to start a secret society with cells all over Russia as the aim and who animates the anarchic tendencies dormant in various circles and persons.

Dostoevsky's interest in explaining by means of fictions violence, anarchy, social alienation, perversion, crime and insanity and all forms of evil, as potentially inherent in men and women and the societies they have made in their own image, turned out to be more useful to the writers of the Revolution and its aftermath than any other model, perhaps because Dostoevsky selected from real life situations and actions he prophetically recognized as representing Russia's future society. But the conflicts in Dostoevsky's novels, though shown more in psychological depth, are still those between parents and their shocking children, between classes, and with the author's sympathy for the underdog, and between people holding conflicting philosophical or political theories. Dostoevsky's novels are not constructed on a system of balances and contrasts as are those we have seen by Pushkin, Lermontov, Turgenev and Tolstoy. *Crime and Punishment* (1865) is a salvationist novel like *Great Expectations* (published 1861 – I would like to know whether Dostoevsky had read it – it would be a useful critical exercise to compare the two novels) and a case-history – evidently the model for Conrad's *Under Western Eyes* – elaborated and entered into to reveal the moral and psychological effects of a crime, chosen as the ultimate in crime, deliberate murder. Raskolnikov, a wretchedly poor law-student, tormented by family troubles and maddened by the injustices of society, decides to murder a money-lender, an old woman who preys on the poor for whom Raskolnikov feels a fellow-sympathy. The murder is to prove to himself that he refuses to accept conventional morality but can judge and act freely as morally independent and superior to the code that the unjust society has established. Though nothing associates him with the murder (or two murders, for her innocent sister runs in and he has to murder her too to save himself, which distresses him), Raskolnikov, under the pressure of the conscience he had denied, falters in his moral self-confidence, becomes subject to fantasies and delusions, as he becomes a prey to psychological tensions, and he is sent to prison in Siberia. Here his moral re-education begins, as his fellow-convicts shun him and he suffers from the new realization of himself and his relation to others. The last chapter is beautiful and convincing in its picture of the beginnings of regeneration in the prison as Raskolnikov takes the first steps toward self-knowledge and contrition, when he sees the Siberian spring breaking up the ice-bound earth and life re-born.

It is as well that the Soviet government, surprisingly, has kept Dostoevsky's and Tolstoy's novels in print, for we can see that their novels were of the greatest use to novelists like Pasternak and Solzhenitsyn who have tried to explain what has happened to Russia since 1917 in human terms. Prison is now the most suitable microcosm for the novelist, it seems. Driven hither and thither by the winds of change as the opposing armies and factions sweep over Russia after the Revolution, Zhivago, poet and doctor (dual vocation of artist and healer) tries to keep himself and his family and his talent and skills alive in this nightmare world. A large-scale novel without padding, the prose of Dr *Zhivago* is rich and vital without being 'poetic' in the rhetorical sense. Yuri Zhivago starts with 'his loyalty to the revolution and his admiration for it, the revolution in the sense in which it was accepted by the middle-classes and in which it had been understood by the followers of Blok, in 1905'. Then came the War of 1914 'with its bloodshed...and the worldly wisdom which it taught'. It became evident that the revolution of 1917 onwards was 'not the one idealized in student fashion in 1905' but 'born of the war, bloody, pitiless, elemental, the soldiers' revolution led by the professionals, the Bolsheviks'. And Pasternak tells us the truth about this revolution – which required considerable courage in Soviet Russia and for which he paid the price he must have envisaged.

There are two leading figures in this nightmare – Yuri Zhivago a doctor, and his great love Lara a nurse, a strong and devoted woman but a complete woman as a mother and wife. Yuri meets at the start in a railway carriage one of the intellectuals of the nihilist type in Dostoevsky – arrogant, short-sighted and doctrinaire. '"All this destruction", he says, "is the right and proper preliminary stage. Society has not yet disintegrated sufficiently. It must fall to pieces completely, then a genuinely revolutionary government will put the pieces together on a completely new basis." Yuri felt sick.'

As a doctor, Yuri is a scientist, as a poet an artist. He thinks of these two opposite methods of progress – 'Progress in science follows the laws of repulsion – every step forward is made by reaction against the delusions and false theories prevailing at the time. Forward steps in art are made by attraction, through the artist's admiration and desire to follow the example of the predecessor he admires most.' And he reflects 'What is it that prevents me from being useful as a doctor or a writer?' – for since the Revolution he has been unable to write and hampered in his medical work. And he turns to Pushkin, the first great Russian writer and poet, as the corrective. And he examines his attitudes about sex: 'He did not believe in "free love" or in the "right" to be carried away by his senses. To think or speak in such terms seemed to him degrading.' Yuri is like Nabakov's Pnin, the heir of traditional pre-war Russian culture.

Yuri is kidnapped by the partisans to replace their surgeon who is killed. At their meeting, honoured figures among them are 'old workers, veterans of the revolution of 1905. Numbered among the gods at whose feet the revolution had laid its gifts and its burnt offerings, they sat silent and grim as idols; they were men in whom everything alive and human had been driven out by political conceit.' We see that Pasternak was a realistic observer and never the victim of simplistic idealization of the workers like Pavese, Vittorini, etc. Pasternak sees the ruins of the pre-war world as a disaster for humanity. Lara says to Yuri, 'You and I are the last remembrance of all that immeasurable greatness which has been created in the world' by the efforts of mankind in thousands of years to raise itself from savagery. She remembers her childhood, when 'it was taken for granted that you listened to reason, that it was right and natural to do what your conscience told you. Murders happened in plays and detective stories, not in everyday life.'

At the heart of the novel is the period when he and his love Lara and her child find a refuge in an old house in the country in winter, where between chopping wood for the fire and contriving to get enough food to keep them alive, he sits up at nights having found the conditions for writing poetry again – inside with him those he loves, in precarious safety, and outside he can hear the threat from the wolves – the howls of real animals and the metaphorical wolves of the winter storms and ice, the partisans fighting over the countryside who may break in, and the wolves that bring death by starvation and cold. These pressures upon him are the stimulus to write and we are caught up in the excitement, as his powers return, of his 'trying to convey by means so simple his feeling of mingled love and anguish, fear and courage in such a way that it shall speak for itself'. He had found that since the Revolution he had been unable to write, from a moral disgust at what had happened in this age of 'mass insanity, daily legalised slaughter' with the loss of faith in the value of personal option and hence 'the power of the glittering phrase'. People, he says, must not live by 'the official tune' and he is sickened by 'the power in our day of rhetoric, of the cliché – all this "dawn of the future", "building a new world", "torch-bearers of mankind"'. To think or speak in such terms seemed to him degrading. The poet, imprisoned in a society where the only tools, words and thoughts, have been degraded, loses his creativeness. Pasternak lets us into the process of creativity in novels, by describing Yuri Zhivago's method of composition and style – he aimed 'to write with an originality so covert, so discreet, as to be outwardly unrecognisable in the disguise of current, customary forms of speech. All his life he had struggled after a language so reserved, so unpretentious as to enable the reader to master the content without noticing the means by which it reached him.' Having 'tried to convey by means so simple his feeling of mingled love and anguish, fear and courage in such a way that it should speak for itself', he found that he 'needed a connecting theme to give unity to the lines, which were incoherent for lack of it'.

Pasternak can diagnose the disease of revolutionary Russia to its centre – 'It was the disease, of the revolutionary madness of the age, that in his heart everyone was utterly different from his words and the outward appearance he assumed. No one had a clear conscience.' Yuri notes as a doctor the new psychological illness – 'its causes are chiefly moral. The great majority of us are required to live a life of constant, systematic duplicity', and he tells his friend who had been 're-educated politically' in prison by his interrogator and is now a pious Communist: 'I found it painful to listen to you when you told us you were re-educated and grew up in jail. It was like listening to a circus horse describing how it broke itself in.'

The image is not sought after, it is spontaneous and *right*, it clinches Yuri's point. Marxism is denaturing and inhuman. Yuri elsewhere has told the partisan leader who has had him kidnapped and for whose company he acts as doctor for two years, that people like him who cant about 're-shaping life' are 'people who can never have understood a thing about life' – 'Life is never a raw material, a substance to be moulded and reprocessed by them.' 'If you want to know, life is the principle of self-renewal, it is infinitely beyond your or my theories about it.'

An Eastern European writer – Arthur Koestler – also deals with the theme of the inhuman denaturing character of Marxism. *Darkness at Noon* follows the pact of Russia with Hitler and the engineers' trial and the wiping out of the Old Bolsheviks, the heroes of the Revolution. It made England and

Western Europe comprehend how these horrors could happen, and the lies be endorsed, in public trials, and show what Marxism does to even decent and talented men like Rubashov, the protagonist, and how it has produced a breed of what Rubashov calls 'Neanderthalers' – men like Gletkin the interrogator. There is first-hand experience behind this analysis, for Koestler, formerly an active Marxist, knew victims of the Moscow trials who are synthesized in Rubashov the eminent Commissar, Revolutionary hero and Party loyalist who after committing crimes for the Party and betraying at its behest innocent and honourable people, is himself at last accused, framed, tried and executed in the usual way. He has not been without a conscience – a repressed sense of guilt had produced an unvarying torturing dream – and in his cell, between interrogations, he recalls his life in detail as a Party agent and argues with himself, and his accusers, the ethics of his actions and their position. He accepts the need to bolster up the Party by signing a false confession and holds to it at his public trial. 'But when he asked himself, For what actually are you dying? he found no answer. It was a mistake in the system; perhaps it lay in the precept in whose name he had sacrificed others and was himself being sacrificed: in the precept that the end justifies the means.' And Koestler has a quotation – hailing from a fifteenth-century Catholic Bishop – that 'when the existence of the Church is threatened, she is released from the commandments of morality...For all order is for the sake of the community, and the individual must be sacrificed to the common good.'

Koestler thus intimates that the same ethical question is not peculiar to the Marxist situation, it has arisen in the past, whenever an institution or government is determined to keep power at whatever cost. Nevertheless, Rubashov wrote in his diary: 'We have thrown overboard all conventions, we are sailing without ethical ballast.' It is too late for Rubashov to undo his past, the ruin he has connived at for humanity he can only pay for by his death – though in fact, dying after endorsing in court the false confession, he cannot be said to have paid, he has merely helped to the last to keep the Neanderthalers in power. Koestler had himself been imprisoned, fought, and knew at first-hand the devious history of the Party and its crimes, and shows us the minds of the successive generations of officials.

Victor Serge in his novel *The Case of Comrade Tulayev* (1951) is a predecessor of Solzhenitsyn. Written in French out of personal experience it recounts the Russian trials, prisons and exile to Siberia, the Russian betrayal of the Spanish opposition to Franco, and the extermination of the Old Bolsheviks by Stalin. The basic irony of the novel is that an impulsive assassination in the street at night, by a good young man, of a particularly vicious power in the Communist establishment, leads by the domino principle to the execution of more and more leading Party men, good and bad, some of whom had nothing to do with the murder but whom Stalin is glad to get rid of; and though the young man who fired the shot ultimately feels obliged to send in an anonymous letter of confession, it was not opened till the faked trials and the deaths of the innocent men had occurred, and the new Public Prosecutor, who opens it, feels that the only thing to be done now is to burn the confession before it creates another excuse for Stalin to immolate more bureaucrats, and indirectly the new Public Prosecutor whose predecessor has also been executed for inadequate zeal in the case. We see that, as in *The First Circle* and *Cancer Ward*, bitter ironies are basic to the social situation in Communist countries as they were in Tsarist Russia too, and it is only by the control of such monstrous inhumanity and mass injustice that *irony* provides, that a novelist can make such material manageable. His natural horror, indignation and disgust are channelled into irony. And the irony of Communist history – in its successive changes of front and line and always without admitting inconsistency or guilt – therefore offers itself inevitably as a weapon for the novelist in his need to present the truth.

Solzhenitsyn has used two metaphors of prison in his novels: one is Russia seen as a cancer ward in the novel of that name, which is in the tradition (in Russia a dangerous one) of Tolstoy's novel *The Death of Ivan Ilyich*; and in the other, *The First Circle*, he studies the plight and fate of the intelligentsia of science arbitrarily herded into a prison (the first circle of Hell as invented by Dante) where they are obliged as slaves under Stalin to put their inventiveness to uses they deplore. This novel is brilliantly witty as well as painful and moving. In both these novels Solzhenitsyn is asking the same question as Tolstoy: What do men live by? and he shows their human

needs – for friendship, their wives, family life, self-respect in
one's work – and how they sustain their morale by their
memories of these things and of literature, music and religion,
and by their constant exchanges of ideas and satiric jokes and
by defiance of the authorities even though this requires
audacity and heroism, thus keeping themselves from succumbing to despair. It is in the surprising sensibility to poetry and
music of these engineers and mathematicians and the high
value they put upon books that we recognize a Russian
characteristic that has survived even scientific materialism. It
seems natural therefore that Solzhenitsyn should devote parts
of each of his novels to discussing the function of literature and
its representatives in the Communist society. He satirizes
literature as officially sponsored and directed and correlates the
state of society with the *trahisons des clercs*. When Solzhenitsyn
was accused by the official critics that he had produced an
unjustified caricature of an arriviste writer in Aviette, the
daughter of a poisonous official, he was able to reply: 'There
is not a single word of Aviette's that is my own – she uses only
words spoken in the last fifteen years by our most important
writers and literary critics.' She is guilty of the crime of
degrading the function of literature, and as Solzhenitsyn shows
in drawing her attitudes and literary notions from the
approved writers and critics, she is what the state has decided
literature should be. In the same novel we are given a glimpse
of the teaching of literature in high school and university where
literature is ground through the mill of Marxist analysis and
students are advised not to read Tolstoy's novels and those of
the great novelists because they would only confuse the clear
ideas learned from reading the approved critical studies of
Tolstoy. Solzhenitsyn is like Pasternak and Sinyavsky in the
great Russian tradition which has known since Pushkin that
it is literature that matters *most*, for communication depends
on its quality. Solzhenitsyn has given us as positive the image
in *The First Circle* of Kondrashov the artist (like Zhivago
writing poetry all night with the wolves at the door) in prison,
a painter whose stint is to turn out a picture a month to adorn
officials' rooms. Actually he will paint only what he chooses
so they have to put up with it: 'with a sigh they took what there
was'. With a landing as his studio (at least as good a studio as
he could afford when outside) he is quite happy because he is

free to practise his art – the only free man in a prison world is the creative artist, we find. The world of the prison as a true microcosm was, among other things, the means of integrating the primitive and the sophisticated elements in Russian culture, in art, which is one of the achievements of the Russian novel. The image of life as a prison or the state as imprisoning, seems to come naturally to Russian novelists for good historical reasons, and the discovery of oneself in prison, as a benefit of the system, almost a mystique. 'Where else but in prison could one get to know people so well, where else could one reflect so well on oneself?' 'Time to sort yourself out, to understand the part of good and evil in human life. Where could you do this better than in prison?' 'Where else can you argue if not in prison? You'd soon be put inside if you tried anywhere else.' It is ironic but a statement of fact, that prison was the only place in Russia where speculation and discussion of ideas and views could take place – again, we see the paradox that only prisoners are free in such a society. The philosophical tendencies of the Russian novel from Tolstoy to Solzhenitsyn are thus very different from the intellectuality of French novelists, where theories are preconceived and the novels framed to illustrate them, imposing on life an arbitrary image of the human. The genius of the great Russian novelists is to reveal to us life in its fulness, by confronting life with death, and thus deduce the answer to the novelist's question: What do men live by? The theory that Solzhenitsyn developed from his conception of the novelist's duty led him to adopt a theory of the treatment of his characters similar to Dostoevsky's practice.

Solzhenitsyn gave a Slovak journalist in 1967 an interview in which he said the writer's principal task is 'not to overlook a single mistake in the social development of his country' and declared

Because he observes the world with an artist's eye and because of his intuition, social developments reveal themselves to a novelist earlier than to others. This constitutes his talent. And from his talent springs his duty. He must inform society of what he has seen, especially about everything that is unhealthy and cause for anxiety.

But the duty to society is not enough. Solzhenitsyn also said that 'a writer's mission' is also to fulfil 'his most important obligation to each individual', adding that 'An individual's life is not always the same as society's'. He therefore believed that each individual in his novels should receive equal attention, so that 'each person becomes the main character when the action involves him in particular. The author must understand and make valid every character he has created.'

Solzhenitsyn called this 'the polyphonic novel', a term formerly invented to describe Dostoevsky's novels though it also describes Tolstoy's as well. In fact, the Russian novelists were able to go on working within the territory staked out and explored by their classical novelists – with their themes, methods, techniques and system of moral values – a moral apprehension of life and a responsible idea of the novelist's function as social critic and prophet to go on working on the same lines even in the apparently new Russia of the mid-twentieth century. And thus their great nineteenth-century novelists have still been available to the Russian people, whereas we see in America and England that the ordinary readers have lost touch with the classical novels of their past.

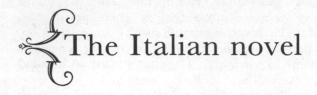

The Italian novel

Having seen how a novel tradition was established and developed in other countries we must ask: Why did Italy not produce a distinctive novel of its own? The radical changes in a nation's history such as emancipation from a foreign government, unification, the development of a post-feudal society – that is, either modern, democratic or industrial – none of these factors produced in Italy a growth and development of a national novel. Why did not the same literary results follow in Italy from the same causes as in the countries I have discussed? Surely the *Risorgimento*, the unification of Italy, and development of the Fascist state, with its challenge to the consciences of the men of letters, the last war, fought tragically on Italian soil with partisan risings against both the German and the Italian armies, the post-war reconstruction, the growth of the Communist party in Italy and its challenge to Catholicism – are all themes crying out for examination through the novel. There have also been socio-economic changes such as the movement of the workers of the South into the factories of the North, changes which I would have thought would have produced sociological-type novels like those of the Industrial Revolution in England.

Of course one sees a number of possible explanations. There is the late unification of Italy and an incomplete one at that since extreme regionalism survived even after the war. There was no religious tension in Italy such as Protestantism provided in Northern Europe, and Jansenism provided in France where it was succeeded by the Enlightenment and revolutionary anti-clericalism. There was in Italy a complete separation of classes which divided the country into peasants, a nationally-minded urban bourgeoisie and a nobility without a function: neither the class mobility of England nor the democratic re-organisation by revolution as in France and America. Derek Traversi, a sensitive literary critic, a Catholic intellectual and half-Italian by birth, wrote that 'We need to remember that the retarded achievement of national unity in Italy coincided with a period of abject spiritual poverty and coarse materialism from which all Italian literature from Pascoli to D'Annunzio downwards, has been trying to escape': and he points out 'an historic gap between political realities and a genuine national consciousness' in consequence.

But we remember that Italy had early established, through Dante, a language finely developed for poetry, and Dante had also written about the problems facing writers who should develop a literature in the vernacular. There seems no reason why a prose art should not have accompanied the development of poetry in Renaissance and seventeenth- and eighteenth-century Italy. There was in fact an Italian tradition from the early days, very successful in its kind, and truly popular and widely practised as by Boccaccio and his contemporaries and successors. This was the *novella*, a form which combined the interests of the courtly classes (love and war) with popular elements crudely satiric and comic that appealed to lower-class tastes. I suppose it was a genuinely native development of fiction corresponding to the English and Spanish picaresque novel, but the *novella* didn't prove in Italy as hospitable to serious development as a higher vehicle as the picaresque novel did for Fielding and Dickens; or perhaps Italian writers of fiction hadn't the stamina, the constructive power and the ability to develop a complex theme that is required of the novelist. One can see that the *novella* has remained the congenial form for Italians – Pavese's *The House on the Hill* and *The Moon and the Bonfires*, Calvino's *The Path to the Nest of Spiders*, Vittorini's *Conversation in Sicily* and *Tune for an Elephant*, acclaimed post-war successes in fiction, are all *novellas* and not one is a novel; and Moravia uses this form all the time. The modern Italian novelists' attempts to write a longer-scale novel such as Vittorini's *Women of Messina*, Pratolini's *A Tale of Poor Lovers*, Moravia's *Two Women* are, as regards construction, merely episodic and can't be taken seriously as novels at all. On the other hand Italians didn't contribute to what we recognize as the art of the short story – their stories read each like a fragment of some *novella* that didn't get written.

One asks why this should be – why, having mastered this rather simple form, the *novella*, Italian writers didn't extend it as the all-purpose vehicle we found the novel to become in other countries, the natural form for expressing the aspirations and disquietudes and achievements of a society. But this function posits an inner life, an inwardness of experience and a self-scrutiny, that seems visibly lacking in Italian literature and life, even in its religious life. Stendhal, who lived in Italy as French consul, noticed this in his fine novel *La Chartreuse de Parme*; the heroine, an enchanting Italian duchess, having impulsively had the ruler of Parma poisoned because he was a menace to her beloved nephew, in post-Napoleonic Italy, now finds the nephew has been imprisoned by his successor and that the governor of the fortress intends to get rid of him by the traditional Italian means of poison. Stendhal writes: 'She didn't make this moral reflection, which could not have escaped any woman brought up in one of those Northern religions which require self-scrutiny, the thought "I employed poison first, I shall perish by it."' In Italy, continues Stendhal, 'this sort of reflection, in moments of passionate feeling, would seem very poor-spirited'. No one who reads Italian fiction of any period can fail to notice this absence of conscience or awareness of moral values, in the characters. It makes Italian fiction less interesting than that of every other country I know, giving its novels characteristically a heartlessness and meaninglessness that only the exceptional Italian writer avoids. The *commedia dell'arte*, an equally crude and popular form like the early Italian *novella*, evolved in Molière's hands into a fine and subtle dramatic art, but in Italy it only produced the heartless comedy of Goldoni and his school. This makes one think, also, that Italian opera, however splendid, is never in the same class as Mozart's. It has no *Fidelio* or *Magic Flute* or *Don Giovanni*. And it was Verdi's operas that were the focus of national feeling, not any novelists' work.

But what was inimical to the development of the novel in Italy was the national taste for opera. Opera appeared first in Italy, and though aristocratic in content and origins (like the French novel) became popular with all classes, not only with the wealthy as in other countries; and so did drama. Humble companies of both actors and opera-singers travelled Italy, even into the smallest towns in remote regions of the South, until the cinema superseded them. Drama, particularly tragic drama, with or without music, seems to have fulfilled a need of the Italian people for imaginative identification. Both D. H. Lawrence and Carlo Levi, among others, report seeing in recent times performances of tragedies (*Hamlet*, and D'Annunzio's respectively) in out of the way places in Italy, performances in which the peasant audiences participated emotionally and seemed to understand instinctively. In line with this is the Italian success as film makers, the cinema following the stage as entertainment. Now opera, like film, is a much simpler thing, as regards characterization and action, than a major novel, even when the opera is based on a novel or poetic tragedy (for example, *Lucia de Lammermoor*, compared with the original novel, Scott's tragic romance *The Bride of Lammermoor*, or even Verdi's *Otello* with Shakespeare's; the opera libretto is *necessarily* a crude reduction of Shakespeare's tragedy and with simplified type-characters. One concludes the frequentation of opera as a national entertainment is inimical to the effort of grappling with and possessing a serious novel. Whereas a Puritanical English eighteenth-century public that fought shy of the theatre had, with its training in listening to long sermons and in discussing them, developed the mental stamina necessary to follow, say, Richardson's *Clarissa* through all the volumes relating her scruples of conscience and refinements of feeling, and so later produced a public capable of following Dickens along the increasingly difficult way, for a reader, from the easy knock-about of *Pickwick Papers* to his demanding later novels, and thus preparing a readership for the really difficult English novelists who followed such as George Eliot and eventually Conrad. No such novelists seemed to have existed in Italy. Nor has the *novella* been used for really ambitious purposes as the *nouvelle* has in other countries, where it has proved capable of substantial masterpieces, such as Thomas Mann's *Death in Venice*, Melville's *Benito Cereno*, G. Griffin's *Tracy's Ambition*, Constant's *Adolphe*, Camus' *L'Étranger*. But these have a moral and philosophical interest as well as in each case a compelling and thoroughly understood social context. Such works have engaged serious writers and cost almost as much, one feels, as a novel. The only such Italian *novella* I know is Silone's *Fontamara*, for Verga's *I Malavoglia* seems to me an Italian pastoral in an impersonal tragic key.

Italy had a late start in prose literature, like Russia, in fact later than Russia's. The great classical Russian novelists had the benefit as *contemporaries* of the Victorian novelists and also Stendhal's and Victor Hugo's and Balzac's novels, contemporary and therefore related to their needs, suggesting forms and modes of expression adaptable for their critical approach to the problems of Russian life and society. But nineteenth- and twentieth-century English novels were no use to so regional and archaic a society as Italy's. The Italian intelligentsia naturally turned to France, related to them in language and religion, for models. Hence Verga was for long set on a wrong track, writing French realist novels about city life, which were quite unsuccessful, before he thought of writing about the Sicilian peasants of his own locality and with whom he had spent some part of his boyhood, and enriching Italian language and literature by bringing into it the speech and sentence forms and life style of Sicilian shepherds and fishermen and villagers. Even so, Lawrence's explanation as to the second-rate quality of Italian creative writers holds: 'They seem to have a borrowed outlook on life'; that Verga's is borrowed from the French and Manzoni's is Germanic while D'Annunzio and Pirandello, he feels, 'always seem to be acting up'. Even their nineteenth-century ideas of democracy were borrowed from the Northern nations, he feels, and were never grafted onto Italy. Thus, as Lawrence says, though Manzoni was hailed as a classic, he hasn't survived like Byron and Scott whom at the time he was supposed to rival.

Manzoni is the first Italian novelist and is like Pushkin in being the father of colloquial prose in his country, deciding to write his novel in the Italian language which previously, he says, 'was never written as it was spoken' and was 'a language never used to discuss great questions verbally'. Therefore, as he explained, 'to write a novel well in Italian is one of the most difficult things'. But Manzoni had originally undertaken to write a novel not for the benefit of the Italian language but in order to inculcate moral lessons. Stendhal, a very good critic, didn't admire *I Promessi Sposi* and anti-clerical Italians of the period very naturally detested Manzoni's novel for its submissiveness to clericalism. The intention to emulate Scott meant a historical novel; *I Promessi Sposi* is therefore set in the early seventeenth century so that it is an historical romance, but the romanticism does not get, as in Scott's better novels, a corrective in realistic sociological analysis. Nor has Manzoni Scott's feeling for moral realities and distinctions; even an admirer like Traversi admits that Manzoni's plot is artificial and that the novel shows 'a rigid and pre-determined framework to which experience must conform'.[1]

Manzoni had spent his formative years in post-revolutionary Paris and reacted to the scepticism of the *salons* in moral philosophy – but his reaction was automatic and not thoughtful. He opted for the conventional position of Catholicism. His thesis is that goodness is possible for all if they will choose it and act under the direction of the Catholic Church and that this alone can avert anarchy, the ever-present threat to society. Lucia the peasant heroine is saved by prayers and submissiveness, in every crisis, whereas the betrothed Renzo, who can't take injustice lying down and tries to resist it, is shown to be a rebellious spirit who is almost ruined by his obstinate assertions of his right to seek justice by his own efforts. Similarly, all bad characters die of the plague but all the good ones recover from it and the plague gives the saintly friar an opportunity to make a noble death while tending its victims. There are awfully wicked noblemen who die as they deserve, and one who appears at the end simply in order to reward the virtuous peasant characters; and the Unnamed One who, though he has passed a consistently wicked life, is converted by Lucia's tears and chastity vow. There is an unbelievably saintly cardinal and other good clerics, and a cowardly parish priest is there to provide comic relief. As Henry James said of some other novel, this surely belongs to the infancy of art. Manzoni's selection of characters really tells us nothing about Italy; it only falsifies it by showing it as a picturesque melodrama with a happy ending provided by Providence and not achieved logically by events.

But Verga, as a realist who inherited from Balzac and his French successors, and as a landowner who managed his family estate, was considerably better suited to come to grips with Italian society and its shortcomings. After his simpler experiment in *I Malavoglia* he wrote a more considerable novel, *Mastro don Gesualdo*; in this he showed the peasants in the entire social context of a small Italian town and its economic hinterland (as in George Eliot's novel *Middlemarch*) by taking us through the life-story of a very able man of the people moving upwards socially as he prospers, with universally tragic consequences that are felt to be inevitable as things were.

Nevertheless, Verga felt unable to continue with the ambition he had had of following up these two novels with three more which should systematically range over the whole field of Italian social and political life from the peasants to the aristocracy and government, a series to do for Italy what Balzac had done for France in his *Comédie humaine*, but to be called *The Cycle of the Doomed*. He wrote only two chapters of the third novel of the cycle and then gave up – perhaps not such a loss for Italian literature as one might have supposed. For he was still the victim of 'looking at life through borrowed vision'. His poor devil Gesualdo is seen externally and offered as a spectacle as if he were Balzac's Père Goriot, whose situation his resembles, but Gesualdo belongs to a different world from Goriot's and unlike him is a really pathetic character whom one can respect and feel sympathy for. But Verga does distil into his novel a disgust for the Italian grasping mentality and the exploitation of Gesualdo, a social innocent, by the degenerate nobility and small-town gentry; and Verga is compassionate towards the tragic victims of the poverty and disastrous conventions of the South. He shows a refreshing absence of that contempt for women which is so characteristic of modern Italian novelists and which is in itself a disqualification for their writing novels worth reading – after all, the relations of men and women, and parents and children are necessarily the subject-matter of the novel, and fineness of sensibility in handling them an essential qualification in a novelist.

D. H. Lawrence thought *Cavalleria Rusticana* (1880) the most interesting of the Verga books. Verga is himself an interesting person, with a remarkable history as a narrator, and better qualified by nature to be a major novelist – a proud, passionate, emotional man, and though poor and provincial, a gentleman whose family owned land in southern Sicily so that he had a relation by birth, upbringing and tradition with the peasantry, since in his maturity he had to manage the family estate, during which he gained his experience of the dolours of peasant life. He had imagination and feeling enough to feel sympathy with them, and this led him to give up writing novels about city life, influenced by Goncourt and Maupassant, and

write about the passionate, primitive, tormented lives of the
unfortunate Sicilian peasants, whose lot as farmers was cast
in an uncongenial climate and soil and who were socially and
economically ill-used by man as by nature, yet nevertheless had
real passions, real sufferings, real pleasures, religion fascinating
in its pagan foundations only slightly overlaid by Christian
ritual, and which supported a backward gentry, suffocated by
its social code – all rich material for a novelist, and at that time
not yet explored.

Verga does not idealize the peasants as George Sand did –
he was not under the influence as she was of the theories of
the French Revolution – but he does not show them as
Maupassant does his Norman peasants as being wholly odious.
Verga sees that they are human and not by any means merely
brutes. He never forgets the handicaps of their lives and ap-
preciates the mark of unselfish maternal and paternal feeling
of devotion to the family's interest that mitigates the inevitable
selfishness and money-grubbing of the lives of these deprived
people for whom life is a perpetual struggle with relentless
Nature. They are despised by the gentry who often have
similar or worse vices with less justification, we are shown,
and deprived even when their abilities and industry have
enabled one of them (for example, Mastro don Gesualdo) to
marry into and emulate the life-style of the gentry, so that it
is a tragedy for him to have surmounted his humble origin.
Society is seen to be even more relentless an enemy of the
Sicilian peasant than Nature, with her droughts and blights.

Lawrence, a most sensitive reader and intelligent critic,
rightly saw Verga's great superiority to his master, the pretentious arid moralist Zola, whose characters, outer histories and
actions are constructed to illustrate a pseudo-scientific theory.
Lawrence points out that whereas for Zola people are merely
'physical/functional arrangements...without any "higher
nature"', Verga's people are always *people*, and though
unsophisticated socially and naïve mentally, they have the
virtues of spontaneity and uniqueness and they have souls and
passions – men are proud, self-respecting and touchy and the
women wisely resigned and long-suffering. And Lawrence
makes another valuable point that Verga was wiser than
Tolstoy who valued the Russian peasant as an example of the
virtues of poverty and humility and loaded the idea of the

peasant with a spiritual mystique. We can see that Verga valued the peasant for qualities of spontaneity and passion that he found no longer present in the effete gentry of Sicily. But he was wise, not self-deceiving; he saw, as Lawrence says, and as other novelists have seen to be a rule in life in other classes, in other countries, that 'the vulgar and the greedy are always destroying the sensitive and the passionate' – I would add Verga also shows that if the sensitive do not let themselves be trodden down by the vulgar and greedy they have to become greedy and remorseless too. Lampedusa sees this too, but wrongly and with resignation, even as a joke; Verga sees it with a noble indignation and pity.

Lampedusa wasn't a professional novelist, he was obviously and essentially an amateur. He spent goodness knows how many years on his one novel but he never even unified it in style and tone, much less integrated the parts, each of which very evidently was written in (probably unconscious) imitation of a different novelist. So much so that it might better have been four separate tales. Undoubtedly the best and only entertaining part is the first where his material is original – he found it in his family archives and traditions and thoroughly sympathizes with it and so enters into it imaginatively. Yet he sees it as Stendhal saw the Italian nobility and his tone is that of the witty and ironical style of *La Chartreuse de Parme*, which combines so oddly in Lampedusa with Stendhal's romantic feeling for the aristocratic life-style, though he is not so capable as Stendhal is of handling political realities. The second section is the courtship of the Prince's nephew and only slightly related to the previous section through the uncle's problem in trying to accept the impossible *nouveau-riche* father of the fiancée – this is quite like a Hogarth tableau. This section soon dissolves into an excuse for an exercise in imitation of Proust as the affianced couple explore the castle – it's really a self-indulgent pastiche, for Lampedusa had said all he had to say in the first section that leads up to the betrothal. The next part too is a pastiche of Verga and has really no place in this novel: Father Pirone's peasant sortie into the world of Verga's stories is a short story on its own and is not related to anything else in the book. The fourth part, the death of the Prince, is again Proustian, and an unpleasant appendix in the manner of the Norman Douglas–Lytton Strachey or International Bloomsbury.

Lampedusa satirizes the former young ladies, now aged survivors living in a dead past and the prey of religious charlatans, winding up with a cheap gesture of the kind so familiar in such novels – the end of the family is symbolized by throwing out on the dust-heap their mangey stuffed dog. One can well believe the author was steeped in the European and English literatures, as we are told by Lampedusa's admirers.

Verga was much better than that. He was not a willing victim of nostalgia like Lampedusa but was possessed by a genuine sense of the tragic nature of the life of the poverty-stricken South of Italy, where the government and society are as relentless enemies of man as nature is with its droughts for the peasants and the cruel sea for the fisherfolk.

This, the best line in the Italian novel, was carried on into the peasant world under Fascism by Silone in his first novel *Fontamara*, truly original in conception and form and something with which we might profitably associate Carlo Levi's prototype of a novel, his account of his experiences in Lucania when exiled there as an anti-Fascist before the War, *Christ Stopped at Eboli*. By both these writers – Silone and Levi – peasants are seen as ordinary human beings, now deprived of even their feudal rights by an exploiting central government and bureaucracy. Silone shows the effects of the Fascist state on the peasants' lot with the maximum impact by giving through peasant narrators their reactions, first of bewilderment then of incredulity and finally helpless passion as they find themselves brutally manipulated by the officials and deserted by the Church to whom they appeal for support. The novel is told in the peasants' own words and ends with their having to accept the only leadership available, that of the Communists, to organize themselves against intolerable injustice. Silone was an artist of courage and integrity. He next, in his more ambitious novel *Bread and Wine*, proceeded from the simple *novella*, that confined itself to the peasants' viewpoint, to offer a more comprehensive insight into the social condition under Fascism. Embodied in the title is a genuine symbolism – bread and wine are both the material food of life and a sacrament – and in consonance with this the devoted and hunted organizer of the people who has adopted a priest's garb as disguise and protection, finds himself obliged to fill a religious role, and the novel develops a spiritual mystique that is certainly far from usual in Italian novels. *Bread and Wine* ends in tragic despair, with the triumph of the wolves and the snowstorm, understood as symbols of the realities of Italy under Fascism.

Silone became disillusioned with the Communists and Verga dried up as a novelist. Italian novelists didn't seem to have solved the problem of an alternative to Fascism because they themselves lack a conception of the satisfactory society or belief that there is one. Having lost religious faith they have no positives, other than the hope that once lay, apparently, in Communism, soon lost by novelists like Silone and Vittorini whose intelligence saw Communism was in practice not really an alternative to Fascism.

And when in Calvino's much admired *The Path to the Nest of Spiders* (1947) – really only a *novella* – we are offered a positive allegedly emerging from the Civil War, it is surely implausible. The experience of a true comradeship emerging from the partisan conflicts in North Italy is symbolized as that of Pin, a boy from the gutter – an Italian city version of Huck Finn – who yearns for grown-up men friends he can admire, and finding himself in the partisan camp develops affection and respect for some of them and is seen at the end going off with a leader, known only and of course symbolically as 'Cousin'. But we can't help seeing the partisans have nothing in common with each other *except* opposition to the old Italy – drawn from all classes, from student intellectuals down to social outcasts, and of all political views (or none), they are so precariously held together that even in the face of the enemy they quarrel over politics and women and mutiny against their officers. We are told they are fighting for 'redemption', 'to create a world that is serene, in which no one has to be bad', something that certainly doesn't seem to have been an object in post-war Italy.

The title of the novel refers to Pin's secret discovery by the river of a place where hunting spiders have made little tunnels in the ground with doors at the openings made of dried grass. He has to break up their nests and torture spiders and insects – we are told he hates them because they copulate. No doubt this is a symbol, but not a symbol that adds anything to the meaning of the novel, for Pin's attitudes have already been profusely accounted for by his relations with his sister – who at least feeds and supports him and shows some kindness, though she (mindlessly) takes up with German soldiers. There are only two women in the novel, both promiscuous and irresponsible.

In Italian novels from Svevo to Moravia onwards the lives of the Italian well-to-do classes are exhibited as empty and depraved. *The Confessions of Zeno*, Svevo's most ambitious attempt at a novel, seems as amateur as *The Leopard* – both written for the author's amusement and to satisfy the desire to explain or account for himself to himself, with no artistic control or sense of an organized whole. It is unfortunate that Svevo's life and personality provided the novelist with none of the richness, variety and glamour that Lampedusa's family did. It is hard to understand Joyce's enthusiasm for Svevo who can't be made to fit into any Italian tradition, such as the late Italian *Verismo* or into the French realist school of Flaubert, but rather is seen as sharing the characteristics of Austrian novelists writing in German, such as Kafka, Musil, Schnitzler and such. After all Svevo was an Austrian until 1918, when Trieste was transferred into Italian jurisdiction and he shared an Austrian rather than Italian culture, like Germans, Czechs and other Slavs educated under the Austrian Empire, which was a unifying and civilizing influence. But Svevo has none of the intellectual and imaginative power of Mann or Kafka, his characters and their actions lack interest and they seem to have no realized background to their lives. Of course this is true also of *Bouvard et Pécuchet*, Flaubert's novel expressing disgust with the petty bourgeoisie, but in Flaubert's case the effect is intentional, whereas Svevo is not detached from his fictional world but of it, and though dissatisfied with it he has no imaginative grasp of any other kind of life. He does not seem to feel the pathos of the wasted lives he charts, even the sexual scenes are parts of a case-history and have no passion or emotional validation. Like Flaubert he was a man whose life was penurious emotionally and spiritually, the very opposite of D. H. Lawrence, and unlike Verga where the society exhibited in his novels is one of primitive feeling, strong passions, violent action, and moving tragedies of people who speak a splendidly virile dialect, who are not ineffective, insincere and defeated by moral cowardice, like the rather bloodless and unattractive characters of Svevo. His Freudian preoccupation is a disability rather than a strength or a help – for psychoanalysis is inevitably reductive.

One understands the boredom (for me at any rate) of a series of novels whose characters and motifs are compulsively, it seems, repeated, none in themselves attractive or worth the interest one is expected to take in them. The weariness one feels of jealousy, love that is only physical and women who exist only in relation to men's appetites, men who are psychological cripples – all this seems to me to be the emanation from a man who wants to be a novelist without having the necessary grasp of life in its fullness and depth, of satisfactory human relationships – Svevo seems to deny the possibility of such. The failures in living he always adopts as his heroes don't arouse the reader's sympathy, they are not tragic or pathetic or even shocking – the novelist himself being without the imaginative powers that could oblige us to be concerned for his personae. Why is Svevo supposed to be the exponent of Trieste? It might be any city with a narrowly conventional money-minded bourgeoisie. It doesn't live for us as Thomas Mann's rich bourgeoisie do in *Buddenbrooks* or Joyce's Catholic Irish in *Ulysses*.

Moravia's first and comparatively promising novel, *A Time of Indifference*, too shows a society of depraved and unhappy but materially rich people, a vision of despair like Hell with no future but total disaster. All Moravia's subsequent novels restrict themselves to clinical accounts of sexual experience, pathological rather than pornographic. I think the apology for him by some critics, that his 'art' belongs with the heartless Italian comedy tradition as in Goldoni, has some basis; but entertainment of this kind doesn't entertain for long (who can read a Moravia novel twice?) and this lack of entertainment is degrading and dehumanizing (like Kingsley Amis's novels).

Disillusion with what Fascism, anti-Fascist ideological movements, the Italian bourgeois values, Communism and all other solutions or formulae offered, must have been inevitable from the start, when the country succumbed to Mussolini; and one asks: can good novels come out of despair and social, political and moral bankruptcy? The Catholic Church, as we see in *Fontamara*, deserted the oppressed peasantry and supported the state (the opposite was, of course, true in Ireland, where the priesthood traditionally supported Irish nationalism and so kept its authority with the peasants and gave them something to live by). We note that post-war West Germany recovered better than Italy and from something more evil even than Fascism and Mussolini, and one wonders whether this was connected with the strong stand taken against Hitler and Nazism by the Lutheran Church, whose pastors thus kept alive something other than the cynical materialism evident in Italian novelists by giving a moral lead.

Vittorini's *Conversation in Sicily* is intended as an anti-Fascist novel. The references to political events, and to Fascism in particular, are so distant and obscure that you would not notice them if you were not told and were looking for them. The surface life of the story – the return of the narrator to his mother Sicily and his origins, is wholly inadequate as a reflection of the opening theme.

Primitivism – the admiration for the simple life of the peasant farmer and the comforting self-sufficiency of the village community – is a day-dream for civilized modern man and impossible for an intellectual. It is also impossible for a Marxist, whose system requires the peasants to be exploited for the benefit of the city and the factory workers. To give primitivism any respectable content it is necessary to establish its human validity. Vittorini's Sicily is extremely unattractive not because of its material poverty but because, unlike Verga's Malavoglia family and their friends, poverty is unaccompanied by moral dignity.

Vittorini's one ambitious novel, *Women of Messina*, suffers in the same way from the novelist's lack of positives, and not having something to construct from and for. It starts with a Robinson Crusoe interest, a community being spontaneously built after the disasters of the war; the deprived peasants and other refugees from the war take over a deserted and ruined village and gradually rehabilitate it (symbolically starting by turning the Church into cubicles to house the people) and restore the land to agricultural uses, they also regenerate themselves in the process. The Robinson Crusoe part is convincingly done and touching in its human details. However, their troubles begin when they have a prosperous commune and the bureaucrats come down on them – what title have they to the land, taxes must be paid, etc. Worse, the buried past of the community is excavated and Ventura, an engineer and so the mainstay of the Development, is threatened as a former Fascist and though now repentent of his misdeeds or rather crimes, is shot (in the original version: in the final version he is seen as a failure and the experiment has failed too, as men deserted for jobs in the city and the women plant grapevines for an easy living). Everyone is now for himself and the old capitalist system has returned – Vittorini then was dying of cancer and his bitterness at the failure of post-war Italy to fulfil the hopes of the anti-Facists is evident. He is another of the Italian novelists who would have been better if they hadn't read and imitated the tough between-the-wars school of American novelists. Dos Passos, whom they could have profited by, and *The Great Gatsby* of F. Scott Fitzgerald, show how to expose a decadent society *novelistically* with economy and without pretentiousness.

Tune for an Elephant (1947), a later work of Vittorini's, though short and straightforward, is really moving. It's a tribute to the culture of the working-class family in Italy. We see a typical working-class family smitten by the post-war depression so that the four generations, crowded into a little flat, have only one member with a steady job (bicycle repairer) to support them all. He gives his wage-packet to his mother who can only afford to buy them bread, which she rations and supplements by wild green stuff picked in the woods and made into hot-water broth. However, standards of decent living are maintained because the mother insists on them for the grandchildren and she pretends they are eating a proper and different imaginary dinner every day and in a civilized style. The touching pretence of normal prosperity is bound up, we're shown, with the self-respect of the would-be workers who hope to get jobs again and thus maintain their morale. The worker's father is the elephant of the title – a huge ancient, a legend as a worker and craftsman, strong as an elephant (the little children of the family believe he built the pyramids and the Great Wall of China and the Cathedral); the bread rations have to be supplemented by buying extra for his elephantine needs, though he is now helpless and can hardly even hear. However, when a worn-out road-worker who is about – uncomplainingly – to go into hospital and die, comes to say goodbye they share their pathetic dinner with him, to which he donates his sandwich with its solitary anchovy; everyone has a smell of the anchovy, then it is put on the grandfather's plate. Having been told that the old man is an elephant, the road-worker remarks how when elephants grow old and feeble they go away to die in secret so as not to be a burden. Grandfather has been listening and insists on having it explained to him; and next day one of the children sees him walk out into the woods (no one can think how he managed it) and is never seen again. The roadman has played them a tune on his reed pipe, making the 'reed return to what it had been in its youth, when it stood among other reeds, and reeds were like an organ and the world itself'. This symbolism doesn't need any explanation. The reeds are the culture of the working-class which in a depressed war economy has no roots.

Vittorini here is exceptional in having found a form and metaphor which embody suitably his thesis, and a thesis which is not merely academic – that is, a theoretical concept – but represents a true feeling about humanity. This is the more remarkable since Vittorini, like Pavese, did translating from the American novelists who had such an unfortunate effect on post-war Italian writers. They translated Faulkner, Dreiser, Steinbeck, Hemingway, Caldwell and such, whose coarseness and crudity and their simplification of people and issues and brutalizing cult of violence, made them undesirable and misleading models. The American South and its social and economic problems were surely not those of Italy at all, nor its negroes to be equated with Sicilian and Calabrian peasants. Nor did the culture of the American Middle West bear any likeness to any Italian society, and no American city was at all like Rome or Florence. I think it very unfortunate that they did not instead frequent Conrad and D. H. Lawrence, who could have taught them some at least of what they needed.

A firm conviction of what could lead to personal happiness, soul serenity and trust and respect between human beings individually, seems absent from the Italian literary scene. Silone's disillusion with the realities of Leninism and his exile from Fascist Italy prevented his further development as the novelist who could be 'the conscience of Italy'. This is a function Italian novelists did not or could not supply for Fascist Italy. Carlo Levi after exile to the South as a critic of Fascism was obliged soon after release to flee Italy with his family when Hitler's anti-Semitic laws were ordained in Italy, and his only novel – but that is a very interesting one – takes up the Italian experience towards the end of the war. *The Watch* is refreshing after the feeble and scrappy attempts to deal with the same phase of Italian life in the novels of Pavese, Calvino and others – because Levi's firmly human values and outward-going sympathies made him appreciate the possibilities inherent in the partisans' underground organisation and also to understand why these sources for a future reconstruction of Italian society would be frustrated by circumstances. *The Watch* is an extended parable of the Italian situation at the end of the war as Levi perceived it, and has many points of interest worth drawing attention to. It opens with the narrator in Rome 'a few months after the liberation', listening at night to the sound of the city – the sound of lions roaring 'in the night desert of houses', a wild and cruel sound, perhaps caused by factories and cars or perhaps, he says, a sound from the depths of memory–history – when wild animals roamed between the hills and woods. He had listened to it for the first time years ago coming through the grating of a cell in the prison (where, as we know, the author was imprisoned for six months early in the Fascist régime for his anti-Fascist views). He hears it now from a room high up such as the many temporary shelters he has had and worked in since the storm had broken 'over the bitter lands of Europe and had carried men like leaves stripped from the tree…Now after seven years of pain and slaughter the wind had fallen, but the old leaves could not return to their branches and the cities looked like naked woods, waiting for the haphazard flowering of new buds.' All Levi's images seem to arise spontaneously and are appropriate to the situation or concept he has to express and he has immense fertility in them – he's a truly creative writer.

The next important passage is when the narrator undresses to go to bed and puts out his watch, the symbol from which the novel gets its title. It is a very beautiful watch of the best make, a gold chronometer that did not miss a second, given him long ago by his father as such watches are, he says, given on an important occasion at a decisive moment in a young man's life – 'It is then that we receive from our father the watch that will be with us always, that will follow all our hours…that will start its life in the dark depths of the pocket, chained to us as we to it, and we are perforce obliged to fall into step with its ticking.' If the watch is an image of tradition it is thus seen in one aspect as not wholly a good thing. A disquisition on the passage of time follows. He falls asleep and dreams that the watch his father gave him has been *taken* (not *stolen*) from him, and he has to attend a tribunal, presided over by the philosopher Croce, to decide to whom the watch that has disappeared legally belongs. He miraculously recovers the watch, in his dream, but though the mechanism is still working the dial and case and glass are missing. He awakes, drops the watch as he dresses, and 'it was all as in the dream' – broken that is. So he chases about the city trying to find a watch-shop able to repair it, without success. This is Fascist Italy. He tells how in Florence he had successfully edited a newspaper 'that had to be created by immediate and spontaneous collaboration, clarity of ideas and community of will. Everything went marvellously.' In Florence 'everyone still lived in the stimulating atmosphere of the Resistance... this active and creative freedom, like all miracles, lasted only a short time'. Later on Florence sends a representative all-classes committee to Rome to explain their plan for keeping this freedom and unity by allowing them to manage their own affairs instead of being administered by a remote, alien, arbitrary bureaucracy. Of course their plea is refused. The regions, it appears, hate Rome and its government as the enemy and during the war said of the bombers 'It's to Rome they should go – they shouldn't leave a stone untouched. Rome is Italy's disaster.'

The printing press in Rome can't work its up-to-date machines and modern equipment because of the lack of electric current in 1945. They therefore set up the paper by hand-type and print the copies on a flat press run by an improvised motorcar engine, with the aid of an old publishing house famous for fine printing who bring their traditions of noble book-production to 'this unfamiliar and hurried work', helping them to deceive the authorities by printing more than the authorities allowed, with smuggled-in sheets of paper. This is a convincing symbol of what Levi wants – to combine the best of tradition with freedom from the chains of the past. At the end of the book the narrator goes at great risk to Naples to visit his beloved dying uncle, 'Uncle Doctor', teacher, father and friend who has devoted his old age to biology and philosophy. He leaves his nephew his gold watch, similar to the one his father had given him, and leaves him also his hundreds of notebooks in which 'he had for fifty years described the world, expressed his thoughts and searched for truth'. How, the author reflects, could he ever read them through and communicate them to others? The narrator has wide experience of Italy and registers the regionalism that survived the war because of its strong traditions. 'This town's all right for the Pope but we should have cleared up the mess and moved the capital to Milan', the judge from Novara says; there is a lawyer from somewhere else with 'a dry and noble face' who had fought for two years to protect the valleys. A worker from Bergamo says at the time of the first air-raids of Milan 'if you spoke Italian nobody would answer you. In the darkness you might have been a spy. But in dialect you could say whatever you wished and they'd answer you from the darkness and not mincing words either! ...They applauded the bombs, even those that crashed into their houses', because they were bombing to free Italy. There is a moving scene showing how the illicit printing of each number was watched and cheered on by the mechanics, intellectuals and partisans thus temporarily united in action but the narrator notices that they collect in regional groups which talk privately in their dialects. There is no sympathy between the regions except in hostility to the central government and the material interests of the regions are against each other and all the peasantry against urban society. Levi ends the novel showing that the arrival of peace meant the closing of the partisan's press and the dispersing of the solidarity and unity which was necessarily precarious.

In contrast, we can look at Pavese's *The House on the Hill* (1948). The narrator here is a 40-year-old defeatist whose problems are personal and nothing to do with the war – chiefly the problem of finding himself isolated and in particular of being unable to establish a permanent relation with any woman. His experiences of the war – mostly secondhand – have not changed him and what Pavese concludes about war, in his final pages, is nothing but clichés. He meets a woman who has been his mistress formerly and she has a boy who might be his. He feels perhaps fatherhood would solve his problems, and if the boy were his son he would marry the mother, he tells her, but, understandably, she refuses to tell him and wants no more to do with him, and by the end of the book he has lost sight of both mother and child. It's hardly a sufficient subject for a short story and makes a boring and repetitive *novella*. This is the case even with Pavese's more pretentious but still very short novel, *The Moon and the Bonfires*. The only point in the novel is the return of the Americanized Italian to visit the scenes of his boyhood, when he was desperately poor and an ill-used orphan (he is now rich and one assumes his wealth was acquired in some sinister way). He has no feeling for war-torn Italy and the reminiscences of his former cronies, but his concern centres on the lovely girl Santina's story, who was first a Fascist spy, then lives with partisans as mistress and fighter and gives them information about the Fascists, and finally is discovered by the partisans to be a double agent for the Fascists, so they shoot her and burn her body on a funeral pyre. No explanation is given of Santina's irresponsibility and viciousness, nor is the symbolism of the title given any grounding in the theme – the alleged myth which is supposed to justify the book and give it technical interest. The only decent person in the book, the narrator's old friend, a folk-musician, would give advice during the war but always refused to act. The book is, again, only a pointless short story blown up by endless repetition and the impression of a writer who can feel no sympathy with life and exists only for himself.

Pavese wrote that in novels before the twentieth century 'the hero was not the same at the beginning of the story as he was at the end' but that 'in modern novels he remains the same'. This is ridiculous. Superficial eighteenth-century novel characters like Tom Jones, or the heroes of Dickens's early novels, do remain the same; but in mature novels, as in Dickens from *David Copperfield* onwards, the protagonist is subjected to experiences which either break or re-educate him. This is equally true of Prince Andrew and Pierre in Tolstoy's *War and Peace*. Protagonists who remain the same, as in Pavese's so-called novels, in spite of having experienced national and civil wars, carnage and social destruction and moral degeneration on the scale that occurred in the Second World War – such characters are surely monsters of insensitiveness and selfishness, but this seems an Italian tradition in fact.

In the modern Italian novels, from pre-Fascist times onwards, there seems to be a different society from that in the novels of all other European and Western countries. The novels have as characters no intelligentsia except sometimes unpleasant lawyers – no writers or artists or idealists, no thinkers or disinterested politicians, no educationists or churchmen or scientists or even devoted professional soldiers or sailors, to give leadership and significance to the society portrayed, and who populate the novels of Russia, England, France, Germany and America. It is true that the narrator of *The House on the Hill* is a schoolmaster, but one without vocation and who has no satisfaction or belief in his work. Nor does one ever see in Italian novels of this century marriage relationships of mutual trust and sympathy which occur in the novels of other countries (except the recent American novels). Unless men and women are capable of relationships which include loyalty, confidence, mutual interests, and there are people of integrity who can act disinterestedly sometimes, which of course requires courage and faith – people, in short, capable of respect for themselves and each other, I don't see how one can expect that novels worth consideration could be written.

Notes

Hawthorne as poet

1 I find support for this in 'Our Old Home': 'Shakespeare has surface beneath surface, to an immeasurable depth…There is no exhausting the various interpretations of his symbols.'

2 'Poe, Hawthorne, Melville: an Essay in Sociological Criticism', *Partisan Review*, Feb. 1949.

3 This naïve demand should be measured against this passage from *Hawthorne's Last Phase* (E. H. Davidson, 1949): 'The rare springtime beauty of the English scene struck him more forcibly than it could the ordinary tourist, for it represented to him the perfect balance between man and nature. This balance was conspicuously absent in the untamed forests of the U.S., where man was busily engaged in subduing nature and dominating a continent. "It is only an American who can feel it", Hawthorne wrote.'

4 She was banished from the colony of Massachusetts in 1638 for claiming that the superiority of personal revelation exempted her from the authority of the clergy.

5 From a review of Hawthorne's *Mosses* in 1850, before he had met Hawthorne.

6 The significance of the suit of armour is admirably explained by Mr Yvor Winters in his essay on Hawthorne, 'Maule's Curse'.

7 The element of irony in Hawthorne has been even more overlooked than in James. Melville's intelligence made him inveigh against the 'absurd misconception' of Hawthorne as 'a man who means no meanings','a harmless man'. Melville insists on the force of Hawthorne's intellect which implies what he calls 'blackness', but concludes 'Nor need you fix upon that blackness in him, if it suits you not. Nor, indeed, will all readers discern it; for it is, mostly, insinuated to those who may best understand it, and account for it.'

8 '*The Europeans*' by F. R. Leavis, *Scrutiny*, Summer 1948 (now in *Anna Karenina and Other Essays*).

Melville: the 1853–6 phase

1 Now published: 'Melville and Leopardi', *Rivista di Letterature Moderne e Comparate*, XXXIII, No. 1 (Marzo, 1980).

James, Trollope and the American-English confrontation theme

1 This is the solution Howells adopted subsequently for a similarly disparate couple in his novel *The Lady of the Arcostook*, where a cultivated and intellectual American from a superior New England family falls in love with and marries a poor, socially crude, rustic American girl he meets on a boat taking them both to Italy. Though the girl is made less impossible by being exceptionally beautiful, an implausible talent for stylish dress (in home-made clothes!) and a voice worth training for professional singing, Howells avoids the problems that would result from domesticating her in her husband's family circle by sending them off on marrying to farm in California. (Cf. the end of Lawrence's *The Captain's Doll*.)

The institution of Henry James

1 This alone should suffice to explode the 'incomparable Max' myth – an ideal of elegant triviality, the cult of which is historically explicable as a result of Oscar Wilde's impact on Oxford and the higher journalism; though Oxford, King's College, Cambridge, and their Bloomsbury affiliations appear to be still culturally in the Wilde phase, the rest of England isn't, and 'Max' should have been politely pigeon-holed long ago instead of being sponsored by the B.B.C. as the G.O.M. of English letters.

2 'I *have* felt, for a long time past, that I have fallen upon evil days – every sign or symbol of one's being in the least *wanted*, anywhere or by anyone, having so utterly failed' (1885).

'I greatly applaud the tact with which you tell me that scarce a human being will understand a word, or an intention, or an artistic element or glimmer of any sort, of my book. I tell *myself* – and the "reviews" tell me – such truths in much cruder fashion. But it's an old, old story – and if I "minded" now as much as I once did, I should be well beneath the sod' (1899).

'I remain at my age (which you know [72]), and after my long career, utterly, insurmountably, unsaleable... The edition is from that point of view really a monument (like Ozymandias) which has never had the least intelligent critical justice done it – or any sort of critical attention at all paid it – and the artistic problem involved in my scheme was a deep and exquisite one' (1915).

His closest friend, Edith Wharton, noted 'his sensitiveness to criticism or comment of any sort' and explains that it 'had nothing to do with vanity; it was caused by the great artist's deep consciousness of his powers, combined with a bitter, a life-long disappointment at his lack of popular recognition.' *A Backward Glance*.

Henry James's heiress: the importance of Edith Wharton

1 *A Backward Glance*.
2 *A Backward Glance*, pp. 175-6.

Edith Wharton: *The House of Mirth*

1 'But she could not breathe long on the heights; there had been nothing in her training to develop any continuity of moral strength: what she craved, and really felt herself entitled to, was a situation in which the noblest attitude should also be the easiest...Gerty could now smile at her own early dream of her friend's renovation through adversity: she understood clearly enough that Lily was not of those to whom privation teaches the unimportance of what they have lost.'
2 '"You're not very fond of me – *yet* – but you're fond of luxury, and style, and amusement, and not having to worry about cash. You like to have a good time, and not to have to settle for it; and what I propose to do is to provide the good time and do the settling."' He makes this insufferable by airing before her her secret fear: '"as a girl gets older, and things keep moving along, why, before she knows it, the things she wants are liable to move past her and not come back. I don't say it's anywhere near that with you yet; but...what I'm offering you is the chance to turn your back on them once and for all." The colour burned in Lily's face as he ended.'
3 This reminds one to note that Proust was the French Edwardian novelist, the chronicler and analyst of an Edwardian society, which had interesting likenesses as well as differences to that of England, America and Ireland.

The Italian novel

1 Svevo, who alone in Italy wrote the restlessly self-enquiring and socially introspective kind of novels that are characteristic of twentieth-century Austria, Germany and France, was of mixed German and Italian origin and lived in an international port. He had no national appeal for Italians and his reputation was made by James Joyce.
2 Compare, for instance, Lucia with Scott's heroine Jeanie (in *The Heart of Midlothian*). Apparently in a situation even more painful than Lucia's (the trial and condemnation to death by hanging of her beloved young sister for alleged child-murder, with the disgrace of the whole family and the ruin of Jeanie's own prospect of happiness in marriage with her lover,

a minister of religion), Jeanie takes on her own the decision to act in the only way possible to save her sister, by walking all the way to London to beg the king for a reprieve. Nothing seems more impossible, but, by her native virtues of character, fearlessness, simplicity tempered by canniness, an inflexible will which overcomes all obstacles and dangers in her path and true modesty which can preserve itself against vice, Jeanie gains her object and incidentally brings about the fulfilment of all her own views of happiness and success in life. Scott's detailed picture of his highly characterized heroine makes her convincing and interesting as the sweetly docile and stupidly devout Lucia never can be – even the inevitable peasant's disabilities are in Jeanie's case made explicit, for instance her only knowledge of courts and monarchs is derived from the Bible, and she assumes that, as kings did in the Old Testament, the King of England will be sitting at his gates seeing justice done in person. When told this is not so nowadays, that the king will be in his palace she says that in that case she will have a silver coin ready to fee the servant so that he will show her into the throne-room. In fact, she walks most of the way from Scotland, and having an introduction from her lover to her clan chief, the Duke of Argyle, she so impresses him with the pathos of her sister's case that he brings her to a private meeting with the Queen, on whom Jeanie's character and artless pleading make a similarly favourable impact. Scott was not romanticizing, like Manzoni, for he heard the tale in outline as having actually occurred to a Scotswoman, then only recently dead, and Jeanie's adventure and character were factual, truly Scottish, and typically so in that the character and abilities Jeanie showed were the normal products of Scottish social and religious history, true to life as it was in an eighteenth century Scott thoroughly knew and realized without romanticizing. Manzoni's seventeenth century is a century and a half before his own time and his novel has all the disadvantages of being an historical novel, a suspect *genre* to which Stendhal's two major novels and Scott's best novels do not belong in that sense. And neither Scott nor Stendhal has the disadvantage of being in thrall to a religious system which hampers the novelist in honestly reproducing experience, and which compresses it into a theoretical preconceived framework to point a moral, which is to many readers an unacceptable theory and moral. Manzoni's cannot I believe be said to be a great novel.